Antisemitism in the Third Reich

HERMANN GRAML

Translated
by Tim Kirk

BLACKWELL
Oxford UK & Cambridge USA

First published 1988
English edition first published 1992

Blackwell Publishers
108 Cowley Road
Oxford OX4 1JF
UK

Three Cambridge Center
Cambridge, Massachusetts 02142
USA

British Library Cataloguing in Publication Data
A CIP catalogue record for this book is available from the British Library.

Library of Congress Cataloging-in-Publication Data
Graml, Hermann.
    [Reichskristallnacht. English]
    Antisemitism in the Third Reich/Hermann Graml : translated by
Tim Kirk. — English ed.
        p.   cm.
    Translation of: Reichskristallnacht.
    Includes bibliographical references (p.   ) and index.
    ISBN 0–631–17209–2. — ISBN 0–631–18506–2 (pb.)
    1. Jews — Germany — History — 1933–1945. 2. Germany — History
— Kristallnacht, 1938. 3. Antisemitism — Germany — History.
4. Germany — Ethnic relations. I. Title.
DS 135.G3315G7313   1992
943'.004924 — dc20   91–38283
                                                                              CIP

Typeset in 10 on 12 pt Garamond
by Times Graphics, Singapore
Printed in Great Britain by TJ Press (Padstow) Ltd, Padstow, Cornwall
This book is printed on acid-free paper

Contents

Introduction: the Subject

This book is an attempt to tell the history of the Nazi persecution of the Jews. It is, however, impossible to deal adequately with a historical process which culminated in a plan to murder all the Jews living in territory either directly controlled by Germany or in the German sphere of influence, and which claimed almost six million victims between its inception in 1941 and the end of the war in 1945. The language and terminology at the historian's disposal for 'normal' subjects will not suffice here. Equally, such a past obviously cannot be 'mastered' by description and analysis, in so far as mastering the past implies deleting it in some way.

Nevertheless, we cannot avoid dealing with the subject: the Nazi persecution of the Jews happened, and consequently it is a part of German history. To suppress it would be a further crime against the European Jews who were mistreated and murdered, and against Jews living today; and to suppress it would also inevitably give rise to new dangers to the intellectual and emotional state of the nation. To be able to live with a burden like the one imposed on the German people by the rulers of the Third Reich we must at least have recognized the mistakes and the wrong turnings which culminated in such political criminality, and acknowledge the guilt arising from them.

For this reason the following work seeks firstly to illuminate the origins of the Nazis' hostility to the Jews in the political and ideological traditions of German nationalism, and on this basis to find an explanation for its peculiar intensity. Only by examining specific flaws in the German national consciousness and in the national movement in Germany can we understand how, just as German Jews were being emancipated and assimilated, a malicious form of antisemitism developed in sharp contrast, which was able to recruit increasing numbers of supporters until it finally became the principal element in the ideological arsenal of the strongest political force in the land: the Nazi movement which, under the leadership of Hitler, took over the government of Germany in 1933. It should be borne in mind, however, that ideologies, or *Weltanschauungen*, as the Nazis themselves put it, do not develop in a vacuum. A study of the spread of Nazi antisemitism also requires an examination of the part played by the military defeats, political upheavals and economic crises which shook Germany in the years before 1933 – disasters for which the German nation itself must, of course, share some responsibility.

In the following chapters, which deal with the persecution of the Jews as such, many details have had to be omitted for reasons of space. The main aim here was to show how the Nazis, although by no means in possession of a carefully worked out anti-Jewish programme in 1933, were propelled by an ideological single-mindedness, which permitted not a moment's respite from antisemitic activity. Their campaign against German Jewry developed a systematic momentum in accordance with its own internal logic, progressing from the removal of Jews' political rights in Germany to their isolation and expropriation.

It will also be argued that one of the essential elements of Nazi antisemitism, was an inability – of which even the Nazis themselves were initially unaware – to tolerate a limited solution to the 'Jewish problem' they had created, a solution depending on German–Jewish coexistence. No measure of discrimination against the Jews could make such coexistence possible in the long term. The remorseless logic of Nazi radicalism behind this antisemitism led to the murder of Jews even before the war, and after the outbreak of war the most consistent theorist and practitioner of antisemitism in the movement, Adolf Hitler himself, managed to take Nazi Germany's 'Jewish policy' over the last hurdle, beyond which there was only the 'final solution' to the 'Jewish question', and this was nothing less than the extermination of European Jewry.

Part I

Reichskristallnacht

1

November 1938: the 'Night of Broken Glass'

Assassination

At 9.30 on the morning of 7 November 1938, less than six years after Hitler came to power and the beginning of the Nazi persecution of the Jews in Germany, a young man entered the German embassy in Paris. The visitor reported to the receptionist and asked to speak to the ambassador or one of the legation secretaries. He had already asked for the ambassador at the entrance to the building, where he had encountered a man who, although rather casually dressed, was nevertheless strikingly elegant. However, this gentleman, who was none other than Count Welczek, the ambassador himself, had directed the naïve youth to the porter. He was then taken to embassy counsellor vom Rath. As he entered his office he took out a revolver and, without saying a word, fired several shots at the diplomat, who was sitting at his desk. He then allowed himself to be arrested without protest by two embassy assistants, Nagorka and Krüger, and handed over to the French policeman who was posted outside the building.[1]

One bullet had grazed vom Rath's shoulder, and another had penetrated his spleen and injured the stomach wall in two places. He was taken to hospital immediately, and operated on by Professor Baumgartner, a specialist at the Alma clinic. Although the operation went well, the condition of the wounded man remained serious: the possibility of his death could not be discounted, and on the afternoon of 9 November Ernst vom Rath did in fact die.

There has been a great deal of speculation, both at the time and since, about the assassin's motives. Herschel Grünspan was seventeen years old and came from a family of Polish Jews who, despite their Polish citizenship, had lived in Germany since April 1911. Grünspan's father – in Poland, of course, the family name had been spelt Grynszpan – had worked as a self-employed tailor in Hanover since 1918. He had just about survived the depression years from 1929 to 1934 by running a second-hand shop, although he had also occasionally been forced to claim unemployment benefit.

Born on 28 March 1921, Herschel was the sixth child of Sendel and Ryfka Grünspan. In a world which was far removed from that of the Bleichröders, Warburgs and Oppenheims, the depression brought grinding poverty, and even when the economy began to pick up again, the Grünspans, and other families like them, were prevented from escaping the poverty trap by the incipient Nazi persecution of the Jews. Younger and more restless members of such families left Germany altogether. Herschel himself joined the Zionist Misrachi Organization in Hanover. In 1935, after leaving an elementary school he had obviously disliked, he attended a Talmud school in Frankfurt, before going to stay with his uncle Wolff in Brussels in 1936, and moving on from there to his uncle Abraham in Paris. He was unable to find his feet in either Brussels or Paris, and he had no opportunity to emigrate to the United States, Australia or Palestine.

In the Europe of the 1930s, which was still suffering the aftermath of the depression, there were few openings for young German emigrants from the Jewish underclass, especially those without a useful school education or an apprenticeship. Jobs were few and far between, work permits difficult to get, and the lack of money and education made it virtually impossible to emigrate further, to a new life overseas.

So Herschel Grünspan was neither a Nazi *agent provocateur*, as the French communist press immediately claimed, nor a tool of world Jewry in its allegedly unceasing war against all Germans and everything German, as the press and radio in Nazi Germany claimed with equal alacrity. Rather, he had suffered the bitter fate which Hitler's party, the NSDAP, had already visited on the Jews of Germany by September 1938. In Germany the Nazi persecuted the Jews, and their propaganda was relentless in its mockery of everything Jewish, while outside Germany, on the other hand, there was virtually blanket condemnation of Nazi antisemitism, and the reaction of both Jewish and gentile German exiles writing in the press was particularly vehement. All this created an atmosphere in which violent gestures of resistance and terroristic acts of revenge became inevitable. Two and a half years previously, on 4 February 1936, David Frankfurter, a Jewish medical student from Yugoslavia, had shot Wilhelm Gustloff, the director of the Swiss section of the NSDAP Foreign Organization in

Davos. Grünspan, too, felt that his personal misfortune was a direct result of the Nazi persecution of the Jews – and with good reason.

In the last few days before the assassination there had been a rather dramatic deterioration in the already miserable condition of those Jews still living in Germany, among them Herchel's own family. Grünspan had been particularly affected by this development and had become very restless. At the end of October his parents and his two surviving sisters had been deported to the Polish border by the Gestapo, along with 17,000 fellow victims. All the deportees were Jews with Polish citizenship but had lived in Germany for some considerable time. The measure was a Gestapo response to pressure from the German Foreign Office, which in turn had been alarmed by Polish government threats to withdraw the citizenship of Jews in Long-term residence abroad, thereby preventing their return to Poland. The deported Jews were forced to wait at the border, where they vegetated for several days in dreadful conditions, because Poland initially refused to allow them entry, while the German authorities refused to allow them to return home. Grünspan learned of his family's fate on 3 November when he received a postcard in Paris from his sister Beile, written on 31 October. The shock of this news was all the greater since he himself had had no valid German or Polish papers since the beginning of the year, and on 11 August 1938 he had received an expulsion order from the French authorities, dated 8 July, which had come into force on 15 August. For months, then, he had lived illegally in France, always facing the prospect of the same fate which had now actually befallen the rest of his family.

On top of everything else, an angry quarrel broke out between Herschel and his uncle Abraham on 6 November, and he felt obliged to move out. With 320 francs in his pocket he left his uncle's flat and took a room in the Hôtel Sucz on the Boulevard de Strasbourg under the name of Heinrich Halter. Bed and breakfast was 22.50 francs, and he was able to calculate precisely how long his money would last. The next morning he bought a revolver and bullets from a gunsmith called Carpe for 245 francs, and made his way to the German embassy. At least one representative of the hated Nazis, who were responsible for all these disasters, would perish.

The Pogrom Begins

Herschel Grünspan's deed evoked sympathy in some quarters outside Germany, but never approval. It was after all a crime: murder. And after Hitler's attempts to annex Czechoslovakia, which had caused six months of nervous international tensions, what the world needed now was calm.

War between the Third Reich and the Western powers had been avoided only at the last minute, with the Munich agreement of 30 September 1938, i.e. with the surrender of the Sudetenland to Nazi Germany. Above all, the people of Europe were wondering if the Nazi regime would use Grünspan's deed as an excuse for a new offensive against the Jews. On 9 November the London *Times* wrote: 'The 400,000 Jews who still remain in the Third Reich await tonight in fear and anxiety another attack upon their race, which, if the tone of the officially controlled press can be taken as an indication, will exceed in violence and thoroughness any Jewish "purge" of the previous five years.'

Certainly, a number of Nazi leaders, including Joseph Goebbels, Minister for Popular Enlightenment and Propaganda with responsibility for press control, had greeted Grünspan's shots with the same enthusiastic outrage with which they had reacted to the Reichstag fire in 1933, an incident which had made the consolidation of the Nazi dictatorship much easier. They also reacted with the same solemn satisfaction that would characterize their response to Count Stauffenberg's assassination attempt of July 1944, which provided them with the opportunity of liquidating the old German ruling elites.[2] The *Völkischer Beobachter*, the Nazi party's official national newspaper, set the tone with a leading article on the first news of the incident from Paris. It contained the following words:

> Obviously the German people will draw their own conclusions from this latest act. It is an impossible state of affairs that within our borders hundreds of thousands of Jews still control whole shopping streets, frequent places of entertainment, and as 'foreign' landlords rake in money from German tenants, while their racial comrades abroad agitate for a war against Germany and shoot down German officials. There is a clear line from David Frankfurter to Herschel Grünspan . . . The shots fired in the Germany embassy in Paris . . . will mean the beginning of a new attitude to the Jewish question in Germany.

Clearly, such words could not have been printed in such a place without the knowledge and approval of the Propaganda Minister. Although the leading article gave neither the ruling Nazi party nor any agent of the state a veiled order for a pogrom, Goebbels must have been aware that the article and the nationwide press campaign, which was conducted in the same tone throughout Germany, make individual anti-Jewish incidents not just possible or likely, but certain. The words were strong enough to prompt some of the radical minor functionaries of an antisemitic party like the NSDAP (Nazis) to take matters into their own hands, especially since the propaganda line conveyed the impression that party leaders were not against such violence, and would see to it that the incidents were covered up afterwards. The incidents of the evening of 8 November tended to follow the same pattern everywhere: first there would be a meeting in the evening with a rabble-rousing speech by the *Ortsgruppenleiter*, who was generally also the local mayor; after this the synagogue would be set on fire or demolished, Jewish homes and businesses destroyed and plundered, and individual Jews would often be manhandled. Although there is no doubt that local party leaders were the ringleaders, it is equally clear that they never acted on explicit instructions from above. When the incidents were dealt with in court after 1945 none of the accused political leaders claimed to have acted on higher orders. They sought only to defend themselves by arguing that the riots had not been organized at all: they had occurred spontaneously.

Although this was not true in most cases, non-Nazis played no small part in the pogroms of 8 November. It is impossible to tell, of course, how far this participation was a result if latent antisemitic tendencies unleashed by Grünspan's deed, and how much simply due to the pleasure of rioting, and the urge to go on the rampage which occasionally surfaces in such strictly regimented societies. Certainly, in some places the popular response and the activity of Nazi organizations were so inextricably interwined that it is impossible to attribute the initiative to the party. Yet whether pushy local party leaders took the lead, as generally happened, or whether it was one of those rare incidents which can be attributed as much to popular agitation as to party initiative, the spur to action was invariably the press and radio propaganda, i.e. rabble-rousing by senior party leaders.

The situation changed on 9 November. Here and there strangers turned up in villages and small towns, presenting themselves to local party officials and SA leaders, and trying to spur them to action against the Jews. Thus the mayor and *Ortsgruppenleiter* of the village of Schupbach near Limburg told his duty constable that 'somebody' had been there and made trouble because no measures had been taken yet against the local Jews; it was impossible to establish who this 'somebody' was. In other cases outside agitators operated independently of the local Nazi party and its associations, starting pogroms on their own. Such was the case in Münzenberg, near Giessen, where the drivers of a government car from Darmstadt and a car from the local government offices in Friedberg delivered wildly anti-semitic speeches at the local market, inciting the locals to storm the synagogue.

There were still no clear instructions from the senior party leaders. Nevertheless, there was a hardening of attitudes during the course of the day among agitators from the middle and lower ranks of the party, who had been mobilized by the propaganda. They became gradually less

inclined to keep an anxious eye on their superiors as they had done in the
past, in spite of their radicalism. Those already involved endeavoured to
persuade others to join them, and attempted to co-ordinate the hitherto
sporadic activities. In the absence of intervention from above, their
instructions grew sharper and more decisive. On 8 November most of
those summoned to the pogrom had turned up at synagogues and Jewish
businesses as they were, in much the same way as they had turned up at
the rallies beforehand: some in uniform, and some in civilian clothes. On
9 November those wearing uniforms were generally sent home to change
into civilian clothes. Whereas on the previous day there had been a degree
of spontaneity in the proceedings, it was now clear that orders were being
given.

The political leaders – which meant Nazi party officials – now formed
small detachments of party members and stormtroopers, and set themselves clearly defined tasks, whereas on the previous day instructions had
often still been relatively vague. Pressure was put on unreliable party
members who hesitated to join such raiding parties, and they were
exhorted to behave in a manner befitting National Socialists; and occasionally, in some places, such as in Gross-Zimmern, near Darmstadt, the
tone of such warnings was very menacing. While on 8 November there
had still been no discernible differences between the various Nazi associations, clear differences began to emerge on the following day between the
party, the National Socialist Motor Corps (NSKK) and the Hitler Youth
after they had received their common instructions. However, the starting-
point of the individual pogroms was still a rally. And, of course, rallies
were being held everywhere to commemorate the abortive Hitler putsch of
9 November 1923. The sequence 'rally – incitement – orders – pogrom'
was modified in only a very few places, such as Beienheim, near Giessen.
Here there was neither a rally nor the usual rabble-rousing speech, just a
simple command. At first, of course, this happened only in the case of SA
units, where such a procedure was more compatible with the military
nature of the organization.

On both 8 and 9 November disturbances generally occurred only
where the local branch of the Nazi party or the local SA unit had for
some years been led by a radical antisemite. Such functionaries were
obviously the most likely ones to react to Grünspan's deed and the
incitements of the press and raido by staging their own little pogroms. It
was also clear that the anti-Jewish agitation they had practised over a
number of years had not been without influence on their subordinates.
For the stormtroopers on the other hand the timing of the incident on 9
November played an important part, since the day was dedicated to the
memory of the Nazi putsch attempt of 1923 and the 'time of struggle',

i.e. the virtual civil war conditions which had characterized political conflicts before 1933.

The hard, warlike 'spirit of the stormtroopers' of those times was recalled annually in solemn ceremonies which fostered a mood of boastfulness mixed with sentimental nostalgia, an atmosphere redolent with the creation of a new Nazi tradition, and one which thoroughly encouraged the stormtroopers' violent tendencies. The SA had lost a great deal of political clout since 1934, which made it all the easier to arouse in many such party veterans the desire to restore the self-importance and informal camaraderie of the old days. In such a mood many stormtroopers were only too prepared to lash out against the Jewish 'enemy'.

By the evening of 9 November then, without senior or middle-ranking party leaders needing either to act or to assume responsibility, there had been apparently spontaneous pogroms against Jewish citizens in several parts of Germany. In reality, of course, they were not the popular demonstrations they purported to be. Persistent agitation over the years combined with the intensity of the regime's propaganda on 8 and 9 November, and the fortunate timing of the assassination had set the apparatus of the Nazi party and its affiliated organizations in motion without any need for instructions from above. Of course, such spontaneous eruptions of antisemitism were necessarily restricted to individual cases in smaller communities, where local Nazi functionaries had succeeded in gaining influence outside the local party leadership. Above all, it would still have been possible at this point for national leaders to distance themselves or to force the affair to a close.

The Unleashing of the Nationwide Operation

9 November saw the symbolic annual re-enactment of the march on the Munich Feldherrnhalle, dispersed by the police in 1923. Everybody who was anybody in the Third Reich had come to this event in the Bavarian capital, which the regime's masters of ceremony had developed as one of the most important of Nazi demonstrations. Such a gathering of the Nazi leadership was a unique opportunity to further the plan hatched by Joseph Goebbels. The 'old guard' of the Nazi movement met on the evening of 9 November for a reunion in the chamber of the old town hall. Hitler was also present. Shortly after the meal, at around 9 p.m., a messenger arrived and informed the Führer in a whisper that embassy counsellor vom Rath had died from his wounds. Hitler then spoke briefly with Goebbels, who was sitting next to him. His tone was urgent, but he spoke so quietly that not even his immediate neighbours could

follow the content of his conversation. He then returned to his Munich apartment without having addressed the other guests, as had been the custom in previous years.

Shortly after Hitler's departure, at around ten o'clock, Goebbels got up, announced vom Rath's death, and delivered a wild tirade against the Jews, during the course of which he also mentioned that in Kurhessen and Magdeburg-Anhalt there had already been spontaneous popular reprisals, and that further outbreaks of popular anger were to be expected throughout the Reich. As the Führer had decided, such demonstrations were not to be organized by the party, but neither were they to be discouraged if they broke out spontaneously. He described the incidents in such positive terms, formulated the instructions to be passed on to party members with such subtle cleverness, incited such hatred against the Jews, and spoke so passionately of revenge that none of the assembled party leaders and stormtroopers could have been in any doubt as to what was expected of them. The party Supreme Court later submitted a report on the events of 9 and 10 November to Hermann Goering, second-in-command in the Third Reich. It stated unambiguously: 'The clear understanding of the oral instructions given by the Reich Director of Propaganda to all the party leaders present was that although the party should not outwardly appear to be the instigator of the demonstrations, it should in fact organize them and carry them out.'

The rationale of the dress rehearsal of 8 and 9 November was now made clear by Goebbels's speech: the references to the disturbances which had already taken place, combined with his own inflammatory words, served to indicate the desired course of action. If the first demonstrations had been prompted by propaganda, then the same propaganda machine now exploited those original incidents in order to encourage further demonstrations. Goebbels's speech was by no means an impromptu performance, especially as he himself had set in train this interdependent sequence of words and deeds. The speech was obviously part of a carefully worked out plan prompted by the combination of hysteria, brutality and cold calculation which was the essence of Nazism, and which characterized all its activities. Hitler aside, the Reich Director of Propaganda was the most professional tactician to exploit such gut reactions.

Only Hitler himself could have played this part better than Goebbels. At the decisive moment, however, Hitler had delegated responsibility to his propaganda chief. Goebbels neither took the Führer by surprise, nor presented him with a *fait accompli*: Hitler's own involvement is beyond doubt. Even if he had not been given detailed information of the plans for the great pogrom before, he was informed at the latest during the reunion, before Goebbels's speech, and his complicity and responsibility are beyond question. His animated conversation with Goebbels just before the announcement of vom Rath's death can only have been concerned with the planning of the operation.

Around midnight, after leaving the old town hall, and without any further contact with Goebbels, Hitler himself gave instructions to the *Reichsführer* (Reich Leader) of the SS and Chief of the German Police, Heinrich Himmler, which were based on a detailed knowledge of the plan. So he must have discussed the proposed course of action during his conversation with the propaganda chief, made the final decisions then, and confirmed Goebbels as head of the operation. As head of state he himself remained so far in the background that he could not be identified as the originator of the pogrom. In this way he also left open the possibility of making Goebbels a scapegoat, and exposing him to the anger of such paladins as Himmler and Goering, who objected to the pogrom on tactical grounds. The same night Himmler dictated the following: 'I suppose that it is Goebbels's megalomania – something I have long been aware of – and his stupidity which are responsible for his initiating this operation now, in a particularly difficult diplomatic situation.'

Hitler's cautious approach also contributed to the fiction of a 'spontaneous' popular response to Grünspan's assassination of vom Rath. If the pogrom was not to be exposed immediately as an organized party initiative, then there could be no Führer order proving any connection between him and the party's actions, which were meant to create the impression of popular indignation. Certainly, this illusion of spontaneity could only be strengthened if the leader of the movement, with his absolute power of command, had not said a word in public which might have unleashed or encouraged the disturbances. For the party rank and file it was enough to replace such an unambiguous Führer order with the less explicit, less tangible, but equally potent 'wishes of the Führer' which were passed on to the middle and lower ranks.

Goebbels's own speech was a further attempt to reinforce the impression of spontaneity. It contained neither a 'Führer order' nor any other kind of instruction. The speech was more of a rallying call, which sought, by suggestion, to have the same effect as the press campaign of 8 and 9 November. Of course, Goebbels's task was easier in that he was able to address his appeal directly to the assembled party leaders sitting directly before him in Munich, rather than having to appeal indirectly to a faceless mass of officials through the press. It was not difficult for the propaganda chief either to rouse the ideological convictions of the 'old guard' assembled in the chamber of the old town hall, mobilizing them for immediate action against an enemy stereotype, nor for him to appeal to the personal bonds of loyalty between each of these faithful followers and his

'Führer', i.e. to exploit their readiness to fulfil the obvious wishes of the 'Führer'.

After Goebbels had finished speaking, the meeting broke up. The senior party leaders immediately set about giving instructions to their own subordinate organizations in accordance with the speech they had just heard. Yet these instructions varied considerably, both in their explicitness and in the degree of commitment they demanded.

The swiftest reaction was that of the NSDAP itself. The speech by the Reich Director of Propaganda was directly binding on the party, and no intermediary was brought into play. *Gauleiters* and *Gau* propaganda directors dashed to the nearest telephone, called their local offices, and attempted to get hold of somebody there who could set the party machine in motion. The Gau staffs were alerted at 10.30 p.m. It was they who were to pass on the instructions to the *Kreisleiter*, and the *Kreisleiter* in turn who were to instruct local groups. Goebbels was suspicious of relying entirely on the telephone, and besides he wanted to make sure that the influence of his propaganda offices was decisive. So at about 1.40 a.m., following telephone instructions from the party leaders. *Gau* propaganda directors received telegrams directly from Goebbels, in which the gist of his speech was summarized. The propaganda officers could now consider themselves empowered to co-ordinate the actions of the party and its affiliated organizations.

The sequence of events in the SA was rather different. Viktor Lutze, the chief of staff, called together the leaders of SA groups immediately after Goebbels's speech, while they were still in the chamber, and submitted to an urge to instruct the stormtroopers by making a speech of his own, obviously in the hope of following Goebbels's example. Lutze, too, avoided issuing a clear command, and chose instead to give a rallying speech. However, he lacked both the passion and the articulacy of the propaganda chief, and it is also quite possible that basically he was opposed to the planned action – he was neither a fanatic nor a rabble-rouser. Certainly, his call for anti-Jewish activity was mixed with some words of criticism of the excesses which had already taken place, and by the time he had finished he had made a speech which could be interpreted either as an instruction for the stormtroopers to take part in the pogrom or, just as easily, as an instruction to keep out of it. Be that as it may, none of the group leaders made use of the let-out clause which Lutze's speech provided. They drove off to their headquarters at the Hotel Rheinischer Hof, where all of them passed on explicit orders to their local offices. These telephone calls took place between 11 p.m. and midnight. From the local SA group staffs the instructions were then passed on via the brigade leaders to the standard leaders, and so on down to the rank and file stormtroopers.

While the SA leaders were already on their way to the Rheinischer Hof the heads of the SS and the police had still not been informed either of what had already happened, or of what was planned. There had been hardly any representatives of the SS at the reunion meeting in the old town hall, and it is certain that neither Himmler nor other important SS leaders had heard Goebbels's speech. Heydrich, the head of the Security Police and the Security Service of the SS (SD), had been in the Hotel Vier Jahreszeiten at the time. He was informed at about 11.15 p.m. – when the first instructions had already been given by the party and the SA – by the State Police office in Munich, whose duty officer asked what orders Heydrich had for the security police and the Gestapo. Heydrich, visibly surprised, gave no instructions at all at first. He wanted to ascertain Himmler's decision, and to this end he sent off SS *Gruppenführer* Wolff to find him.

Wolff tracked Himmler down at half past eleven, when he was with Hitler at the latter's flat in the Äussere Prinzregentenstrasse. He briefed Himmler, and requested orders both for Heydrich, and for the SS and the police. Himmler then spoke to Hitler, but before he could get in touch again with Heydrich and other senior SS leaders he had to go to the Odeonsplatz and attend the traditional midnight ceremony of the swearing in of SS recruits. At about one o'clock he went back to his hotel, the Vier Jahreszeiten, and there he finally drew up instructions for Heydrich, directing the police to 'act according to the wishes of the propaganda offices'. The overall control of the exercise was in the hands of the *Gau* propaganda offices, and with these instructions Himmler acknowledged the leading role of the Reich Director of Propaganda. Since he disapproved of the operation, however, this would also enable him to hold Goebbels responsible, if necessary. Himmler, as Reich Leader of the SS then informed the regional SS leaders, who were also staying at the Hotel Vier Jahreszeiten, of his instructions to the Gestapo, adding that the SS itself should keep out of the affair entirely, and come to the assistance of the Gestapo only in an emergency. Finally he dictated a memorandum to Wolff's personal assistant, SS *Hauptsturmführer* Schallermeier, in which he presented all this as a result of his conversation with Hitler, thereby giving it the character of a Führer order.

At 1.20 a.m. Heydrich in turn sent a telegram to the regional State Police office, in which he made it clear that the task of the Gestapo, and of the police in general, was the protection of non-Jewish life and property, and that this meant that synagogue fires should be prevented from spreading. He also gave the Gestapo an order for the arrest and removal to concentration camps of as many Jews as it was possible to accommodate: they should be healthy, male and preferably well off. In fact the State Police offices had already received such an order an hour and twenty-five minutes earlier from the Gestapo office in Berlin. The director of the Gestapo office, SS *Standartenführer* Müller, probably warned by the Munich Gestapo, had already been active, but without yet having been in contact with either Himmler or Heydrich, and at 11.55 p.m. he had sent a telegram to regional head offices which anticipated the essence of Heydrich's later instructions. However, it differed in three notable ways: firstly, there was no reference to vom Rath's death; secondly, more precise figures – twenty to thirty thousand – were given for the number of arrests to be made; thirdly, Müller seemed to want to claim overall control of the operation for the Gestapo. Clearly, Müller had simply been following a contingency plan available in the Gestapo office for just such an occasion as this. The plan had to be modified, however, in the light of Heydrich's instructions following the discussion between Hitler and Himmler, and not least in view of the cautious approach adopted by the latter.

Night of Broken Glass

On the evening of 8 November the *Kreisleiter* of Hanau, like other local Nazi party functionaries, had received a secret order from Sprenger, the *Gauleiter* of Hesse, forbidding individual initiatives. As a result, his command area had remained quiet during the night of 9–10 November. However, Sprenger's instructions were superseded by a telephone call from the *Gau* propaganda office in the early hours of the morning of the 10th, ordering merciless reprisals for the death of vom Rath. All Jewish property was to be completely destroyed by means of a pogrom to be staged and directed by the party, but without the party appearing as its instigator. The *Kreisleiter* understood what he had to do and, instead of calling out all party members, he merely summoned to a meeting his subordinate functionaries, along with the local SA, SS and SD leaders. At this meeting he announced the order and allotted the assembled men their tasks.

Then, on the morning of 10 November synagogues and Jewish businesses were damaged in swift, anonymous attacks. Naturally, the commotion attracted a number of curious bystanders, and party officials, who mingled with the ever-growing crowds, cleverly provoking them into a mood of sullen agitation and increasing the intensity of the atmosphere with their loud and increasingly virulent interventions, until it seemed only natural when the stones they had brought with them smashed through the windows of a shop or a synagogue. This broke the spell, the crowds rampaged through synagogues, shops and houses. A destructive frustration had been manipulated and released. The public responded 'spontaneously' to vom Rath's murder, and yet only an hour before they had given little

Destruction of Jewish store, Berlin, November 1938
(Wiener Library, London)

more thought to Grünspan's deed than they would have given to an earthquake in Japan.

By avoiding the deployment of the majority of party members and using the carefully instructed political leaders of the NSDAP and its affiliated organizations, the *Kreisleiter* of Hanau had acted precisely according to Goebbels's conception of the pogrom. Party and SA agitators had instigated and led the demonstrations, spurred people on and directed them towards the desired objectives, serving as the catalysts of the pogrom. They had neither operated in closed formation nor had they pretended to belong to the 'people' themselves. In this way a certain level of popular participation was attained, and the appearance of a 'spontaneous demonstration' had been more or less successfully achieved.

Such a precise implementation of Goebbels's wishes was, of course, a rare exception. Even the *Kreisleiter* of Hanau failed when he tried to apply the pattern which had been used so successfully in the town to the rest of the district. He used a routine policy meeting convened by the district council to inform the local mayors, all of them naturally also Nazi *Ortsgruppenleiter*, of the instructions for the pogrom, and to sketch out the desired sequence of events. However, the *Ortsgruppenleiter* were unequal to the task of following such demanding instructions. Thus, on returning from the meeting, the mayor of Gross-Auheim promptly alerted all the party members he considered reliable, simply gave them their orders, and led them in closed ranks against Jewish houses, making no attempt at all to contrive a 'popular' demonstration or incite riots on the Hanau model. Gross-Hanau was typical of the course of events in villages and small country towns. This is where Goebbels's plan of campaign fell down; his plan proved to be unrealizable in such places, in that it overestimated the intelligence of the lower party officials. While the middle and lower ranks of the Nazi party did not lack brutality, especially in response to orders from above, it was not matched by the necessary dynamism, flair and tactical skill. They succeeded in mobilizing the party, but not in disguising the mobilization or rousing the population. So they deployed their party formations as the 'people', and even when members of the public joined it was already clear that the disturbances had been organized and initiated by the party.

If, as occasionally happened, the party followed Goebbels's example and used a rally rather than a series of explicit commands to issue its instructions, then even party members might remain too inactive. The *Kreisleiter* of Erbach, near Darmstadt, for example, was at a loss what to do about the ambiguous instruction which had come from his superiors at *Gau* level, so at first he did nothing at all. He also failed to react when he heard radio reports of 'popular anger' in other places. Then on the morning of 10 November a civil servant came from the district council office and was surprised at the inactivity of the *Kreisleiter*: after all there had been an order from Berlin forbidding police intervention to prevent acts of violence. After this the *Kreisleiter* could no longer be in any doubt that a nationwide party operation was under way, and that the *Gau* propaganda office was expecting him to participate.

In spite of this he still did nothing: he had, of course, received no orders. Only when he was informed that outside agitators had stirred up trouble in several places in the area did he resolve to undertake his 'official duties'. He sent for his *Ortsgruppenleiter* and made a speech. Vom Rath's murder, he declared, necessitated certain measures, but the party should hold back. The scene in the chamber of Munich's old town hall repeated itself on a smaller scale, but with the difference that Goebbels had known what he wanted, while the District Leader was as uncertain as ever. His speech emphasized neither the call to action nor the appeal for caution. Not unexpectedly, his even-handedness was reflected in the results: the more active *Ortsgruppenleiter* interpreted the speech as an order for a pogrom, and acted accordingly, while the passive ones read it as an order for calm, and did nothing.

The fact that Goebbels and some of his subordinates in the *Gau* staffs did no more than hold rallies was used by some party officials as an opportunity to ignore deliberately the demand for a pogrom, or even to act against the rioters, although they themselves were by no means uncertain of the intentions of the leadership. In Bad Nauheim, for example, there were clashes between rioting stormtroopers in disguise ('Räuberzivil') and uniformed party leaders, who were trying to stop the pogrom. Such attempts could be successful only when the party official trying to prevent the pogrom had sufficient authority to countermand the explicit orders of the *Gau* Propaganda Director or an SA *Standartenführer*. Basically, only a *Gauleiter*, responsible directly to Hitler for what happened in his *Gau*, could prevent the pogrom with any degree of success. *Gauleiter* Kaufmann of Hamburg, for example, strictly forbade the pogrom. Kaufmann had not been in Munich on the evening of 9 November, and had not heard Goebbels' speech, so it was naturally easier for him to dissociate himself from it. Pogroms did take place on Kaufmann's territory, but they had to be started by commando units from neighbouring *Gaue*.

In other places too agitators were sent from neighbouring command areas. For the most part this method served to remind dilatory party functionaries of their duty. Such was the case in Steinheim, where the *Ortsgruppenleiter* sat in his office and did nothing, despite an explicit instruction from the district leadership in Offenbach. He hoped that his superiors would not notice. However, the district leadership was informed of his inactivity, and sent three SA *Standartenführer* from Offenbach to Steinheim. The SA leaders threatened and insulted the *Ortsgruppenleiter*. With the three emissaries from Offenbach looking over his shoulder, he now summoned all the party members and stormtroopers in Steinheim, and delivered an intensely antisemitic speech. To drive home the effect of his words, he not only reminded them of the personal oath they had all sworn to Adolf Hitler, but made them all symbolically take it again. Only one of those present failed to raise his hand for the oath — a non-party member who felt that he was not included. After this the operation took its course to the satisfaction of the SA leaders.

In rare cases agitators were sent in from outside because some resourceful character in the *Gau* staff or district leadership wanted to go one better in disguising the role of the party. In these cases local political leaders were deliberately left without orders or information. Consequently the actions of the outside agitators took them completely by surprise, and it was clear to everyone that local officials had not been involved. If they joined in the pogrom, they they were merely being carried along by their 'justifiable indignation' at the assassination. If they did not join in, or even took steps to oppose the outside activists, then the ploy came fully into its own, and really began to work. For how could the party have organized the pogrom when the local party functionaries were opposing it? Of course, nothing they did stopped the pogrom. By the time the local *Ortsgruppenleiter* intervened, the outside agents had already done their work, and the pogrom was already well under way. And yet this tactic failed in practice, in that the role of agitator always fell to the best motorized sections of the SA, so that the SA did not so much send in undercover agents as shock troops. The sight of thirty to fifty men leaping from one or two lorries to storm a synagogue was unlikely to give the impression of a convincing 'spontaneous demonstration'. Such tactics only made more obvious the complicity of the senior party leaders.

In any case the SA had its own distinctive approach. In the countryside and in small towns, party influence was predominant. In such communities it was the political leaders who represented the Nazi regime and set the tone rather than the leaders of the affiliated organizations. Furthermore the leaders of local SA units were thinly spread over large areas, and were generally of a lower rank than the party functionaries, so that an *Ortsgruppenleiter*, for example often faced only an SA *Truppenleiter*, in other words an officer of junior rank. In addition, the more senior SA officers in the countryside found it difficult to bring together the men under their command quickly. On the whole, therefore, the SA units scattered among the villages were alerted not by their own superiors but by local party leaders, which usually meant that the part they played in the pogrom was within the framework of a party-directed operation.

The situation was quite different in larger towns and cities, where the position of the political leaders was weaker, while the SA, thanks to their tight military organisation, could mobilize very quickly, and bring together larger units much faster than the NSDAP. In the towns the SA retained its autonomy over its own chain of command. This not only meant that the mobilization of the SA and the formation of commando units took place independently of the party, but that once they were in formation the shock troops acted alone and independently, taking not the slightest notice of the instructions or intentions of the *Gau* propaganda offices. The SA fell only too happily back into the habits of the years before 1933.

In the towns there were many SA leaders, now sitting in offices, for whom the 'time of struggle' was still a lively memory and the decline of the SA from the status of the movement's paramilitary wing to that of a veterans' association a source of bitterness. The orders from Munich presented these office-bound hooligans with an unexpected chance to release those energies so firmly suppressed by Hitler with the liquidation of Röhm and numerous other SA leaders in 1934. They seized the opportunity enthusiastically, and turned on the Jews. Their use of language was

correspondingly telling. Instructions and orders were characterized by the callous and euphemistic jargon of the street battles and other illegal activities. Thus the SA donned 'civvies' ('Räuberzivil') as in 1931 or 1932, and talked about 'the night of the long knives'. The police were informed that the SA would be 'going for a stroll this evening'. On the other hand, however, they often did not even bother with such games. The leader of SA Group Nordsee, for example, gave the following order from Munich:

> All Jewish businesses are to be destroyed immediately by stormtroopers in uniform. After their destruction an SA guard is to be posted to ensure that no valuables are removed. The administrative leaders of the SA will safeguard all valuables, including gold. The press is to be invited.
>
> Jewish synagogues are to be burnt immediately, Jewish signs are to be put in safe keeping. The fire brigade is not to be allowed to intervene. Only the homes of Aryan Germans are to be protected by the fire brigade. Adjacent Jewish living accommodation is also to be protected by the fire brigade, but all Jews must be moved out, so that Aryans can be moved in during the next few days.
>
> The police must not intervene. It is the Führer's wish that the police should not intervene.
>
> The identification of Jewish businesses, stores and warehouses is to be conducted in co-operation with the local mayor or lord mayor; the same applies to itinerant trade. All Jews are to be disarmed. In cases of resistance they are to be shot. Signs bearing the following text are to be placed on the businesses, synagogues etc. which have been destroyed:
>
> > Revenge For The Murder Of Vom Rath
> > Death To International Jewry
> > No Compromise With Jew-loving Peoples
>
> This can also be extended to freemasonry.

Such aggressive language, expressed both an ideological hatred of the Jews and a sheer delight in brutality, and was bound to provoke the most radical interpretation of the ambiguously worded instructions. Slogans of hatred, such as 'Death to international Jewry' were succinct and easy to understand, while resistance, and with it the right to shoot, could be taken for granted. The staff leader of SA Group Nordsee later explained to the party Supreme Court that he personally had not composed the sentence in such a way, but had to admit that other SA leaders had understood the message very much in this sense, and had acted on it accordingly. Further communication by telephone served to make the instruction – radical as it already was – all the cruder and more brutal. The following conversation, for example, took place between SA Standard 411 (Wesermünde) and *Sturmphauptführer* K. (mayor of Lesum, and leader of the SA unit there):

'Standard 411 here. *Truppenführer* S. speaking. Have you received any orders yet?'
'No.'
'Major alert throughout Germany. Reprisals for the death of vom Rath. By this evening there are to be no more Jews left in Germany. *Sturmbannführer* R. is to be informed.'

K. repeated the order and then, very surprised by what he had heard, asked: 'What exactly is to happen to the Jews?' S. replied: 'They are to be annihilated.' K. then informed his superior *Sturmbannführer* – a *Sturmbann* corresponded roughly to a battalion – and as both of them found the order from the Standard rather dubious, the *Sturmbannführer* called the group staff headquarters in Bremen: 'I've received a crazy order here. Is it true, anyway?' he asked. The duty officer replied: 'Yes, in Bremen the night of the long knives has already begun. The synagogue is already on fire!' So a combination of antisemitism and nostalgia for the 'time of struggle' had given the instructions a sense beyond that of the original command, and as a consequence three Jews were shot in the course of the operations of the Lesum SA *Sturm*. The party Supreme Court, which later investigated the murders, commented: 'The feeling . . . that night in the Café Wendt, where the witnesses (the staff of Standard 411) were sitting, was that the time for the final solution to the Jewish question had come at last, and that the few hours before morning must not be wasted.' It was also understood that if there was the least resistance, shots might be fired without consideration for the loss of Jewish life. All the leaders taking part understood clearly from the Standard Leader's statement that although there was no written authority the Jews could, and should, be tackled in this way, that this was the intention of the highest authorities, and that they had not expressed themselves more clearly because they did not want to create a difficult legal situation by issuing an explicit order.

The mood of the meeting, which then spread to the entire SA Standard, was so radical that Goebbels's plan failed completely. It did not suit the stormtroopers anyway, as is clear from the opening words of the instructions from SA Group Nordsee, which ordered the destruction of Jewish businesses by 'SA men in uniform'. Even though this particular instruction was not followed anywhere, in that all the group's units wore 'civvies', it nevertheless proves, as does the rest of the order, that the SA were not, and could not be, concerned with the precautions considered necessary by the party leadership. The SA were useless as *agents provocateurs* and were unable either to simulate or to stimulate a 'spontaneous popular reaction'. They mounted a brutal, frontal attack on the appointed enemy, without concerning themselves with the co-operation or approval of the public.

Basically, the SA leaders saw themselves as political soldiers; they liked to think in military terms, and looked on the public as 'civilians', whose role in this exercise was that of camp-followers or marauders. In several cases the stormtroopers forcibly prevented other people from taking part in the pogrom. In Heppenheim, for example, an SA pioneer unit broke into a synagogue, set it on fire, and then turned on Jewish businesses and homes; yet when a section of the population wanted to join in, they were immediately chased away. Under the circumstances, the SA were simply striking poses and indulging in pure farce by turning up in 'civvies'. With this distinctive approach, the SA undermined the impression that Geobeels had wanted to create abroad of a spontaneous demonstration on the part of the German people. Thanks to their enthusiams, energy and organizational superiority, it was the stormtroopers who determined the image of the pogrom in the towns, and it was in the towns that foreign observers lived, whether as guests, as journalists or as diplomats. The stormtroopers' behaviour ensured that none of the organization behind the pogrom was hidden.

Where the party took charge of the pogrom it passed off relatively lightly. Although the political leaders set synagogues on fire and destroyed anything they could find in Jewish businesses or homes, they stopped at Jewish individuals. They were by no means sparing with insults, but only in rare cases did they beat up their victims, or inflict other physical torture. However, where the SA was in charge there was uninhibited brutality. The stormtroopers dragged numerous Jews from their beds, and mercilessly beat them up in their homes; with the tried and tested subtlety of the 'time of struggle', they hounded Jews half to death through the city streets, dragging them out of sanctuaries provided by friends and neighbours. Where the police or Gestapo had beaten them to it, and arrested and imprisoned Jewish men, putting them in prisons which were little more than transit stations on the way to concentration camps, it was quite possible that the SA would break into the prison, force their way into the cells, and indulge in an orgy of violence. In their relentless persecution of everything Jewish, the stormtroopers did not stop at beating up individuals and plundering their property: they also raped and murdered. SA men stabbed, shot or beat their victims to death, and also threw Jews into rivers or canals, where they drowned.

When there were shootings, they did not take place in an attack of blind rage, but by order. A hesitant stormtrooper might even be forced at gunpoint to carry out his superior's orders. In Lesum, for example, an SA *Scharführer* who had been ordered to murder a couple named Goldstein, refused until he himself was threatened with being shot. Then he went into the bedroom where Dr Goldstein and his wife, terrified by the noise and

Mass arrest of Jewish men in Oldenburg 10th November 1938
(Archive Stadt Oldenburg)

disturbance, were already standing by their bed. The *Scharführer*, with pistol in hand, said, 'I have been instructed to carry out a difficult task', but still hesitated. Frau Goldstein replied calmly, 'Please aim well, sir!' and then he fired.

SA leaders who gave orders to shoot believed that they were acting according to the unspoken will of the senior Nazi leadership, and rightly so. To be sure, there were often misunderstandings when lower-ranking SA leaders ordered Jews to be murdered, but all that had been misunderstood was the direct order of their group or brigade leaders, who had not generally intended to mount a murder operation. On the other hand the result accurately reflected the wishes of the director-in-chief in Munich. Goebbels himself provided confirmation of this when, at two o'clock in the morning of 10 November, the murder of a Polish Jew was reported to him, and he was asked to do something to prevent a degeneration to this dangerous level. His response, which the party Supreme Court recorded, was that one should not get so excited about a dead Jew, and that shortly thousands would have to 'come to terms with it'. Those responsible were then first extracted from the normal judicial procedures through the intervention of the Deputy Führer, and subsequently acquitted by the party Supreme Court. No one was ever prosecuted for arson or the demolition of property; it was clear from the outset that these acts had been in accordance with the wishes of the leadership, and that no one could be reproached on any account. Yet those who had beaten and murdered Jews also went free, as long as they had not offended 'discipline' by plundering, or committed a 'racial crime' by raping a Jewish woman. The party Supreme Court justified its leniency with a statement to the effect that the offenders had merely 'correctly interpreted and acted upon the – admittedly rather unclear – wishes of the leadership'.

The result of the combined efforts of the party and the SA was frighteningly impressive: several hundred synagogues were burned down across Germany, and about a hundred were demolished; at least eight thousand Jewish businesses were destroyed, and countless homes were devastated. Heydrich assessed the total material damage in the entire territory of the Reich at several hundred million marks. The psychological torture endured by all Jews was immeasurable, and an incalculable number were badly manhandled and injured. Several hundred perished in Dachau, Buchenwald and Sachsenhausen in the months following the pogrom. The Gestapo had dragged off some 30,000 Jews to these concentration camps.

To this extent Goebbels could be satisfied that one of his objectives had been met. However, his intention to disguise the organization behind the pogrom had not been realized. Both the party and the SA stood too clearly in the foreground. In comparison, the other Nazi organizations played only a small part. The NSKK was frequently not alerted at all, and where it did take part it did so under the command of the SA. The Hitler Youth was generally informed by the local party leadership, and requested by the latter, and sometimes by the SA too, to lead its support. It was employed in Bad Nauheim, for example, to remove Jewish clothes and furnishings from houses and burn them in the street. Occasionally it also served as an auxiliary force for the Gestapo, 'safeguarding' books and documents from synagogues, and taking them to the Gestapo offices. Here and there, of course, where the Hitler Youth had active leaders 'trained in antisemitism' it participated quite enthusiastically in the actual destruction. This was the case in Laubach bei Giessen, for example, and in Königstein (Taunus).

Himmler had ordered the SS not to get involved. Not, of course, because he considered the pogrom an injustice, but because the time did not seem right, and because his bureaucratic sense of order was horrified by the undisciplined behaviour of the SA. He saw the SS as the regime's police, and their task as the discreet exercise of a cold bureaucratic terror. In fact the essential difference between the SA and the SS was simply that the SA was a force to be deployed openly against political enemies in civil war, while the SS served to consolidate the regime's authority after the conquest of state power, and to realize Nazi ideology by 'eradicating pests'.

In any case Himmler's instructions, passed on by the heads of regional offices, were generally implemented. Where the SS did take part in the pogrom it was on the initiative of the local leaders, whose hatred of the Jews was stronger than their discipline. In some cases it was because the party and the SA chain of command had functioned better, and operated more quickly than that of the SS, which in any case had been informed hours later. By the time Himmler's order to hold back was received, the pogrom was often already under way, with the participation of local SS men organised by the *Kreisleiter*. In the few cases where – as in Darmstadt – the SS leaders themselves encouraged their men to attack the Jews, either ignoring Himmler's instructions or believing they were following his true intentions, they too did nothing to disguise the organization behind the pogrom, beyond pointlessly dressing up in 'civvies'. In fact SS men were called up and deployed in much the same way as the SA.

According to the instructions issued by Heydrich and Himmler, the SS were supposed to assist the Gestapo with the arrests which were to accompany the pogrom. Yet even here it did not play an important part. The Gestapo, which actually had too few men for so unexpected and large-scale an operation, generally enlisted the support of men from the SA, the party and the NSKK. Remarkably, while the SS remained in the background even in this exercise, SA and party leaders needed no prompting, and acted on their own initiative. The police and Gestapo needed only to step in later and take charge of those who had been arrested. The leader of SA Group Nordsee who, like the others, had alerted the area under his command shortly before midnight, gave a further order by telephone at two o'clock in the morning to arrest as many Jews as possible and take them to concentration camps.

The part played by other Nazi organizations was even smaller, although *Kreisleiter* and SA *Standartenführer* did appoint local farmers' leaders, Labour Front officials, and – ironically – fire chiefs, if the local party or SA dignitary could not be reached. On the whole, however, there was no spontaneous initiative or co-operation from those sections of the population outside the NSDAP or the SA. Of course, the 'people' did not remain passive everywhere. Both in the country and in the towns there were cases where people followed the example of the party or the SA. Sometimes antisemitism played a part, whether of a Nazi stamp or a more traditional kind; in other cases animosity directed against affluent Jews was class-based, while in yet other cases private and personal grievances were avenged. Sometimes there was a mixture of all these elements.

In the towns in particular, inquisitive bystanders would form a mob and eagerly plunder Jewish homes and businesses. The police did not intervene in such cases: they had been ordered not to intervene in the pogrom itself, and since it was difficult to distinguish between the party operation and the plundering of property they had little opportunity to prevent it. Margraf of Unter den Linden, the famous Berlin jeweller was ransacked, causing 1.7 million Reichsmarks' worth of damage. Goebbels was by no means displeased at such incidents: 'At least the little people of Berlin were able to help themselves to some decent things for a change. You should have seen how they enjoyed it: ladies' furs, carpets, expensive fabrics – and everything was free. The people were so enthusiastic. A great success for the party!' But the NSDAP and the SA had to set the example; without their guiding role as instigators and organizers nobody would have raised a hand anywhere in Germany.

Furthermore, although a minority had followed the Nazis' example in a number of places, the majority had not only refused to join in, but expressed their opposition to the pogram quite unambiguously, and in terms of vocal indignation rather than silent disapproval. In some villages and market towns almost the entire population brusquely opposed attempts by Nazi officials, whether from the locality or from outside, to get the pogrom going. The criticism and indignation also extended to the obvious involvement of the Nazi leadership, and the fact that large-scale criminal violence was now evidently part of the leadership's repertoire of official policy.

Goebbels naturally tried to stick to the story of a 'spontaneous demonstration'. On 12 November he wrote boldly in the *Völkischer Beobachter*: 'It is being said that the spontaneous reactions of the German people were carried out by organized teams. What little idea of Germany these scribblers have! What a reaction there would have been if it had been organized.' But his rhetoric made no impression anywhere. The party Supreme Court confirmed internally that 'The public know to a man that political initiatives such as that of 9 November are organized and carried out by the party, whether it admits it or not. If all the synagogues are burnt down in a single night, there must be some organization behind it, and only the party could have organized it.'

The official version of 'the spontaneous response' of the German people prompted mockery in Berlin, where the black humour of the ironic term *Reichskristallnacht* (usually translated as 'night of broken glass', but literally 'Reich crystal night') alluded directly to the nationwide and uniform character of the antisemitic operation and the complicity of the party leadership. Nor were foreign observers fooled, whether journalists or diplomats. They reported unanimously that incidents had taken place in

Germany for which 'there was scarcely any precedent in any civilized country since the Middle Ages', but they did not attribute responsibility to the people. They all agreed that the Jews in Germany had been the victims of 'an exercise which had obviously been planned and carried out with great precision', and a British diplomat wrote that he had not spoken to a single German who had not sharply criticized the pogrom. The British Consul General in France even went so far as to say that the indignation of the German people was such that if they were free, then 'they would be so carried away by their indignation that wherever possible they would stand those responsible against a wall and shoot them.' Nor was there any doubt, despite the lack of more specific information about the events in Munich on the evening of 9 November, that those responsible were to be found among the leaders of party and state. The London *Times*, which normally adopted a cautious and diplomatic tone, referred to the incident as 'an act of the Reich government'.

Yet it was precisely the Nazi leadership's obvious complicity in such a lapse into the crudest barbarism which made it so difficult for observers, both at home and abroad, to understand either the reasoning or the purpose behind the pogrom. Most of the world's press admitted that, since it had obviously been an act of government policy rather than a spontaneous – and as such perhaps understandable – outbreak of popular feeling, they did not know how to explain it. This was particularly so since the Nazi leadership stuck rigidly to its line that the pogrom had not been organized, and yet at the same time officially declared that the matter would not rest with the pogrom, but that the regime's own revenge for the Paris assassination was yet to come. Indeed, unsettling noises were to be heard from Berlin, and in fact on 10 November the Nazi press had issued a 'strict order to the whole nation to desist from any further demonstrations or antisemitic activities of any kind'.

On 12 November Goebbels confirmed in the *Völkischer Beobachter* that 'the German people has obeyed the government's request willingly and with discipline. Demonstrations and other activities came to a halt within hours.' Even if Goebbels's assertion was not entirely true – it was not so easy to stop the party machine once it had been set in motion, and there were minor disturbances on 11, 12 and even 13 November – the pogrom nevertheless slowly petered out. But on 11 November the *Völkischer Beobachter*, in a report on anti-Jewish activities in Stuttgart, wrote that 'the Jews should certainly be aware that the German people's bitterness at their behaviour is by no means assuaged by broken windows or the smoking ruins of synagogues.'

Goebbels himself wrote on 12 November that 'in this question law and order can be ensured only if the solution fulfils the wishes and requirements

of the German people', and on 13 November he drove his point home in a speech to the volunteers of the *Winterhilfswerk* (Winter Relief Fund) in the Germania Hall in Berlin: 'I am convinced that the German government and the German people are in complete agreement in this matter! The Jewish question will be resolved as soon as possible in accordance with the will of the people. That is what the German people wants, and we merely carry out its will!'

What was behind such words? It was certainly clear from Goebbels's speech that the Nazi leadership itself saw the pogrom merely as a stage, a dress rehearsal for the 'real' solution to the so-called 'Jewish question'. Is such an assessment correct? And if so, in what sense? How can we answer the question put by contemporaries and asked again and again ever since: what were the origins of the *Reichskristallnacht*? What was its significance for the development of the regime's Jewish policy? How – and this is the most urgent question – could a pogrom without precedent in European history take place in Germany? Why did the Nazis persecute the Jews? What was the impetus behind the development of their persecution during the twelve years of the Third Reich, and what were its effects?

Part II

The Persecution of the Jews in the Third Reich

2

Modern Antisemitism in Germany

On 30 January 1933 Hitler was appointed Reich Chancellor: the leader of a radical antisemitic party had became head of the German government. Furthermore, the Nazi movement which now assumed power in Germany was a 'community founded on faith and struggle', and one whose declared antisemitism lay at the very heart of its political programme. The Nazis themselves referred to this program as a *Weltanschauung* (view of the world). They preached a sermon of salvation through a biological racism which, they argued, would save the sick and poisoned German nation, by removing the poison which had entered its arteries and infected it with a disease which would ultimately prove fatal: the Jewish spirit and Jewish blood. The nation would be cured both physically and mentally, would gain enormously in strength, and would enjoy a future of material prosperity, cultural riches and political power – almost a quasi-religious redemption on earth – if it waged a holy war against the Jews living in its midst and dealt out with relentless thoroughness the fate which these most dangerous enemies of Germandom deserved.

The sudden emergence of antisemitism as government policy and state religion in twentieth-century Germany is one of those historical events which, although unpredictable before they occur, seem with hindsight to be the logical and inevitable outcome of a clearly discernible process. Such a contradictory view of the accession to political power of antisemitism in Germany is based on the fact that in no other European state were relations between Jews and non-Jews determined by such contradictory tendencies as in the German Empire founded in 1871 (and in the German parts of Austria-Hungary and its successor states).

Prehistory

The emancipation of western European Jews from the discrimination, isolation and frequent persecution which they had suffered at the hands of pre-industrial Europe's Christian society up to the late eighteenth century was a natural part of the development of the modern constitutional state. The revolutions in England, the United States of America and France saw the triumph of ideas and political principles which ensured that a group of citizens could not for long be denied political and legal equality on the grounds of their ethnic origin. The triumph of humanism, liberalism and parliamentary democracy cleared the decks for a further stage. America and the nation states of western Europe were founded on values so revolutionary and possessed of such creative political force that they eventually became a more significant feature of the national consciousness of those states than factors such as common origins, common history, even a common language.

Nationalism in Britain, France and above all America was characterized more by the expression of political convictions held in common and embodied in the constitution than by expressions of community based on descent or blood ties. It was in states founded on this basis that the newly emancipated Jews were most fully accepted, and this applied not only to Jews who had left the Jewish community and were fully integrated into non-Jewish society, whether Christian or secular, but also to those who continued to live in the Jewish community, so long as they accepted – either by formal acknowledgement or through their behaviour – the social values and political principles which were fundamental to the constitution of the nation in which they lived.

Although antisemitism did not disappear altogether in western Europe or the United States, the residual hostility towards the Jews remained for the most part politically insignificant. In Britain and the United States the arrogance of the established political, economic and cultural elites did make it difficult for Jews, or for that matter Irish and Italian, newcomers, to gain acceptance. Such 'social climbers' might, for instance be refused membership of clubs. However, such attitudes were neither explicitly political nor easy to politicize. Wealth or political power, but above all a combination of both, have generally been sufficient to open such doors.

In France too, since 1789, antisemitism has for the most part been almost a spent force. That is not to say, however, that it is entirely absent, and a virulent and politically ambitious antisemitism has persisted among certain social groups. It is no coincidence that several of the classic racist and antisemitic texts orginated in France, and became best sellers there. In 1853–5 the Comte de Gobineau's *Essai sur l'inégalité des races humaines*

('Essay on the Inequality of Human Races') appeared, arguing that the race question is the key to history, and declaring the 'Aryan' or, more closely defined, the 'Germanic' race the noblest and most creative branch of humanity; in 1886 Edouard Drumont published a two-volume work, *La France juive* ('Jewish France') which described the racial subversion of the French nation by parasitical Jews, and demanded a strict isolation of the Jewish parasites amounting to a reversal of emancipation.

Yet although Drumont's publisher managed to sell 100,000 copies within a year, this sort of antisemitism remained restricted to a minority in France. Indeed, whether antisemitism was espoused by anti-republican monarchists or anti-liberal Catholics, whether it surfaced as an aspect of the doctrine of 'integral nationalism' espoused by Charles Maurras's monarchist and anti-liberal organization, Action Française, or whether it was propagated by the extreme right and, later, fascist movements such as the Parti Populaire Français of Jaques Doriot, French antisemites, vociferous as they were, always found themselves outside the mainstream of the nation.

The majority of the French clung to a revolutionary tradition dating from 1789, which was felt to be central to true French nationalism and the basis of the constitution. And French nationalism not only never opposed humanism and rationality, liberalism and democracy, it remained resolutely committed to these principles, entered, indeed, an indissoluble union with them. The French subordinated nationalism and chauvinism to the principles of liberty, equality and fraternity which became such essential elements of their national identity, and consequently could not then impede the integration of the Jews into the nation – whether as a religious community or as an ethnic minority. Nor could they at any time deprive the Jews of their political and civil rights.

The decisive conflict between French antisemites and the liberal republican majority had already been resolved before the First World War. In October 1894 an officer of the French general staff with a Jewish family background, Captain Alfred Dreyfus, had been arrested on suspicion of spying for Germany, and after an irregular trial had been sentenced to exile for life in Cayenne by a military court whose judgement had clearly been affected by the antisematic prejudices of its members. The conflict which arose after the trial over Dreyfus's guilt or innocence, condemnation or rehabilitation, gripped and divided the entire nation.

On one side were ranged all those whose antisemitism prompted them to believe, or at least to pretend to believe, that Dreyfus was guilty: anti-republican and anti-liberal circles in the army, and, among the Catholic clergy and the bourgeoisie, forces which found organizational expression with the establishment of Action Française in 1898. On the other side were the combined forces of all those demanding justice for

Dreyfus. They interpreted the wrongful judgement, particularly since it was influenced by antisemitism, as a blow to the principle that all French citizens were equal, and as such to the revolutionary tradition itself. On this side were the liberals and republicans of the political middle ground, still clearly dominant among the bourgeoisie, along with more radical middle-class liberals and socialists. From 1898 these forces too had their organizations, with the formation of the 'League for Human Rights' and the 'Bloc Républicain', in which intellectuals and writers like Emile Zola, representatives of the republican petty bourgeoisie such as Georges Clemenceau, and socialists like Jean Jaurès worked together.

After a long and often very bitter civil war in the French press the quarrel was finally resolved by the election of Clemenceau as Prime Minister in 1906, when he defeated the antisemitic and anti-parliamentarian enemies of the Republic, who never recovered. It was not until decades later, when France was militarily defeated in the summer of 1940, and occupied by German troops, that the last fellow-travellers, the ideological descendants of those defeated at the turn of the century, could regain any influence – borrowed influence exercised on borrowed time. Alfred Dreyfus was fully rehabilitated in 1906, decorated with the Cross of the Légion d'Honneur and promoted to the rank of major. It is significant, perhaps, that for Clemenceau and his allies French national pride required not only the moral and legal rehabilitation of a Jew, but his triumphant return to the bosom of the nation as well: following his promotion to the rank of lieutenant colonel, Dreyfus played an honourable part in the First World War.

In eastern and southern Europe on the other hand, where modern constitutional states of the Western type failed to emerge during the eighteenth and nineteenth centuries, the fate of the Jews was characterized not by emancipation and acceptance as members of the nation but by lack of rights, and by isolation, discrimination and sporadic persecution. The political systems of those countries, and particularly Tsarist Russia, even prevented the emancipation of the majority of the Christian population and any political development towards nationhood in the Western sense. Under the prevailing political conditions the national movements of the region were for the most part dominated by a minor gentry with little democratic feeling, and a weak and rather unassertive middle class. Nationalist movements, although prompted by Western examples, developed very differently. They never completely lost sight of the goal of liberalizing and humanizing the political system, but as long as this goal seemed unattainable they instinctively, although not without some guidance from above, directed their force and aggression towards imperialist objectives abroad, and against members of other national groups at home.

Their nationalism degenerated into a mystic glorification of their own community, based on common blood and common ancestry and, almost invariably on the Christian religion as well; and this community operated in a manner which was extremely hostile to minorities.

Nationalism of this kind was characterized not least by a hostility towards the Jews which was bequeathed undiminished to the nineteenth century. An inherited religious antisemitism was compounded with a more modern aggressive nationalism which isolated outsider groups, a nationalism which became a sort of surrogate redemption where religion declined, or reinforced religious sensitivities where they remained alive. Romania was a classic example, and the Romanian government was supported passionately by the politically conscious sections of its own population. At the Congress of Berlin in 1878 Romania rejected outright the demands of the western and central European powers for the introduction of political and legal equality for its Jewish population, and in subsequent years the Romanians employed every form of chicanery imaginable to circumvent such demands despite the threats of the great powers to deny recognition to the new state, which had just gained its independence from Turkey. That the Jews could expect nothing from the national movements of eastern and southern Europe was confirmed repeatedly, not only in Romania, but also in Russia, in Poland, in Slovakia, and in the German parts of the Habsburg monarchy. Although they were gradually able to increase their economic freedoms and extend their political influence, these gains always remained insecure and precarious. Quite how precarious can be measured by the frequency of the extreme antisemitic outbursts which even such modest gains provoked.

It seemed to be the socialist movements of the region which were most serious in their commitment to the social and political ideas of western Europe, and it was for this reason that many Jews placed their hopes in them. Great numbers of Russian, Baltic and Polish Jews were drawn to parties of a Marxist orientation, and often played a prominent role in them – one need think only of Trotsky, Radek or Rosa Luxemburg – not because Jews had a particular affinity to socialism and communism, but because as a disadvantaged minority they were strongly attracted to political doctrines which promised emancipation, even if that promise could not yet be fulfilled.

Many eastern European Jews, however, looked elsewhere for a future with dignity, and right up to the first decade of this century many of them emigrated to Germany; indeed, the states of the German Confederation and, subsequently, the German Empire, were among the preferred destinations of Jewish emigrants.[1] In fact at the beginning of the nineteenth century the German states seemed to offer Jews similar opportunities to the states of western Europe, and this was not just true of the Rhineland, which had been subject to French influence during its occupation by Napoleon, and where the position of the Jews had been improved in accordance with the ideology of the French Revolution. Of course, none of the states which were occupied by Napoleon's armies or subjected to French influence managed to produce a successful popular movement capable of liberalizing and democratizing the political system, and the embryonic German national movement was not remotely strong enough, in the face of opposition from the monarchies and principalities of the old empire, to create a German national state and organize it along liberal lines, granting equality to German Jews and offering them a role in the nation. Everywhere a combination of feudal-corporative, authoritarian and absolutist elements persisted.

This did not mean, however, that the spirit of humanity, the Anglo-Saxon conception of freedom, the French notion of equality, made no impact at all on Germany. Liberal middle-class groups followed Western examples, and writers such as Gotthold Ephraim Lessing – whose play Nathan the Wise (1779) proclaimed the equal validity of Judaism and Christianity – preached a new concept of human dignity with far-reaching implications for the relations of the two communities, and this doctrine was bound to have some influence on both the political climate and the social order. Indeed even the bureaucracies, the organs of the authoritarian states themselves, accepted enough humanism, liberalism and, above all, rationalism to instigate enlightened and progressive reforms reflecting the spirit of the age, and they did so on their own initiative, without pressure from below – often, indeed, in the face of resistance from broad sections of the population.

Their approach to the 'Jewish Question' was similar. Senior civil servants in the states of central Europe began to accept that the Jews, no less than other citizens, should be seen first and foremost as human beings, endowed with the universal human capacity for development, and they argued both on humanitarian grounds, and for the greater good of the state, that the Jews should be released from the ghetto, and should be given normal educational opportunities and the chance to engage freely in economic activity. As early as 1783 Wilhelm Dohm, a Prussian and a Christian, had outlined these basic ideas for the emancipation of the Jews from above in his essay 'On the Improvement of the Jews as Citizens', and in 1812 they were put into practice by Hardenberg, the Prussian State Chancellor, and Wilhelm von Humboldt, one of the greatest German humanists. It was by edict from above, then, that Jews in Prussia attained legal equality, albeit a qualified equality that did not extend to the state service, or beyond the Prussian heartlands. Furthermore, Prussia persisted in its chosen policy, even when most other states in the German Confederation repealed the emancipatory measures imposed by the French, in defiance of the Federal Acts of 1815, which guaranteed the principle of equality for the Jews. The process of emancipation which Prussia had initiated from above could, however, now no longer be checked, no matter how long it took, and no matter how many such damaging reverses it suffered.

In the decades of emancipation (1812–71) the Jews in Germany were able to use the gradual extension of their freedom of movement impressively. In 1820 around 270,000 Jews lived in the territory of the future German Empire, over half of them in Prussia. In those Habsburg territories which belonged to the German Confederation, including Bohemia, there were 85,000. Although a consistently large proportion of the German emigrants to North America were Jewish, their numbers in Germany increased to 512,000 (1.25 per cent of the population). The numbers of Austrian Jews increased at an even faster rate, to 200,000 (1.5 per cent of the population). This corresponded to a no less remarkable change in the social structure from the 1840s onwards. In 1848 around 65 per cent of Jews in Prussia, and 90 per cent in the rest of Germany, were still scraping a living just above the bare minimum, generally as small traders. By 1871 60 per cent of Jews living in Germany had already managed to rise into the middle and upper taxation levels.

To be sure, the non-Jewish population had also benefited from the scientific and technical progress which accompanied Germany's industrialization. Yet it was unmistakably the Jews, restricted for centuries by the Christians around them to financial occupations and various forms of trade, and therefore considerably more mobile, who were particularly well prepared to profit from industrialization, from the extension and increasing interdependence of the markets, from the expansion of trade, from the growth in financial transactions and capital requirements, in short from the spread of the capitalist system, and from the modernization of Germany.

After the founding of the German Empire the pace of industrialization and modernization increased dramatically. Despite various crises and recessions it was to prove unstoppable for decades. Again the Jews were prepared. They streamed in from the countryside to the rapidly expanding cities, seizing with both hands the opportunities in the new industries and service sectors, founding businesses of all kinds, and exploiting the opportunities offered by the expanding banks. Although the Jewish proletariat did not disappear altogether, most working-class Jews were now recent immigrants from eastern Europe. The majority of native Jews rose to join the lower middle classes, but many others went further and entered the prosperous bourgeoisie or even the upper middle class. Some, who had already been well off by the time the process of emancipation was complete, were able to amass huge fortunes in the stormy boom years which followed the founding of the Empire.

A steadily increasing number of Jews took the step from emancipation to assimilation. However, until the last three decades of the nineteenth century this was not – or seldom – combined with a conversion to Christianity. In an increasingly secular society, they often by-passed this stage and went further. Many Jews, once they had left both the physical and the intellectual ghettos they had inhabited, eagerly embraced Germany's cultural heritage, whose classical expression they had found in philosophy, literature and music, and they did so with an expectant curiosity and a spontaneous sympathy, which eventually grew into a deep and abiding love of German culture. German Jews were affected by a deeply felt sense of close inner affinity as they entered the intellectual and musical landscape which had been shaped by Kant, Hegel and the brothers Schlegel, by Lessing, Wieland, Schiller and Goethe, by Haydn, Mozart and Beethoven. The humanism of German culture seemed to promise an additional protection against the threat of malice and persecution, and seemed to indicate that the future could only bring about a further liberalization of Germany.

So quickly did the Jews come to feel at home with Germany's national culture that very soon they were no longer satisfied with affirmation and passive enjoyment, but instead took an active and creative part in the cultural life of the nation themselves. Their diverse contributions enriched German cultural life, and were honoured accordingly by many Germans. Such acknowledgement in turn reinforced the Jews' feelings of belonging to German society, so that even a political career soon no longer seemed to be an affront to the German nation as in the past. The strength of Jewish participation in national political life had its roots in this consciousness of belonging, and this was evident not least in the fact that no specifically Jewish party or grouping emerged to represent sectional interests. Instead the Jews immediately aligned themselves with whichever of Germany's political movements suited their individual persuasions and interests.

Naturally, many Jews were attracted to liberal parties and associations. As a guarantee of the emancipation which had been achieved, and as a vehicle for further assimilation, liberalism corresponded to a Jewish group interest which was still keenly felt, but it also corresponded to the specific professional interests of many Jews: bankers and businessmen for example, or doctors and lawyers. Jews constituted a progressive element, too, in literature and journalism, where they were often associated with those circles campaigning for the further liberalization of the state, or furiously denouncing illiberal conditions. Yet Jewish writers and politicians were by no means only a feature of the liberal or even the socialist and democratic left. The majority of German Jews were drawn to the bourgeois political centre, as was to be expected from their cultural and economic position, and not a few were attracted to the right. Berthold Auerbach's 'Village Tales from the Black Forest', and his novel *Barfüssele* were far removed from the impatient and biting social criticism of Ludwig Börne; Heinrich Heine and Friedrich Julius Stahl, the first great ideologue of German-Prussian conservatism, occupied very different political positions, both from each other and from important National Liberal figures such as Eduard Lasker and Julius Bamberger, not to mention Karl Marx.

With the founding of the Empire this process of intellectual and political assimilation gathered pace and increased in intensity. Completely emancipated, German Jews could only benefit from Germany's modernization, acquiring a standard of living which outstripped that of the rest of the population. They sent a disproportionate number of their sons to senior schools and universities. Since some branches of the public service, including the officer corps of the army and navy, were for a long time reluctant to admit Jews, and since those who were accepted suffered discrimination in their careers, an exceptionally large number of Jewish graduates entered the free professions. The proportion of Jewish doctors and lawyers was well above the proportion of Jews in the population as a whole.

Emancipated and assimilated Jews also played a prominent part in the expansion of the press, literature and the theatre, not only as journalists, writers and playwrights, but also as publishers, directors and managers. In publishing one need think only of Samuel Fischer, in newspaper publishing of Mosse and Ullstein. Similarly many Jews established themselves in universities and research institutes, where they turned above all to the expanding new sciences: medicine, physics and chemistry. Their achievements in these disciplines were entirely disproportionate to the number of Jews in the population – about twenty German scientists from Jewish backgrounds won Nobel prizes, among them such great research scientists as Paul Ehrlich, Heinrich Hertz, Fritz Haber and Max Born. The discoveries of such Jewish geniuses as Albert Einstein and Sigmund Freud changed the consciousness both of their contemporaries and of subsequent generations. The humanities too were enriched by significant contributions from German Jewish scholars, such as the philosophers Hermann Cohen and Edmund Husserl, the philosopher and sociologist Georg Simmel, the literary historians Albert Bielschowsky and Friedrich Gundolf, and the constitutional lawyer Hugo Preuss, who was one of the fathers of the Weimar constitution in 1919.

In view of such material, political and intellectual success it is not surprising that many German Jews looked upon their assimilation into

German society as a definitive acceptance into the German nation. This feeling must have been reinforced by the gradual erosion of the Jewish religious tradition which accompanied assimilation, bringing about as it did the progressive deconstruction of a separate Jewish consciousness still based largely on religion. In the decades after 1871 this did not necessarily mean a formal separation from the Jewish community, or the complete abandonment of Jewish customs; after all, among Christians, too, there were innumerable agnostics, who were statistically registered as Protestants or Catholics, and celebrated church festivals. However, it was clear that many Jews now retained only the loosest of ties to the Jewish faith, and that their identification with a separate Jewish community within the nation was becoming increasingly weak, and the final step into the non-Jewish world was frequently accompanied by conversion – sometimes light-hearted, sometimes exaggerated – to a Christian denomination. This was a step which was taken by many thousands of Jews in imperial Germany. At the same time there was a growth in the number of marriages between German Jews – especially baptized Jews – and Christians, and the extent of such Jewish integration into the German population seemed to indicate that a considerable proportion of the German public, at least, no longer had anything against it.

If the number of Germans belonging to the Jewish religious community remained more or less stable between the 1870s and the first months of the Nazi dictatorship (499,682 or 0.8 per cent of the population in 1933), despite continuing immigration from eastern Europe, this was probably because emigration, mainly to North America, had also continued, and because the statistics of 1933 were incomplete, in that they failed to take account of the Jewish population of territories lost to Germany in 1919 at Versailles: the Saarland, Alsace-Lorraine, parts of Upper Silesia, West Prussia, Posen and the Memel area. A more important reason, however, was the incipient and accelerating process of the dejudaization of German Jewry.

Origins

Nevertheless there were always some Jews whose faith in the future of German Jewry was by no means confident. They reckoned that despite the continuous and apparently unstoppable progress of emancipation and assimilation, hostility to this process was also increasing in certain quarters, and that new antisemitic tendencies were developing which, although difficult to evaluate, needed to be watched closely, and perhaps justified concern and even anxiety on the part of the Jewish community.[2]

From a very early stage the German nationalist movement displayed characteristics more akin to eastern European variants of nationalism than to the original Anglo-Saxon or French models. The bonds between the emergent German national consciousness and the social and political values of the West were damaged in their formative stages, during and directly after the Napoleonic period. This happened in two ways.

Firstly the major German states, by driving the French revolutionary armies back to France, managed not only to retain their feudal and authoritarian political systems, but to reinforce them, albeit by modernizing reforms from above. The ruling elites and the bureaucracies in these states were able to impose illiberal and extremely anti-democratic systems throughout the German Confederation. For decades liberal and democratic nationalists in Germany were deprived of any opportunity for development or organization. The ideas and objectives which had originally characterized German nationalism receded over an increasingly distant and unrealistic horizon, and the frustrated will to fulfil them was focused elsewhere. In the political wilderness, in the miserable and restrictive conditions of the apparently interminable Metternich restoration, a yearning for national unity, greatness, prestige and power arose alongside the dreams of freedom and equality. A considerable potential for aggression was built up. Börne and Heine fled from this heavy, storm-laden atmosphere to Paris, where the latter's bleak prophecies foreshadowed the wild eruptions of Germany's future.

A second and much stronger influence on German national consciousness was the association of the ideas of 1789 with the violence which accompanied them to Germany during the French occupation. Both before and during the rule of Napoleon the French revolutionary armies were always able initially to find sympathizers who felt liberated. Yet the establishment of a French garrison inevitably prompted opposition. In time French rule came to represent a slight to German national pride, and became a heavy burden on the areas under French occupation or control. This was especially so as the occupation came increasingly to be exercised according to military requirements, involving the brutal exploitation of human and material resources. Inevitably, too, the reaction against both the occupation and the political ambitions of the French liberators-turned-oppressors developed into a hatred which gradually came to challenge the values and principles of 1789, distorted as they now were by association with the experience of violent subjugation and the burdens of occupation. Before long the rejection of revolutionary ideas in the states dependent on, or threatened by, France ceased to be restricted to the representatives and supporters of the old regime. Some – though by no means all – spokesmen and interpreters of bourgeois national consciousness began to rebel against

French rule, to condemn everything French, and consequently to consider liberalism, parliamentarianism and democracy to be 'un-German'.

Anticipating a development which was later to be echoed in eastern Europe too, notions of national community based on shared political convictions increasingly gave way, in the writings of such men as Johann Gottlieb Fichte, Ernst Moritz Arndt and Friedrich Ludwig Jahn, to an exaggerated mysticism of community based on ancestral German blood ties. Adherence to shared political principles receded before notions of a superior and exclusively German morality inherent in this ancestral German community. Consequently the most important task of the national movement ceased to be the reform of society, and still less its revolutionary transformation. Instead, nationalists would devote themselves to the restoration and constant practice of virtues such as honesty, loyalty, generosity, bravery and, not least, piety, all of which came to be identified as specifically German characteristics. The consequence of this visionary idealism was that the German national state almost ceased to be regarded as a political phenomenon at all; it was rapidly transformed into a vessel for the embodiment of a social order superior to that of other nations.

It also became immediately clear that the emotional element which had now entered the German national consciousness did indeed mobilize aggressive attitudes, and not only against neighbours of other nationalities. It also led to the discriminatory exclusion of minorities unable to prove that they belonged to the ancestral blood community, or who had lived for centuries in isolation from their Christian-German environment. Fichte had already spoken out vehemently against the emancipation of the Jews in an article of 1793, which was republished in 1844,[3] and 'Turnvater' Jahn's book Deutsches Volkstum ('German Nation) placed the Jews on the same level as the gypsies: German blood and the German spirit were necessarily alien to both groups, and neither was welcome in the German nation. That such writers generally considered themselves to be good Christians – that is, in most cases, good Protestants – by no means diminished their aggressive hostility towards the Jews. On the contrary, in the tradition of Martin Luther and his antisemitic polemics, they believed they had the blessing of religion. Indeed in 1819 Hartwig von Hundt-Radowsky, one of the radical nationalist demagogues of those years, wrote that he considered the 'killing of a Jew to be neither a sin nor a crime'. And in a pamphlet entitled Der Judenspiegel ('Mirror of Jews') he unashamedly demanded the castration of Jewish men, adding that 'the best thing would be to cleanse the land of the vermin.'[4]

Nor were such manifestations of malicious antisemitism restricted to theory. Hundt's Judenspiegel was published in a year when a spate of antisemitic demonstrations and riots took place, above all in Franconia, Hesse, Baden and the Prussian Rhineland provinces. This outburst, which was called the Hepp Hepp movement after an anti-Jewish slogan, was a protest, largely by university graduates and students, against the incipient emancipation of the Jews. Tirades such as those collected by Jakob Friedrich Fries, and published in 1816 under the significant title *Über die Gefährdung des Wohlstands und des Charakters der deutschen durch die Juden* ('On the Dangers to the Prosperity and Character of the Germans from the Jews'), served to inflame the situation. Fries was a National Democrat who taught philosophy and psychology, and exercised considerable ideological influence on the student corporations at German universities. The Hepp Hepp movement also incorporated an outburst of blind rage on the part of the peasantry and the lower middle classes, who were unable to accept the part played by impersonal factors in their personal economic distress during the crises of the years following the Napoleonic wars – crises exacerbated to the point of misery by painful government reforms. Instead they wanted to avenge themselves on more tangible culprits.

Such populist rebellions, whipped up by antisemitism, were ruthlessly put down in all the German states. Indeed, in order to protect the Jews, regular troops were called up and deployed alongside the civilian police forces. Some journalists were briefly imprisoned. One such was Hundt-Radowsky, who later recanted, and in 1828 in a *'Neuer Judenspiegel Apologie der Kinder Israel* ('New *Judenspiegel* Apology to the Children of Israel') published a sort of declaration of honour for the Jews. For the first time a paradox emerged which was to govern relations between antisemites and Jews until the fall of the authoritarian monarchies. On the one hand those sections of the population which had originally favoured emancipation and equality for all citizens suddenly and violently turned against the principle of emancipation and equality for one particular group of citizens, a change of attitude brought about by the frustration of their own aspirations. On the other hand the personal security and civil rights of this persecuted minority were guaranteed by agents of political systems whose ideology was fundamentally opposed to the liberal political ideals of 1789. This was because all political activity outside the state power apparatus seemed dangerous and impermissible to such regimes. By suppressing the German national movement, however, they were responsible for the continued accumulation of aggression towards minorities among German nationalists.

Such paradoxes often give rise to strange and contradictory chimeras. And among the journalists and other writers who formed the courageous advance guard of the liberal and democratic legions, skirmishing with authority, and repeatedly dipping their arrows in the poison of social criticism before firing them at the fortifications of the Metternich system, there were some particularly eager sharpshooters who, like Heinrich Heine, were Jewish or from a Jewish background, and this led many a restoration bureaucrat to wonder seriously whether the new-fangled French ideas, the upheavals they had brought about, and the trouble they had caused to the representatives of order, were not perhaps the result of Jewish machinations, and possibly best explained by the innate wickedness of all Jews.

Conversely, antisemitic National Democrats such as Hundt-Radowsky, pondering in their cells over the forces that had sent them to prison, and brooding over the protection which the hated authoritarian state seemed to afford the Jews (a protection which effectively amounted to *de facto* emancipation), concluded – inevitably, as it seemed to them – that the German Confederation, and the illiberal political order of its member states, was the work of Jews. Prince Clemens Metternich himself was seen in a very concrete sense as the paid agent of Jewish puppet-masters operating behind the scenes. For the first time the figure of 'the' Jew emerged as a sort of diabolical demiurge behind totally contradictory ideas and structures. During the restoration period the 'Jew' behind the revolutionary agitation and the 'Jew' behind the forces of reaction were observed separately, and did not come together as two emanations, operating simultaneously, of a putative 'actual' Jew. Nevertheless, for the first time the stuff of future conspiracy theories was there, and such theories were to play an important part in later antisemitic ideology.

However, the bourgeois movement in Germany was to remain under the influence of west European political ideas for decades to come, its aim the creation of a constitutional state; and throughout that time the majority in the German national movement was prepared to concede equality to German Jews and accept them into the German nation. This was demonstrated in 1848–9, when the Frankfurt Assembly resolved to grant equality to the Jews, and even the severe defeat of the liberal and democratic forces, which brought an end to the revolutionary disturbances of those years, did not entirely dispel this readiness to accept Jews into the nation. The political careers of men such as Bamberger or Lasker would not otherwise have been possible. On the other hand the frustration of the revolutionaries' hopes and the return of more reactionary regimes visibly served to strengthen those factions more interested in the unity and greatness of the nation than in the freedom and equality of its citizens. This led to the growth of a nationalism whose adherents saw the nation primarily as a community of blood ties and virtue, a nationalism which inclined to the delusion of German ethical and moral superiority, and whose approach to neighbouring nations was characterized by the same fundamental and enduring hostility and contempt with which they treated those domestic minorities they considered alien and obstructive.

In the years following the failure of the 1848 revolutions a novel was written whose purpose was to console the defeated German bourgeoisie and offer it moral support, and which unquestionably achieved these aims. It was not chance, however, which prompted Gustav Freytag in *Soll und Haben* ('Debit and Credit') (1855) to preach the moral superiority of bourgeois values rather than insist defiantly on the political demands and rights of the Third Estate. He was merely expressing and promoting prevalent contemporary attitudes.

Furthermore this was a serious work of literature by a serious German writer, which presented for the second time a literary portrait of a Jew. Yet Freytag's Veitel Itzig was very different from Lessing's Nathan.[5] This time an extremely intelligent and successful Jewish businessman and financier was depicted by the author as the worst and most wicked of characters, the antithesis of all German and bourgeois values, and therefore by his very nature an exceptionally dangerous and constant threat to the Germans and to Germanness. *Soll und Haben* was the most successful German novel of the nineteenth century; its consciousness-forming force cannot be over-estimated. Right up to the middle of the twentieth century hundreds of thousands of Germans were unable to hear or think of the word Jew without associations, many of them characteristics with which Gustav Freytag endowed Veitel Itzig (the name itself is a masterpiece of propaganda): repellent ugliness, slimy ambition, blood-sucking avarice and megalomania, and finally unscrupulous and destructive use of power once it is achieved. This literary depiction must have been contradicted a thousand times over by reality, yet no matter how often the facts revealed the fiction's deceit, Freytag's message always reasserted itself. And this message was not dissimilar to that of Jakob Friedrich Fries's pamphlet of 1816: the emancipation of the Jews is an insane and illogical threat to the nation.

Development

After the founding of the German Empire this message appealed to the nation with both greater force and greater effect. In 1873 the Berne publishing house Rudolf Costenoble published a work with the alarming title *Der Sieg des Judentums über das Germanentum vom nichtkonfessionellen Standpunkt aus betrachtet* ('Jewry's Victory over Germandom, Seen from the Non-confessional Point of View'). The author was a journalist called Wilhelm Marr. Marr was the first of those anti-Jewish agitators who in the years that followed were to use the hitherto unknown word 'antisemitism'. By 1879, when his essay went into its twelfth impression, Marr had founded his *Antisemitische Hefte* ('Antisemitic Journal'), whose sole purpose was to spread anti-Jewish feeling, and in the same year he founded an 'Anti-Semitic League'.

The previous year, 1878, had seen the birth of the Christian Social Workers' Party, whose clerical founder, court chaplain Adolf Stoecker, sought to win the workers of the ever-growing industrial factories for the state and the existing social order, and hoped to achieve his aim through evangelical Christianity, through a range of social and political reforms and through an initially rather less explicit antisemitism. Stoecker had no effect on the Social Democratic workers, but noticed that his antisemitic remarks had something of an impact on lower middle-class audiences; he accordingly changed the name of his party to Christian Social Party, and in 1879 presented an openly antisemitic manifesto. Although its contents were not particularly radical, it nevertheless demanded the first practical measures against Jewish emancipation, such as restrictions on the professional activity of judges and lawyers.

A little later, in August 1880, Bernhard Förster, a grammar school teacher, and Max Liebermann von Sonnenberg, a junior officer, circulated an antisemitic petition to be presented to the Prussian Diet, demanding the virtual prohibition of all immigration from eastern Europe, and the imposition of binding restrictions on the admission of Jews to certain branches of the state service. By the time this petition, which called for an end to the constitutional equality of German Jews, was presented to Reich Chancellor Bismarck in April 1881 its authors, with the help of several organizations whose sole purpose was to campaign against the Jews, had collected 225,000 signatures, of which no fewer than 4,000 were those of university students.

This striking increase in anti-Jewish activity, and the support it found, is frequently attributed to the economic crisis which Germany suffered during those years. The boom which followed the Prussian-German victory over France and the founding of the Empire was followed by a slump in 1873. The crash which brought the hectic boom and feverish speculation of the Gründerjahre to an end rapidly developed from an economic hangover into a serious and prolonged crisis and, as always in times of economic hardship, there was an increasing tendency to attribute the cause of distress to simplistic explanations and scapegoats, and in particular to blame the Jews for everything since, after all, they played such a prominent and highly visible role in banking. Yet on the whole the economy continued to grow, and certain individuals and groups, who now proved to be particularly susceptible to antisemitic slogans, such as sections of the university-educated middle classes and members of the old Prussian-German ruling class seem to have misunderstood the nature of the economic crisis; Count Herbert von Bismarck, son of the chancellor (now raised to the rank of Prince), promoted an aggressive and political antisemitism which differed dangerously from the contempt for the Jews which his father himself had never quite managed to forget in his dealings with 'his' banker, Gerson von Bleichröder. Only a few years later, in 1890, the young emperor Wilhelm II, also discovered the connections which allegedly existed between the Jews and other enemies of the Reich, such as the Jesuits.[6] The wave of antisemitism probably had more important causes, which had nothing to do with economic developments.

The decisive factor was a further change in the character of the German national movement, and in the very nature of German nationalism, a change which arose from the founding of the Empire, the effects of which were threefold. The victory over France, unification, and finally the intoxicating discovery of the inhabitants of the smaller German states that they were now the citizens of the greatest economic, military and political power on the Continent – all of this was a great boost to national self-confidence, and stoked up national pride to a glowing red heat. Yet this intensification of national pride betokened a further shift away from the original character of European nationalism, and its objectives of liberal and democratic social reform, and this time it was a decisive shift.

German nationalism as a bourgeois reform movement had in any case suffered many years of frustration; increasingly, it had concentrated its energies on the attainment of national unity, a goal it had been incapable of achieving alone. Now, by presenting national unity – albeit only within the framework of a 'little Germany' – as primarily the result of Prussian policy and Prussian weaponry, Bismarck actually managed to force German nationalism into a peace settlement with the combined forces of feudalism and authoritarianism, forces which continued to set the domestic political agenda in Prussia, as in the other German states. A considerable number of liberals expressed resolute, and even enthusiastic support for these illiberal political systems, particularly since the new situation opened up splendid opportunities for business, and since Bismarck himself was prepared to appease their consciences with a few domestic political concessions. The rest of the liberals surrendered to a mood of resignation, continuing with their critical rhetoric, but accepting that the party of progress and freethinking had become too small for practical activity.

The bourgeois national movement had been politically domesticated and at the same time had become much more nationalistic, developments which could only encourage its already quite marked tendency to define the nation primarily in terms of an 'ancestral blood community', whose value lay in the essential excellence of its racial stock. This was a tendency which came to dominate the movement, and which was reflected in the symptomatic attempts of several writers to assert an unbroken connection between the present 'little' German Empire and the long-gone triumphs and tragedies of the Germanic tribes before and during the migrations of the Dark Ages. They promoted the notion that for centuries the Germans had been custodians of a mystical 'Germanness', a quality of the highest and noblest order.

More portentous than the content of this literature was the enormous success which the work of such writers achieved. One need only mention the sixteen-volume epic novel *Die Ahnen* ('Ancestors'), for example, which Gustav Freytag wrote during the 1870s, while he was still very much impressed by the campaign in France and the founding of the Empire, or Felix Dahn's *Ein Kampf um Rom* ('Struggle for Rome'), which appeared in 1876. The reading public was all the more susceptible to such ideas when the authors were respected historians and university lecturers, who lent the stamp of scholarly authority to the mystical nationalism which they had packaged so neatly as exciting dramatic narrative.

Suddenly, then, the warrior kings of the Ostrogoths became the subject of a contemporary literature which was deliberately agitational. Literary distortions of warriors such as Totila and Teja, or Gustav Freytag's Prince Ingo, their careers distorted by 'poetic licence', were readily accepted by countless numbers of the new Germany's citizens as the personification of manliness and the embodiment of specifically German virtues. Middle-class grammar school boys were particularly enthusiastic and saw such figures as shining examples. Clearly the founding of the empire had fundamentally changed the order and scale of German middle-class values. However important other conditions and factors may have been, the unity of the nation and the new German Empire were indisputably the result of victorious war. The prestige and political influence of the military increased accordingly, of course, but the consequences extended much further. By winning glory in France, and dying by the hundred on battlefields such as Saint-Privat, the sons of the Prussian-German nobility not only came to dominate the officer corps of the victorious regiments; their success helped to extinguish for the foreseeable future middle-class aspirations for domestic political reform, and the bourgeoisie was convinced of the superiority and exemplary character of feudal values. Respect for the efficiency and uprightness of the middle classes, for their productive achievements and commercial spirit, virtues which Gustav Freytag had opposed to aristocratic values several years earlier, did not, of course, disappear overnight, but they came to be eclipsed by an ethic which was essentially feudal, and a code of honour which derived from the values of a military elite.

Very quickly the middle classes came to accept that a young man's position in German society, and even his entitlement to be fully accepted as a member of the nation was no longer dependent on honesty and prosperity, professional achievement and economic success alone, but depended much more on his acceptance by, and participation in, the world of this warrior caste. 'The triumph of militarism' is an inexact and inadequate description of these changes in attitudes, of the immense social importance of the institution of reserve officer, of the vital significance for the individual of the words 'Leutnant d. R.' (Lieutenant of the Reserve) on his visiting card. it is scarcely an exaggeration to say that the middle classes of the Empire, whether manufacturers, lawyers or university lecturers, considered their normal, and in material terms often very fortunate, position as unsatisfactory, and not infrequently looked on such success with a slight feeling of contempt; they felt themselves called to nobler deeds, to a harder and more warlike existence; or at least they felt obliged to feel some such vocation. The position of the reserve officer in Wilhelmine Germany marks the subjection of bourgeois values to those of the aristocracy and the military, a domestic victory which was won in France.

Yet on the other hand it was the efficiency and entrepreneurialism of the German middle classes which promoted the further industrialization and modernization of the German Empire. A pre-industrial political system, slightly modified but nevertheless still largely based on feudal and authoritarian principles was reasserting and stabilizing itself in a nation undergoing a rapid process of industrialization, urbanization and civilization. An aristocratic elite whose economic base was agrarian and whose political position was dependent on its military service managed not only to preserve its feudal values but also to impose them on the middle classes.

Countless Germans, therefore, reacted to modernization with deep misgivings, even with anxiety. The basis of the nation's material prosperity stood in stark opposition to its citizens' social values, contradicting all their aspirations; the social structures and political models which Germans were convinced were the greatest guarantee of the nation's 'socio-biological health', and which reflected their highest moral principles, seemed to be in mortal danger. This state of affairs bred a deep-rooted antagonism to industrialization, and the enemies of industrialism and its consequences were by no means content to remain passive. Cultural critiques of modernity and progress, based on the myth of a romantically idealized past and inspired by pastoral idylls, unleashed the hope of a comprehensive counter-revolution, which would reverse the process of industrialization, or at least limit and isolate it. This was a time of backward-looking social utopias, and of demands for the restitution of social relations which removed the threat to Germany's pre-industrial political system and secured the feudal virtues of its military elite, causes which must be taken up by the entire nation. And there were many who were prepared to take up this struggle, to work for the realization of such utopias, with every confidence that the nation still had enough time and energy to carry through such a comprehensive counter-revolution. After all, industrialization was by no means complete, and the countryside especially was still an unshaken bastion of pre-industrial social structures and mentalities.

There is no doubt that countless middle-class Germans, despite the enormous profits and advantages they derived from Germany's industrialization and modernization, accepted an anti-modern ideology and adopted its attitudes, all the more readily because they themselves felt threatened by the consequences of modernization, and above all by the material, social and political aspirations of the burgeoning working class. Although the Empire's political system and dominant ideology excluded the bourgeoisie from equal participation in state power they seemed at least to offer protection against the dangers of socialism and the political organizations of the workers' movement, and this led many middle-class Germans to seek psychological and political security in a radical conservatism, and in dreams of the restoration of a past Gold Age.

However, those committed to an anti-modern counter-revolution and to the restoration of a pre-industrial social structure and value system did not direct their attack against any particular rival political or economic system, least of all against a political party, but against the industrial centres and proliferating cities themselves; it was here that the biological, psychological, moral and political sickness was diagnosed, the source of the poison which had infected the whole nation and brought about its decline. Distinctions between the politically desirable and the politically undesirable were not determined by notions of right and wrong, or justice and injustice, but between health and sickness. A further typical feature of this ideology was the 'recognition' that the only way to get rid of these infectious sores and restore a healthier social order, i.e. agrarian society of villages and small towns, was by successfully winning more space for the nation. In view of the increase in population – widely perceived as 'overpopulation' – more territory was needed for the planned decontamination of the cities.

The intensification of nationalism, the domestication of the bourgeois national movement, which was now bound to an emergent völkisch ideology based on notions of an 'ancestral blood community', the dominance of feudal values, the formulation and dissemination of anti-modern representations of society, the increasing use of biological terminology to describe the socio-political order, the emergence of a claustrophobic awareness of the German nation's lack of space: all of these developments combined to dwarf the other consequences of the founding of the Empire, and to increase the aggressiveness of German nationalism and the German nation. With few domestic political objectives left, German nationalists looked for new fields of activity and new enemies, and these were not always to be found outside Germany.

There was expansionism too, of course, and it took the form of a hectic imperialism which regarded overseas colonies as indispensable and, without any noticeable economic gain, collected such colonies in Africa, in the Pacific and along the coast of China from the 1880s onwards. Germany persistently strove for a 'place in the sun' and 'international standing', and was soon to pour monstrous sums of money into the construction of a militarily useless, economically damaging and politically dangerous war fleet, whose purpose was to symoblize the country's colonial policy and world power ambitions. Finally, potential objects of annexation were selected in Europe itself in preparation for the possible collapse of Austria-Hungary. Yet this aggressive nationalism was also directed with equal vehemence and hysteria against domestic minorities within the state: against the citizens of Alsace-Lorraine, against Poles, 'ultramontane' Catholics and socialist *'Reichsfeinde'* (enemies of the Reich), but above all, and with utter relentlessness, against the Jews.

German nationalism had finally degenerated into a *völkisch* blood mysticism at the moment of its greatest success, and its adherents saw German Jewry as a foreign body which was assimilable at best only with difficulty, and at worst not at all; too small a measure of assimilation provoked imperious and peremptory demands for the Jews to integrate into the German nation immediately, accompanied by threats that they would otherwise be excluded altogether, lose their citizenship, and possibly even be expelled from the state. Yet a greater measure of assimilation only served to prompt nationalists to ask whether the Jews were at all capable of laying aside Jewish feeling, thinking and behaviour, and becoming truly 'German', and the answer 'no' was basically taken for granted. Growing numbers of the middle classes, their political aspirations tamed and their fear of the dangers of socialism sharpened, interpreted the natural tendency of Jews to become involved in political movements with a commitment to emancipation as clear proof of the immutably 'un-German' nature of Jewry, whether they joined the rump of the established liberal and democratic movement or the new socialist movement. The success of many Jews in bourgeois and capitalist professions inevitably prompted the same conclusion; achievement in such fields was now deemed essentially foreign and alien to the nation's feudal values.

An even greater danger to the Jews arose from the domination of German nationalism by anti-modern socio-political models which idealized the social relations of the past as biologically 'healthy'. Increasing numbers of the adherents of this reactionary social utopianism became convinced that the Jews were not just participants or beneficiaries of Germany's industrialization and modernization, but that they had actually initiated the process and continued to control it. There was often an overwhelming temptation to locate the origins of industrialization and the responsibility for its consequences among an identifiable group of individuals, who could then be accused, arrested and charged, rather than to look for objective causes, and this was often overwhelming. Since 'modernity' was increasingly rejected as a poison which brought decay and sickness, its 'discoverers' became creatures who could no longer be regarded as human in the eyes of their anti-modern antagonists; instead they were seen as agents of disease and putrefaction or, in short, in terminology borrowed from modern medicine, as bacilli.

Wilhelmine Germany's most influential historian, a veritable teacher of the nation both as university professor and historiographer, was to become the most eloquent apostle of this new antisemitism, and a symbolic figurehead for the movement. Heinrich von Treitschke regarded German nationalism and the creation of the German nation state as the crowning achievement of the historical process, and could not have been more satisfied with the results of Prussian policy and military prowess in 1871. In his *Deutsche Geschichte im neunzehnten Jahruhundert* 'German History in the Nineteenth Century'), which appeared in several volumes between 1879 and 1894, he recounted the course of political events in Germany in forceful, rousing language as a ballad with a happy ending, and with the same force of persuasion he accorded the emergent Empire the status of a divine creation. Although he was a Saxon, and a liberal of many years standing, Treitschke felt so much gratitude to Prussia for her achievements in the service of national unification that he was quickly able to get over the loss of liberalism to the German national movement in Prussia and make himself at home in the illiberal imperial order without further ado. There can be no doubt: shaking off his liberal beginnings, Treitschke's ardently triumphalist and increasingly aggressive nationalism, which demanded not so much unity as uniformity, could no longer tolerate the Jews as a separate and apparently alien social group. This new attitude is evident countless times in his *German History*, where he presents himself as livng proof that bourgeois nationalism can only be perverted when a bourgeois national movement allows itself to be distracted from its original task of constitutional, social and political reform.

Treitschke, of course, probably did not really see himself as a resolute opponent of Jewish emancipation and assimilation by any means. On the contrary, when he coined the slogan 'The Jews are our misfortune!' in his essay 'Our Views', published, under his own editorship in the November 1879 issue of *Preussische Jahrbücher* ('Prussian Yearbook'), he added 'What we have to demand of our Jewish fellow citizens is simple: they should become Germans, they should quite simply feel German.' Yet despite such an apparently honest invitation to the Jews to join the German nation, Treitschke's attitude was inevitably bound to lead to increased hostility towards them.

It was of relatively minor importance that his imperious demand for assimilation was issued with an impatience which it was impossible to satisfy. With the best will in the world German Jews were unable to shed all evidence of their background and traditions overnight, and simply disappear without trace into their non-Jewish environment. Similarly his assumption 'that many powerful groups of Jews simply lack the good will to become German',[7] was also of secondary importance. Even his thinly veiled demand that the Jews should stay out of sight as much as possible in Germany – rather than draw attention to their achievements as bankers and businessmen, journalists, writers and scientists – was not the most dangerous element in his thinking, although the absurd combination of his insistence that the Jews assimilate, while at the same time forgoing all practical routes to assimilation, unquestionably betrayed a forceful tendency to deny them the possibility of assimilation, and even to withdraw the emancipation of the Jews itself.

For there was a further nuance to Treitschke's antisemitism which was even more threatening. He attributed to Jewish influence all the negative consequences of Germany's industrialization and economic modernization, and not least the negative effects on the nation's intellectual and spirital life of a 'materialism' which was at best uncreative, at worst destructive, and which he characterized almost as a Jewish onslaught on the German mind. By effectively declaring all the contemporary phenomena he considered offensive, damaging, dangerous or diseased to be the product of an infinitely expanding Jewish influence, Heinrich von Treitschke equated Jewish activities – which he thought should be resisted – with an irresistible process; he identified the essentially ineradicable consequences of modernity with a Jewishness which he insisted should be rooted out. In the face of such vicious reasoning the Jews could do nothing to win respect. With seemingly irrefutable logic Treitschke had proved that the Jews and the Jewish mind could not but be enemies of the Germans and of Germanness for the foreseeable future. In other words, if sentiments along the lines of Treitschke's doctrines were to find wider acceptance, then the argument which had determined the attempts of the Prussian bureaucracy to introduce and implement Jewish emancipation over the previous decades, i.e. that the Jews were capable of change and improvement, would be completely undermined.

An antisemitism began to develop which did not reject the traditional hostility of feudal Christianity towards the Jews but combined it with nationalism and anti-modernism, new elements from a secularized age, which threatened to undermine any possibility for the Jews of leading a normal life in Germany; neither baptism nor ennoblement was an adequate defence. There were three virtually insurmountable barriers which this anti-semitism placed around the German nation, and these were tellingly defined by Theodor Mommsen, the great historian of classical Rome, when in 1880 he mockingly responded to Treitschke's article of the previous year: 'and soon we shall have reached the stage where the only citizen entitled to full rights will be one who, firstly, can trace his ancestry directly back to one of the three sons of Mannus; secondly, believes in the gospel precisely as it is explained by the pastor; and, thirdly, can demonstrate experience of ploughing and sowing.'[8] In his unambiguous condemnation of his colleague's arguments, Mommsen affirmed with horror that Treitschke's antisemitism came from someone to whom 'of all their writers the German nation' owed 'the most gratitude in their recent great crises', and to whom they would therefore listen. Furthermore, by adopting them himself Treitschke had made respectable the whole rag-bag of anti-Jewish reproaches and prejudices. Mommsen concluded that the antisemitic movement had been 'de-stigmatized'.[9]

Mommsen's assessment was correct: the brand of antisemitism which Treitschke's authority had helped to make respectable was unmistakably different from that which he had formulated; those who profited from Treitschke's intervention were the more radical antisemites who expressed themselves in a much more dramatic way. Anyone who had been infected by Treitschke's antisemitism could no longer recoil in dismay, when a respected oriental scholar and cultural philosopher such as Paul de Lagarde described the Jews as 'carriers of decay' and wrote in 1887:

> One would need a heart of stone not to pity the poor Germans, who have been bled dry, and to hate the Jews, which amounts to the same thing; to hate and despise those who – for humanitarian reasons! – defend the Jews, or are too cowardly to crush the vermin. It is impossible to do deals with trichinae and bacilli, nor can they be educated, only destroyed as quickly and thoroughly as possible.

Lagarde added: 'Where such a concentration of decay has accumulated as in Europe's Jewry, medicine can succeed only where a surgical incision has first removed the source of infection.'[10]

Such words were, of course, ambiguous. This was not necessarily a demand for the physical extermination of the Jews. Yet such remarks promoted the gradual emergence of a climate of opinion in which antisemitic violence, in the form of a carefully planned social policy rather than pogroms, could make such a possibility first of all thinkable, and then increasingly a familiar subject for discussion. At the very least the language of such important and influential scholars influenced broad sections of the population, by suggesting that the Jews and Jewishness could not be changed, and that they somehow existed at a level beneath that of true human beings; since an unbridgeable gulf separated the Germans and the Jews, the Germans should seriously apply themselves to the task of reversing Jewish emancipation and assimilation.

Although Paul Lagarde claimed that he was not an unconditional opponent of Jewish assimilation, his essay of 1887 could be read as nothing other than a rallying-call to those forces in Germany opposed to assimilation. The title itself, *Juden und Indogermanen* ('Jews and Indo-Europeans'), was further evidence that in another respect too, he had gone a little way further than Treitschke. Against the Jews, characterized now not so much as a religious group or ethnic minority but as a 'race' engaged in negative activity on a global scale, Lagarde opposed a positive force comprising not merely the Germans but the whole family of Indo-European peoples, defined in equally racialist terms. Thus he had raised the antisemitic struggle from the national to the international level, and at the same time had managed, with his pseudo-biological racism, to contribute substantially to the secularization and modernization of religious and *völkisch* antisemitism, although he himself denied that he subscribed to primitive biological notions of race, and thereby to racial determination.

Racial Manichaeanism

Other antisemitic prophets were more consistent. As he put it in the title of a pamphlet published in 1873, Wilhelm Marr interpreted the relationship between Jews and Germans from 'a non-confessional point of view', and popularized the view that it was time to dispense with the idea that the Jews in Germany were a religious minority; instead it must be more widely acknowledged that with the Jews one was dealing with a race immutably alien and irredemably subversive. And of course if antisemitism was to have a political future it needed to make a resolute break with the religious antisemitic stereotypes of the past.

In an era of blind faith in the natural sciences and the secularization of thought, even political ideologies and theories, whether related to identifiable interests or inspired by chimeras, had little chance of social acceptance if they were not presented as the result of serious scientific research. It is conceivable that even *völkisch* antisemitism, let alone the Christian variety, would have lost prestige, had it not adopted the position that antisemitism was the inevitable result of 'racial science', with a scholarly basis combining elements of anthropology and biology to solve all the puzzles of history. This position was not consciously adopted in order to prevent loss of prestige and make antisemitic agitation easier. Marr and similar apostles of antisemitism were true believers. They were, of course, certainly capable of the useful lie in questions of detail: without really believing in them, they spread the gruesome stories of cruel ritual murder recounted by the Austrian theologian August Rohling in his 1871 book *Der Talmudjude* ('The Talmud Jew').[11] But they were not interested in the cynical use of scholarship to disguise their message as science; they were simply accommodating their thinking quite instinctively to the requirements of the age in which they lived.

In 1881, eight years after Wilhelm Marr's pamphlet, the Berlin philospher and economist Eugen Dühring, published a book which completed the pseudo-scientific basis of antisemitism, providing the movement with the full armoury of a scholarly theory. Under the title *Die Judenfrage als Racen-, Sitten- und Culturfrage. Mit einer Weltgeschichtlichen Antwort* ('The Jewish Question as a Question of Race, Custom and Culture. A World Political Response'),[12] Dühring argued that the feelings, thinking and behaviour of human beings were racially determined, and that each existing race must be regarded as a natural, immutable given. 'Here, too, a scientific approach is appropriate.'[13] At the bottom end of the scale of human races were the uncreative, culturally quite worthless, and uninhibitedly selfish Jews, 'one of the lowest and least successful of nature's creations', scarcely human.[14] Eternal parasites, for millennia the Jews had been waging 'a war of oppression and exploitation' against humanity; they were indeed the enemies of all nations, but above all the enemies of the German nation, and of Germany.[15]

The only promise of salvation was tireless and merciless struggle, above all struggle against assimilation and emancipation: since the Jewish question was a question of race, baptism could alter nothing of the Jew's character or nature, and do nothing to change the fact that he was rooted in a dangerously hostile race. Baptism served only to facilitate the Jews' parasitical scrounging: 'It is the baptized Jew in particular who is able, unhindered, to make the farthest inroads into society and politics.'[16] If Dühring considered intolerable the 'infiltration of the nooks and crannies of our national life by racial Jews', and the 'spread of Jewish characteristics' incompatible 'with our best instincts',[17] and if the thought of marriage between Germans and Jews pained him, he was merely giving expression to a hysterical fear that sexual contact between Jews and non-Jews would lead to the contamination of the non-Jewish partner. The classic formulation of this thesis was to be found in Artur Dinter's unusually successful novel *Die Sünde wider das Blut* ('Sin against Blood'), published in 1918, in which a German woman lost for ever her ability to bear German children through her very brief relationship with a Jew.

All later theorists of this racial antisemitism, which was to eclipse all other antisemitic doctrines, faithfully adhered to Dühring's original general framework, which was imitated by Otto Böckel, the first antisemite elected to the Reichstag without Conservative Party support, whose *Die Juden – Könige unserer Zeit* ('The Jews – Kings of our Age'), appeared in 1901. The same is true of Julius Langbehn, a cultural historian who was extraordinarily successful in educated circles, in the relevant passages of his *Rembrandt als Erzieher* ('Rembrandt as Educator'), and *Der Rembrandt-deutsche* ('The Rembrandt German'), published in 1890 and 1892 respectively, and of Theodor Fritsch, who founded the successful leading antisemitic publishing house, Hammer Verlag, in 1887, and reiterated variations on Dühring's theme in his 'Antisemitic Catechism', published in the year the firm was established, and reprinted forty times as a 'manual of the Jewish Question'.

Although by the First World War the antisemitism of Eugen Dühring, who survived the war and died in 1921 at the age of eighty-eight, had not remained unchanged, there was no addition of new elements, still less a radicalization. After all it was difficult to formulate theories more radical than those of Dühring. What Dühring's companions, disciples and imitators undertook was much more a work of clarification. So where Dühring had concentrated on describing the inferior, repellent and dangerous nature of the Jews, other authors placed equal emphasis on a self-indulgent celebration of the status and creative abilities of the Indo-Europeans who were to be found at the top of the ladder of human races, and for whom the term 'Aryans' rapidly became common.

The philologist Friedrich Max Müller had used the word 'Aryan', derived from Sanskrit, simply to denote a linguistic group comprising several European peoples, including the English and the Germans, as he explained in lectures, delivered in England between 1859 and 1861. On the basis of the results of his linguistic research, Müller argued that these peoples were very closely related, and that the original homeland of their common ancestors had probably been in India.[18] The term now suddenly became a mystical designation for the noblest race, indeed for the only one which was truly human. Although the question of who was to be included among the aristocrats of this racial hierarchy elicited differing responses, the apostles of racism were agreed that in Europe the Teutons counted among the Aryans, or even comprised the Aryan race, and that although the German nation somehow managed to remain the most important Teutonic race, Teutons were more Teutonic, their blood purer, the further north they had settled, and the term 'Nordic race' was used with increasing frequency. So it was clear from the outset that not only the Germans counted as Teutons (and therefore as Aryans), but also the Scandinavians, the English, the Dutch, and the Flemings, and every possible synonym was used in journalism and propaganda to describe this category.

The treatment of other western European, and above all southern and eastern European peoples, on the other hand, receded into the twilight of great uncertainty, or simply fluctuated according to the demands of political expediency. And it was just such opportunism that characterized the sort of calculated political stategy which emerged after the First World War, and which prompted Hitler, the most important interpreter of racism at the time, to write that fortunately Russia would easily fall prey to the necessary German invasion because the Russian Bolsheviks had exterminated the Russian nobility, and thereby eliminated the 'Teutonic' element in Russian society.

There was a flexible, tactical approach to the use of terminology, and occasionally the whole racist ideology was quite cynically subordinated to the demands of politics and propaganda, as was the case with Stoecker's decision to shift the emphasis of his programme, but this was by no means an indication of weakness of conviction. All racist writers and journalists believed sincerely and unshakeably in 'Aryan' superiority; if they declared the 'Aryan' race to be the most creative, and very soon the only creative human race, they were simply confirming, in their opinion, nothing more than biological fact, proved by anthropology and history. On the one hand the Jews and their culture, once they were demonstrated to be inferior and dangerous to the rest of humanity, were inevitably subjected to a process of dehumanization, ultimately becoming a combination of demon and vermin; but once the rest of humanity had been devalued to the status of raw material for their cultural and political creativity, Aryans and Aryan culture too were just as inevitably dehumanized, in a process culminating in deification.

The war between the race which personified absolute good, and that which personified absolute evil was, in such a perspective, naturally and inevitably a basic fact of life – in fact the decisive condition of human existence; it was a war which had raged since the beginning of time, the noise of its battles determined the moment, and it would soon have to be resolved – by an Aryan victory, naturally. The introduction of pseudo-scholarship into antisemitism led, then, to a racial Manichaeanism, which served as a key to the interpretation and explanation of all previous history, furnishing a weapon to understand and overcome the political and cultural crises of the present, and promising, a sort of redemption on earth in the form of the imminent victory over the opposing race. This manichaeistic edifice had even less to do with scholarship or science than any of its component parts.

It was not only pamphleteers and sectarian preachers who presented such abstruse racism to the public, but writers and artists who could count themselves among the intellectual leaders of the German bourgeoisie, as was the case with nationalist antisemites such as Heinrich von Treitschke. There were others, of course, such as the Austrian Adolf Lanz, a former Cistercian monk. After knighting himself Jörg Lanz von Liebenfels, Lanz publicized the doctrine he called 'theozoology' in an obscure journal called *Ostara*, where he glorified 'Aryan heroes' who were incessantly called to do battle with Jewish dragons in a way which could only strike even a half-educated German as little more than comical;[19] or Alfred Schuler, a bohemian intellectual living in Munich who, with financial support from Gustav Freytag's son, was able to make an impression on particularly exalted minds in the inns of Swabia and in the villas of upper middle-class Munich families, where he preached his cult of Teutonic blood after the turn of the century.[20] But the same racist gospel was presented in other ways: it was more ambitiously literary, more obsequiously aesthetic, less primitive in thought and argumentation, and clothed itself in a sophisticated and mystical philosophy of culture. If the apostle of the antisemitic gospel embellished the doctrine with a few truths or half-truths, and diluted it with a few observations or considerations which were open to discussion; if, furthermore, he had successfully established a reputation in a quite different field, he could make countless converts with his contributions to the spread of racism and antisemitism.

Julius Langbehn was not the only one who worked in this way; there were many others, above all the Bayreuth circle around Richard Wagner. The master himself instilled the Teutonic cult in the hearts of countless Germans with the material and with the intellectual and ideological message of almost all his operas, and even to a certain extent with the music itself; and he did so as effectively as an exceptionally successful television series would have done in later times. Nor did he shrink from investing the more scurrilous side of racism with his full authority as the most popular German composer of the time, in antisemitic pamphlets, in many of the articles in his *Bayreuther Blätter* ('Bayreuth Journal'), and in countless letters and conversational remarks.[21]

There was also Wagner's son-in-law, Houston Stewart Chamberlain, the sickly and nervous offspring of an English officer's family who was probably prompted by his constitution not only to settle in Germany and learn the German language, but also to make himself at home with his father-in-law's Teutonic mythology and hero-worship. In 1899 he published *The Foundations of the Twentieth Century*, his *magnum opus*, in which he discussed and propagated racial Manichaeanism with such linguistic dexterity, such plausible argumentation and wit, that the book was soon to be found on the shelves of most literate Germans. Finally, Ludwig Schemann, an old friend and ideological soul mate of Richard Wagner, made a special contribution. German antisemitism had so far developed effectively uninfluenced by the Comt de Gobineau's *Essai sur l'inégalité des races humaines*, and Schemann made good this deficiency. In January 1894 he founded a Gobineau Association, and between 1898 and 1901 he published his German translation of the French classic of racism. Apart from anything else, the French count was a much better writer than the German prophets of antisemitism, and his adoption (alongside Dühring) as one of its high priests could only serve to raise the prestige of such pseudo-scholarship.

In the decades between the founding of the German Empire and the outbreak of the First World War the imperialist policies of several European states had led to an enormous expansion of European colonial rule in Asia and Africa. The notion that there were considerable, and possible innate, differences of ability between the different races, and that that these differences, i.e. the superior qualities of the white race, could be politically useful, had become a received idea among Europeans. However, the increasing tendency in Germany to use racist ideas in domestic politics, and against a minority like the Jews, was encouraged rather more strongly by something else.

Deference to science, so characteristic of the times, had encouraged the growth of the conviction that it was both possible and necessary to use the 'exact' natural sciences in particular to discover the natural fundamental laws of human society, and then to orientate the political order of society and international relations according to these revealed laws rather than ideas and ideals. One product of such attitudes was the development of a racist antisemitism based on pseudo-scientific premises. Charles Darwin's dissertation on the origin of species (published in 1859) had completed its triumphant victory over European thought, and the necessarily more specialized question arose: could the Darwinian doctrines of the 'struggle for existence', and the 'survival of the fittest', of 'natural selection' and the gradual development of all living species be applied to the correct organization of human relations, and how?

Scholars such as Wilhelm Schallmeyer and Ludwig Woltmann responded positively to this question, which was popularized by events such as the essay competition organised by Krupp in 1900. A scientifically approved biologization of political thought naturally boosted racism, and with it racial antisemitism.[22] A direct and indissoluble link was forged between 'Social Darwinism' and racism by the notion that the logical conclusion of Darwin's theses was that human beings were capable of, and therefore committed to, the improvement of their own kind through controlled breeding. The adherents of such theories of eugenics argued that a nation's most important political task was on the one hand to eliminate all that was racially weak, sick or harmful from the body of the nation, and on the other other hand to cultivate all that was racially strong, healthy and useful, and to encourage such elements to multiply.

In this way the nation would become constantly more refined, more powerful and more capable of undertaking the naturally determined 'struggle for survival' in its relations with other nations. Racial antisemitism, for so long obsessed with the one-sided weeding out and eradication of inferior and dangerous Jewish elements, acquired with the adoption of Social Darwinist eugenic utopias a more active programme of racial hygiene aimed at refining the species, a programme which gave it a veneer of scholarship and a little more respectability. The haste with which the racial antisemites grasped Social Darwinist solutions raised the suspicion that they were transparently dissatisfied with the racial constitution of the Germans. Strapping Teutons with blond hair, blue eyes and noble, finely chiselled features, reflecting the aristocratic vigour of legendary Gothic or Norman patriarchs, were few and far between in Germany.

In his critique of Treitschke, Theodor Mommsen had cited with pleasurable agreement an author who had written that 'la race prussienne' was 'a mass which had been formed from degenerate slaves and all manner of other human refuse'. So every honest 'Aryan' had to admit that the improvement of the nation through eugenics was nothing more than the bitterest necessity.

Although the Social Darwinist programme of eugenics was clearly a long-term mission, a catalogue of necessary measures could be commenced immediately. Schallmeyer, for example, demanded the strict control of marriage in the interests of racial hygiene, with some marriages prohibited and compulsory quarantine and sterilization for all those considered mentally or physically 'inferior'. Other Social Darwinists called for a stringent examination of the right of new-born children to live.[23] The approach to the question of how to wage the struggle against the Jews was precisely the opposite. On the one hand, it seemed that the danger was immense, and that the swiftest possible action was necessary. Wilhelm Marr had already spoken of the 'victory of the Jews over Germandom', and prophesied the 'world dominion of semitism'. In the title of a pamphlet published in 1890 Hermann Ahlwardt referred to the struggle of the Aryan nations against the Jews as a 'desperate fight',[24] and no pamphlet written by a racial antisemite was without its alarming description of the Jewish conspiracy to attain world dominion, and in particular to subjugate the Germans.

Hermann Goedsche, a conservative journalist, who wrote successful historical-political thrillers under the pseudonym Sir John Retcliffe, described with spine-chilling clarity in his 1868 novel *Biarritz*, how in nocturnal congresses in the Jewish cemetery at Prague the innermost circle of Jewish leaders prepared its sinister attacks on the gentile nations. On the other hand the programmatic declarations of the racial antisemites were for the most part surprisingly vague. Of course it was agreed that the Jewish immigration from eastern Europe, massively exaggerated by Treitschke, must be stopped. In addition, writers like Marr, Fritsch, Langbehn or the orientalist Adolf Wahrmund in his book *Das Gesetz des Nomadentums und die heutige Herrschaft der Juden* ('Nomad Law and the Present Rule of the Jews'), published in 1887, were in no doubt that assimilation must be reversed and emancipation repealed. Nor did they doubt that such measures as these, along with the introduction of a rigid immigration law, which would completely isolate the Jews again, could only be the first steps, which would have to be followed by further measures. What these additional measures were to be, however, was generally left unclear. What was meant by the 'removal of the Jews'? What did Houston Stewart Chamberlain mean when he spoke of the 'elimination' of the 'Jewish infection'?

Some, of course, abandoned such reticence altogether and, when they talked about the 'solution' to the 'Jewish question' (manufactured by themselves), they unashamedly betrayed tendencies inherent in racial antisemitism. Hermann Ahlwardt, for example, who, like Böckel, sometimes sat in the Reichstag, referred to the Jews during a parliamentary debate of 1895 first as 'predators' and then as 'cholera bacilli', and recommended that they should be treated in the way the British administration in India treated the murderous sect known as the 'thugs', i.e. he literally said they should be 'exterminated'; while claiming he would not wish to go as far as the antisemites in the Austrian parliament, who wanted to put a price on Jews' heads, and have the property of a Jewish 'manslaughter' victim pass to his killer, he made it clear in which direction his thoughts were moving.[25]

Three years previously, in 1892, Karl Paasch had written in the Danzig *Antisemiten Spiegel* ('Antisemitic Mirror') that the simplest and most practical solution to the Jewish question would undoubtedly be to kill the Jews; since he doubted that this would be possible in Germany, he had proposed as the next best solution that they should be deported to New Guinea.[26] In fact given that modern racial antisemitism tended from its outset towards expulsion or murder, the murder of the Jews presented the more logical conclusion. This was not only because expulsion implied merely a geographical deferment of the problem, which might even lead to an increase of Jewish influence in other countries, but because the *Weltanschauung* of antisemitism and manichaeistic racism found the mere physical existence of representatives of the enemy race in itself threatening and intolerable, no matter where they were. By its very nature, modern antisemitism could not be satisfied with any limited solution to the 'Jewish question'. Eugen Dühring had already said as much, and with with unmistakable clarity.

Dühring argued that the suppression of all Jewish influence, and the repeal of the emancipation was necessary but insufficient – merely an intermediate stage; he considered the creation of a Jewish state in Palestine as a potentially dangerous strengthening of Jewry, and he even rejected the expulsion of the Jews to the most distant parts, where they might form the seeds of numerous new 'Jewish questions'. 'As soon as this race is truly recognized for what it is', he argued, 'one sets oneself the next goal, which will not be attained without the use of more forceful means.' A 'more energetic future generation' would come to the indisputable conclusion that 'Jewish influence can be removed . . . only with the removal of the Jews themselves.'[27] The young Theodor Herzl was deeply impressed when he read Dühring's essay, shortly after it was published; it was then that his transformation into a Zionist began.

In the decades before the First World War German Jewry found itself in a peculiar situation with no clear indication of the future. A considerable number of non-Jewish Germans tolerated and even welcomed the emancipation, while others characterized the Jews as the originators of national decay, and consequently disputed their right to membership of the nation. They were also indignant at the progress of Jewish assimilation, which provoked them into preparation for battle, since they could interpret increasing assimilation only as the progressive destruction of the nation's body and equate it with an increase in the power of the Jews.

In the meantime antisemitic parties, along with Adolf Stoecker's Christian Socialist Party, were able to achieve real victories at the regional and local level. This was true of the Soziale Reichspartei (Social Reich party), founded by Ernst Henrici in 1880, the same year in which he helped to get the Antisemitic Petition off the ground; and there were successes too for the Antisemitische Volkspartei (Antisemitic People's party), which Otto Böckel organized in time for the Reichstag elections of 1890. For a time (1893) sixteen deputies sat in the Reichstag who had been elected on a purely antisemitic programme. Similar organizations in Austria were even more effective, such as the German National Union (1882), and the Pan-German League (1901) of Georg Ritter von Schönerer, who seasoned his Greater German nationalism, and his 'Germanic' anti-Catholicism with a poisonous racial antisemitism, which by his own admission he had lifted directly from Dühring; Karl Lueger's Christian Social Party became a mass party on the strength of antisemitic propaganda which made its leader mayor of Vienna in 1897 – against the embittered opposition of the emperor – a position which Lueger did not relinquish until 1910.

Such movements, like some of their forerunners in the early years of the nineteenth century, were not without a streak of populism. Since the process of industrialization had had a particularly alienating effect on artisans and other lower middle-class groups and they were hostile to the inroads of capitalism, they were particularly fertile ground for the mixture of racism and anti-modernism preached by the apostles of racial antisemitism, and the interests and attitudes of such supporters gave the antisemitic parties and associations a specifically petty-bourgeois colouring. Of course, the economic and social aspects of the programme never achieved equal prominence with the antisemitism which – with the exception of Lueger's Christian Social Party – remained central and dominated such organizations.

Nevertheless antisemitism proved to be a promiscuous ideology, capable of gaining a foothold in virtually every political faction and virtually every economic interest without losing an iota of force or independence in the process. Finally the anti-modernism which gave rise to antisemitism, and which accepted antisemitism as the solution to every ill, was to be found in the end in almost all political camps. Strong antisemitic tendencies, with a Catholic angle, emerged in aristocratic and bourgeosis circles within the Centre Party, and among nationalist liberals, but above all among conservatives, who preserved the extremely anti-modern outlook of the Prussian-German ruling class in its purest form.

In fact the only social and political organizations in the entire German Empire which remained practically free of antisemitism were those of the working class. There had been a left-wing antisemitism in the very early days of the socialist movement, of which the most prominent example was the harsh critique of Jewish involvement in finance formulated by Karl Marx in 1844. In the Journal *Deutsch-Französische Jahrbücher*

('Franco-German Yearbook') he reviewed two pieces by the Young Hegelian Bruno Bauer under the heading 'On the Jewish Question', one of them Bauer's book *The Jewish Question* (1843), which had also been an expression of this left-wing antisemitism. But since then such elements had disappeared from the socialists' programmes and propaganda. However, the fact that the German labour movement kept antisemitism at arm's length was of little practical significance for the Jews. After all, German socialists themselves were still fighting for acceptance as members of the German nation, and not infrequently from a position of semi-legality.

A more reliable protection for German Jewry was the fact that power in Wilhelmine Germany was not invested in the political parties at all, but in the monarch and the princes, in governments appointed by these rulers, and in a bureaucracy which was at the disposal of the cabinet it served. Parties were effectively restricted to the representation of business interests or lobbying. Their ideological models and more ambitious political conceptions could be put into practice only if the holders of power permitted it in order to preserve the system, to stabilize the domestic 'balance of power', to appease one party or the other. Concessions to antisemitism and antisemites were unlikely to be granted for any of these reasons. Quite the opposite: here was an all-embracing ideological framework which appeared as suspicious to the rulers of the system as socialism itself, especially since it was often accompanied by lower middle-class protests against the establishment. To compromise with it would unleash the most unpleasant political forces in the state, as Bismarck disdainfully commented in connection with Stoecker's activities.

Besides, although the agencies of the state never openly and decisively opposed antisemitism – if one overlooks Bismarck's temporary participation in international pressure on Romania – and thereby repeatedly caused highly placed Jews such as Bleichröder to doubt their resolve, they nevertheless unquestionably felt a duty to protect Jews, and not only because they believed – as Bismarck once put it – that the usefulness of the Jews was on the whole rather greater than the danger they presented. The civil servants of the German Empire continued to personify that enlightened absolutist spirit, combining rationalism and humanism, which had led them to initiate Jewish emancipation, and guided them through its implementation. It was above all this spirit that provided German Jews with a safe refuge. Their progressive assimilation had so strikingly proved the correctness of the fundamental assumptions of emancipation policy. The peculiar path of German liberalism had given rise to a paradoxical situation: if the profoundly illiberal antisemites wanted to achieve political power of any kind, they needed the collapse of the authoritarian state and the transfer of power to political parties within a liberal democratic parliamentary system.

From Eugen Dühring to Adolf Hitler

Certainly, there was no doubt that a powerful and growing group of antisemites was prepared for such a change. The fundamental paralysis which determined the domestic politics of Wilhelmine society could not conceal this fact. It condemned those parties with antisemitic programmes to disappear after flourishing for a short time, because a political party which concentrated too much on ideology and too little on the representation of economic interests was unable to survive in this system. But the disappearance of an antisemitic party did not mean the disappearance of its supporters and their ideology as well. The short-lived German Reform Party of 1881 survived in the shape of reform associations which spread across the whole of Germany, increasing in number from fifty-two in 1885 to 136 in 1890; in Westphalia they came under the decisive ideological influence of Dühring, while in Leipzig, for example, they were dominated by Theodor Fritsch, and in Hesse by Otto Böckel.

Furthermore, in the last decades before the First World War it became clear that, in view of the obstacles that existed, the movement against the emancipation and assimilation of German Jews was seeking ways and means of putting its antisemitism into practice independently of the legislative and executive activities of the state. One solution which was always available was the practice of social 'apartheid'. More and more organizations which were not party political, and sometimes not even political at all, adopted articles in their constitutions excluding Jews from membership. By the outbreak of war virtually all the important student associations, such as the *Burschenschaften*, had an 'Aryan clause', as did such diverse groups as the Farmers' League and the German National *Handlungsgehilfenverband* (Association of Commercial Assistants); the same was true of the Austrian-German gymnastics clubs, which had become involved in antisemitic politics much earlier than the German Gymnastics Association.

The development of the Pan-German League in particular was very significant in this respect. It was here that the intense nationalism of the Wilhelmine bourgeoisie found its characteristic expression.[28] Founded in 1891 to promote the German Empire's colonial policy, the League quickly developed from its overseas imperialism an ideology based on the particular racial superiority of the Germans, and directed against other European nations as well as ethnic minorities at home. Alongside a policy of conquest on the European continent it developed a framework of references for a domestic policy of persecution: terms such as *Herrenvolk* (master race), *Lebensraum* (living space) and *Volksfremde* (aliens in the nation) were invented by the Pan-Germans. With some hesitation at first, and voicing only the demand for the closing of German borders against further Jewish immigration from eastern Europe, the League soon fell under the influence of radical racial antisemites, who asserted themselves once and for all in 1908, when one of their number, Heinrich Class, a lawyer, took over the leadership, which he retained until the dissolution of the League in 1939.

As Class himself put it, he had been deeply moved at the time by Treitschke's slogan 'The Jews are our misfortune', and this had led him to become involved in political agitation. He regarded Paul de Lagarde, the Comte de Gobineau and Houston Stewart Chamberlain as his other three intellectual mentors. After taking over as president of the League, he immediately introduced an 'Aryan clause', and gave his personal friend, Ludwig Schemann, Gobineau's translator, every opportunity to use the League for the dissemination of racial antisemitism. In fact for Schemann this was an exceptional opportunity: in the decade following the turn of the century the League had between 20,000 and 30,000 members, of whom between 20 and 30 per cent were teachers in elementary schools, grammar schools and universities, and could be used to multiply the effects of Schemann's agitation. Equally, Class himself ensured that a racially tinged interpretation of history was disseminated among people outside the League. Under the pseudonym Einhart he published a 'German History' in 1909 which enjoyed considerable success.

A few years later Class published a political pamphlet under the name Daniel Frymann, which attracted great attention and was reprinted five times before the beginning of the war.[29] What was remarkable was less the central and extraordinarily well defined Pan-German thesis with its arguments based on imperialist ideology and notions of 'living space', and the idea of a relentless struggle against the internal enemies of the nation founded on racial antisemitism, but much rather Class's justification for the conquest of this necessary 'living space': it would provide a solution to the 'social question'. In this way the leader of a political pressure group with no workers among its own ranks, had not only assumed the task of integrating the socialist working class into the nation, but at the same time had appealed to citizens both within and outsie the League to assist this integration, and thereby stem the ever-rising 'left-wing tide', without having to make any material, sociopolitical or ideological concessions to the socialist movement.

Such a comforting message attracted a great deal of attention at a time when the Social Democratic Party of Germany (Sozialdemokratische Partei Deutschlands SPD) – recently emerged from underground, where it had been driven by Bismarck's Socialist Laws – was making massive gains in every Reichstag election, and when the threat of a socialist coup had appeared on the horizon. On the other hand Class criticized the Reich government for timidity in both its foreign and domestic policy, which had resulted in a pernicious quietism.

In order to overcome the immobility within the political system, and to make possible, finally, an imperialist and racist politics in accordance with the Pan-German programme, Germany must be swiftly transformed into a nationalist dictatorship. Class, who presided over a bourgeois association, betrayed here an impatience with the Establishment, an impatience brought about only in small part by the increasingly dangerous 'social question'. An important indication of this was that the heady brew of nationalist imperialism and racial antisemitism, which had for some time simmered in the vats of associations like the Pan-German League, was now beginning to rattle against the lid of the authoritarian state itself. Class had given his pamphlet the significant title 'If I were the Kaiser'. Although he sought for himself neither the role of emperor, nor that of dictator, his critique excluded nothing and nobody. The movement which he represented was so frustrated that it was obviously both fully prepared and quite capable, if necessary, to create the conditions necessary for the implementation of its programme by mounting an attack on the existing order.

A growing middle-class awareness of the existence of a 'working class problem' which must somehow be overcome, and an increasing bourgeois impatience with the paralysis of Wilhelmine Germany: both these phenomena surfaced in other quarters as well. The latter emerged in the Colonial Society and above all in the German Navy League, founded in 1898. Launched and supported by the navy and patrons from heavy industry to popularize and finance the building of a huge battle fleet, the Navy League's exuberantly nationalist and imperialist propaganda roused emotions and raised expectations within its own ranks, which it was impossible for official government policy to meet or fulfil. So a discontent grew among the adherents of a middle-class mass movement which had found an organizational framework in the Navy League, and at some point this mood would rebound on the creators and sponsors of the movement.

At the same time, however, as the Pan-German League and the Navy League approached the first peaks of their activity, a German-Austrian party was founded, which contained both the social and imperialist elements and at the same time a critique of the system. The German

Workers' Party (*Deutsche Arbeiterpartei*, DAP), founded in Trautenau in 1904, was consciously conceived as an instrument to win the socialist working class for nationalism, and to integrate the workers into the nation. On the other hand the party's policy sought reform of the authoritarian monarchy and the capitalist economic system, and was not without the odd revolutionary element. The legitimate material and political aspirations of the workers should be satisfied, thus providing the indispensable pre-conditions for their membership of the national community. At the same time, however, the basis must be laid for a forceful nationalistic politics directed against both the external and the internal enemies of the nation.[30]

The German Workers' Party, which organized throughout German-speaking Austria, but was concentrated in Bohemia and Moravia, was predestined for just such a pro-worker outlook and just such a revolt against the Establishment. It accepted refugees and leftovers from the predominantly middle-class Schönerer movement, but had other, equally important roots in the German workers' associations emerging in Bohemia and Moravia as a result of the nationality conflict between Germans and Czechs, which, even on the left, either prevented altogether the formation of supranational or class-orientated political organizations, or at best divided them. Although, despite their name, such workers' associations were predominantly petty-bourgeois in character, they were so close to the working-class milieu that they were able, along with the new party which they had now spawned, to campaign for working-class support and for domestic reform policies in a more serious and credible way than the Christian Socialists of Stoecker, the court chaplain, or the populist, party political enterprises of Henrici or Böckel. It was at this point that the term 'national socialism' started to become a familiar designation for the combination of a critique of capitalism appealing to the workers and a hot-headed nationalism which produced a disrespect for the established political order.

In the German-speaking parts of Austria any German nationalist movement was bound to come up against supranational institutions such as the monarchy, the civil service and the church. The founding of the DAP was, however, symptomatic of a development, which was pushing its way to the surface throughout German-speaking Europe. This was evident – even more clearly than in the activity and writing of Heinrich Class and his Pan-German League – in the emergence of political organizations like the DAP within the German Empire itself. On 7 March 1918, at almost the same time that the DAP changed its name to DNSAP (Deutsch-nationale Sozialistische Arbeiterpartei, German National Socialist Work-ers' Party) Anton Drexler, an intellectually and politically ambitious mechanic from the main railway works in Munich, established a Free

Workers' Committee for a Good Peace, whose direct objective consisted of strengthening the workers' determination for survival and victory, by spreading propaganda for nationalist and imperialist war aims. It was with some justification, then, that it was called a 'popular version of the Independent Committee for a German Peace' set up by the Pan-German League.[31] In its basic political orientation the committee was the exact counterpart of the DNSAP.

In October 1918 Drexler organized a Political Workers' Group along with the sports journalist Karl Harrer, and on 5 January 1919 the two of them, seeking political influence with growing ambition, made the transition to party politics: in the Fürstenfelder Hof, together with twenty-five colleagues of Drexler, they launched a political organization to which, like their Austrian forerunners, they gave the name German Workers' Party. Independently of these events in Munich, a Düsseldorf engineer, Alfred Brunner, had founded a completely identical German Socialist Party in December 1918, which soon had local groups in several major cities. The leader of its Nuremberg branch was a teacher, Julius Streicher. In March 1920 Drexler's DAP again followed the Austrian example and renamed itself National Socialist German Workers' Party (*Nationalsozialistische Deutsche Arbeiterpartei*, NSDAP). By the summer of 1920, following the setting up of an 'inter-state chancellery' by the Austrian National Socialist Walter Riehl, in order to co-ordinate activities, the party had entered a federal relationship with the National Socialists of Austria, which was now an independent republic, and with the DNSAP of Bohemia and Moravia, now part of Czechoslovakia. Although this federation at first remained merely a formal association, it nevertheless ensured the partners an exchange of ideas, political concepts and tactics.

Meanwhile, in September 1919, Adolf Hitler had joined the Munich NSDAP. Hitler was an Austrian, but had lived in Munich since 1913 and served during the war in a Bavarian infantry regiment. He combined an uninhibited lust for power with an enormous talent for dealing with people, a capacity for unscrupulous tactics with unrestricted energy, burning political ambition both for himself and for his organization with an ability to control mass audiences. He very quickly pushed Drexler and Harrer into the background, and on 29 June 1921 took over the presidency of the NSDAP himself. Within a very short time he had led the party out of its provincial niche and forged a 'political community of faith and struggle' of great force, whose almost daily demonstrations left no doubt as to its resolve to disseminate its ideas and realize its objectives. Of course, such a 'political community of faith and struggle' needed a leadership which reflected its avowed *Weltanschauung*. Instead of the president and executive body of a normal political party, its ideology and its necessarily quasi-military principles of organization demanded a political generalissimo with exceptional powers.

The 'leader principle' is deeply rooted in the method of operation of such movements and, under certain circumstances, can lead to the most mediocre figures temporarily being given disproportionate authority, as in the case of Konrad Henlein, the rather conventional leader of the Sudeten German party between 1933 and 1938. When, however, fortune presented the 'community of faith and struggle' with a man who possessed to perfection all the characteristics it demanded of its generalissimo; when somebody proved to be the movement's most representative ideologue and at the same time the most persuasive prophet of its message of salvation – in brief, the most successful and possibly most indispensable propagandist; when he was driven by a will to power, supported by superior tactical ability, then he must be granted an authority which would not only protect him against any attack, but which would eventually deflect all criticism until he would be able to dictate party policy as long as he kept the ultimate objectives of the party in mind.

This is precisely the relationship between Hitler and the NSDAP, even before he had published his two-volume political programme, *Mein Kampf* ('My Struggle'), in 1925 and 1926, and thereby attained the position of protector and final court of appeal in the matter of the interpretation of party ideology, his speeches and newspaper articles had made him the most important NSDAP propagandist. Easily its most successful speaker, in fact a real magnet for the masses, he appeared with good reason to be a guarantee of the party's survival and success. He not only persuasively argued the party's hunger for power, he personified it. At the same time he knew just how to give the impression that he was a politician who combined a fanatical loyalty to the party *Weltanschauung* with an easy-going gift for practical politicking and political tactics. So, as 'Führer' (Leader) he soon had the sovereign power of decision over both the programme and the policies of the NSDAP. And with these same promising talents as a speaker and propagandist, he also managed to channel into one stream all the minor National Socialist tributaries which had sprung to the surface, such as the 'German Socialists', Brunner and Streicher in 1921. Out of the NSDAP's 'community of faith and struggle' he created a mass movement for which the thought of winning power gradually lost its utopian character. By 1926 the Austrian and Sudeten German Nazis had also recognized Hitler's leadership.

The Nazis sincerely believed in the two new goals they had been given: the winning of the workers for nationalism, and the reform of the domestic political order in Germany, to be crowned with the establishment of a nationalist dictatorship; and they campaigned for these goals seriously and resolutely. Yet the concept 'National Socialism' by no means signified any change in the long-standing ideological constructs of German nationalism, much less a synthesis between the political outlook of the bourgeoisie and the socialism of the workers, as was implied in the combination of the terms 'nationalist' and 'socialist'. The *Weltanschauung* of the 'community of faith and struggle' was no more and no less than the latest version of the same anti-modernism which Treitschke, Lagarde, Langbehn and Chamberlain had expounded; that racial Manichaeanism tinged with Social Darwinism which Eugen Dühring, Hermann Ahlwardt and Otto Böckel had instigated and bequeathed to Ludwig Schemann and, again, to Houston Stewart Chamberlain; that imperialism rationalized by an anti-modern view of society and by Social Darwinism, which Heinrich Class and the Pan-Germans had so vociferously preached.

The National Socialists made no claim at all to originality. On the contrary, Austrian and Bohemian or Moravian Nazis such as Walter Riehl, Rudolf Jung and Hans Krebs spoke often and respectfully of the decisive influence which Dühring had had on their thinking. Rudolf Jung, who had long toyed with the idea of devising a separate programme for the Austrian Nazis, wrote a book even before the military defeat, which then appeared in 1919 under the title National Socialism. This, too, offered its readers a classic selection of Treitschke, Dühring and Class.[32] Everything was there: anti-modern utopias based on agrarian society, the war of conquest necessary to solve the 'social question' and realize such utopias, and the Social Darwinist racism with its sharp antisemitic edge, which was woven into all these ideas. Jung made not the slightest attempt to claim any originality for his ideas; his declared aim was to popularize the teachings of the masters in an easily accessible form. Karl Harrer, too, functioned virtually as an agent of the Thule Society, a more or less secret political order based in Munich which practised the Teutonic cult in the style of Gobineau and Richard Wagner as a sort of substitute religion, in much the same way as the related Teutonic Order or the German National Protection League. It would never have occurred to Harrer to minmize such ideological roots.

Other Nazi activists who, as politicians or publicists, helped to form the character of the movement, also began their careers in the Thule Society, for example Rudolf Hess, Gottfried Feder, Hans Frank, and not least Dietrich Eckart, whose journal *Auf gut Deutsch* ('In Plain German'), founded in 1918, was the first official organ of the NSDAP until 1921 and offered its readers a dreary mixture of Dühring, Böckel, Langbehn und Chamberlain. From 1921 until his death in 1923 Eckart, who was a close associate of Hitler's at this time, was the principal editor of the *Völkischer Beobachter*, the first national newspaper of the NSDAP. Two of Dühring's ablest disciples came to the NSDAP from the German National Protection League, Artur Dinter and Theodor Fritsch, and the latter enjoyed almost the status of high priest within the party in recognition of his position as a doyen of antisemitism. The ideological debt to Otto Böckel was acknowledged with similar appreciation. It was only logical that the NSDAP soon started to produce a journal, which issue on issue – from 1923 – offered little more than a tireless repetition of the most vicious and primitive antisemitism in the style of Ahlwardt, Rohling and Paasch. The driving force behind the paper, *Der Stürmer*, was its editor, Julius Streicher, who had come to the party from the German Socialists, and now, as Hitler's 'governor', led the Nuremberg and Franconian branches of the party.

Nor did Hitler himself break this continuity. He had admired Schönerer and absorbed his racial antisemitism while still in Austria, and in doing so had immediately become a sort of ideological grandchild of Eugen Dühring. At the same time he fell under the profound and enduring influence of the music and the ideology of Richard Wagner. In the first years after the war, which had served to confirm his *Weltanschauung*, already formed from a mixture of racism, Social Darwinism and imperialism, he came into close contact with the Austrian and Bohemian-Moravian Nazis who reinforced his manichaeistic racism. For many years Hitler was a drop-out, without a real education or even an adequate schooling, and there were many gaps to be filled with detail, vague opinions to be translated into the firm convictions of a clear consciousness. He was now able to remedy these deficiencies by occupying himself with writers such as Heinrich Class and Houston Stewart Chamberlain, and he now got to know the latter personally.

Meeting so famous a man as Chamberlain, whom to some extent he regarded as a high priest, encouraged Hitler and strengthened his sense of mission. It also served to render superfluous a search for an ideological approach of his own. Similarly, German émigrés from Russia, and above all from the Baltic, such as Alfred Rosenberg, whose first work, *Die Spur des Juden im Wandel der Zeiten* ('The Mark of the Jew through the Ages'), was published in 1919, and whose *Mythus des 20. Jahrhunderts* ('Myth of the Twentieth Century'), which was published in 1930, became one of the Nazi movement's most authoritatively programmatic works, had a significant influence on the reinforcement of Hitler's antisemitism. These émigrés brought with them 'indisputable' evidence of Jewish plans for world dominion, namely the record of a secret Jewish meeting, at which such a plan had been worked out. Translated from Russian into German in 1919 by Gottfried zur Beek, a pseudonym for one Ludwig Müller, under the eye-catching title *Die Protokolle der Weisen von Zion* ('The

Protocols of the Elders of Zion'), this pseudo-document attracted great attention.[33] Hitler, like all the Nazis, was strongly impressed and probably continued to believe in the truth of the 'Protocols', although they were exposed as early as 1921 as a clumsy forgery on the part of the Tsarist secret police. One model among others must have been that scene in the Jewish cemetery in Prague which Sir John Retcliffe (i.e. Hermann Goedsche) had invented for his novel *Biarritz*.

In any event Hitler's earliest comments on the 'Jewish question' reveal him to have been a complete racial antisemite in the Dühring mould. On 16 September 1919, while still observing the political scene in Munich in the service of the Enlightenment Department (Auflklärungsabteilung) of Bavarian Group Command IV, he wrote on behalf of his superior, Captain Mayr, to another agent who had requested material relating to the issue. In this letter he warned expressly against regarding the Jews as a religious community; 'Jewry' indisputably constituted 'a race'. He added darkly that, following the introduction of 'new legislation relating to aliens' (eine Fremdengesetzgebung), the goal of a 'rational anti-semitism' would have to be the 'removal of the Jews altogether', and that this would be 'irrevocable'.[34] In his first major speech on the subject, 'Why we are against the Jews', delivered on 13 August 1920, by which time he was already a propagandist for the NSDAP, he spoke similarly of 'scientific anti-Semitism'.[35]

His own major manifesto, composed during his imprisonment at Landsberg following the abortive putsch of November 1923, showed how comfortable he felt with the ideological structure inherited from Dühring, Gobineau and Chamberlain, how deeply he had been impressed by the words inspired by Dühring and Class, but written by the like-minded Rudolf Jung (like Hitler a South German). Hitler, the naturally talented propagandist, was by now sufficiently experienced to write easily, and often very tellingly, about techniques of mass manipulation, while, at the same time constrained to sell himself as a future statesman, he developed his own views on how to bring about an imperialist German foreign policy. In those passages, however, where he expanded on the Nazi *Weltanschauung* he introduced not a single one of his own ideas. Working without any particular means of assistance, he satisfied himself with simply repetitively dictating the received ideas of his ideological predecessors. In the sections where he elaborated on the anti-modern view of society, proclaimed the 'struggle for living space', and raised racial Manichaeansim to the status of the religion of true National Socialism, *Mein Kampf* ('My Struggle') becomes in parts little more than a wordier version, furnished with various flourishes, of Rudolf Jung's somewhat plainer book. At the time Hitler scarcely bothered to draw attention to his debt to such predecessors. When

Jung and Krebs congratulated Hitler in 1938 on the annexation of the Sudetenland by the German Reich, however, Hitler did speak in warm terms of the debt he owed to Jung's first attempt to present a clear outline of the Nazi *Weltanschauung.*[36]

The Nazi movement became the spearhead of the anti-modern counter-revolution. The Nazis transformed uneasiness with industrial society to radical hostility producing anti-urban blueprints for a healthy and harmonious social order, in which the whole nation would be transformed into a people of warriors and landowners. The flight from the reality of the twentieth century into a mythical medieval past was the most consistent element of their propaganda. Their romantic agrarian view of society, which postulated a sort of refeudalization process had little to do with the real political conflicts in Germany and the other industrial nations. They were also basically indifferent to the great conflict between capitalism and Socialism. Although some Nazi writers, such as Rudolf Jung, introduced clearly anti-capitalist elements, others, such as Hans Zöberlin, struck a more vehemently anti-socialist note.[37]

In reality, however, the Nazis wanted neither to defend capitalism against the socialists, nor to bring about a socialist victory against capitalism; they rejected both these products of industrial society equally, and sought to transcend them in a new order. The German nation, in fact the whole of the so-called Nordic race, was to be raised with an 'iron fist', as Hitler put it, to the rank of ruling class of the new empire they dreamed of;[38] the working class, freed from the Marxist International, would be carried along with the tide, and the old elites, once subjected to the new order, would either be integrated or gradually excluded, according to their usefulness. The Volksgemeinschaft (national community) of Nazi propaganda, which appealed to so many Germans, and which would immediately be realized in a Nazi Germany where class conflict would be eliminated, was essentially nothing other than the anticipation of a future utopia where Germans would be the aristocracy of a mighty empire.

For the Nazis, with their extremely simplistic utopia, were bound to feel more keenly than most the 'shortage of space' associated with anti-modern social thought, and they addressed themselves to it most passionately of all. They transformed a rather burdensome perception of national claustrophobia into a resolve to get rid of it, and this resolve enabled them unashamedly to welcome, and even to demand, the only means available to rectify the situation: a war to conquer *Lebensraum* (living space). Inspired by the wartime policies introduced by the supreme command of the army under Hindenburg and Ludendorff, which had found their first rather sketchy expression in the Treaty of Brest-Litovsk of March 1918, the Nazis located Germany's future 'living-space' in eastern Europe, and more accurately in Russia. The conquest of an empire based on a land mass stretching from the Urals to the English Channel, the possession of which would make possible the realization of utopian Nazi social policies, was to become the most important and practically the only aim of the party's foreign policy. Following Germany's defeat in the First World War, the Nazis were also more or less compelled to inscribe the repeal of the Treaty of Versailles on their banners, and with it the destruction of the European state system founded on the basis of the Paris treaties and the League of Nations. To this extent they found themselves in partial agreement with the foreign policy thinking of virtually all Germans. But in the Nazi programme such aims were merely stations along the road to territorial expansion.

Similarly the Nazis combined the feudal and aristocratic elements of their social utopia in a particularly simplistic and rigid way with contemporary pseudo-biological and Social Darwinist ideas. Ultimately they used particularly naïve and brutal racial criteria to justify the suitability and legitimacy of the Germans and several 'related' nations for the coveted role of imperial class, referring to the superiority and godlike creativity of the 'Aryan' race. Therefore, the dreams with which they deluded themselves, of the preparation and successful prosecution of a war of conquest, and of the social utopia to come after it, were dependent on immediate and energetic racial policies. Such dreams depended on the improvement and refinement of the German nation itself; in a public speech of 1929, faithfully reported by the *Völkischer Beobachter*, Hitler spoke of the strengthening of the nation which would follow from a period of hardship, when in each year only the racially best 10 per cent of births each year were allowed to survive.[39]

Later plans foresaw the 'planned cultivation and reproduction of good stock' among adults as well, by 'eliminating the feeble-minded, sexual offenders and the socially incapable (asocials)', in fact by 'orientating the national community' according to the 'principles of breeding'.[40] But above all the removal and destruction of 'racially alien pests', had to be achieved, especially the Jews, that subhuman and diabolical race of enemies, which sought to achieve world domination, and in particular the subjugation of the Germans by means of creating and controlling industrial societry, and by poisoning the 'Aryan' race through assimilation. More clearly, then, than other, related groups, the Nazis complemented and clarified their dogmatic ideological racism with a totally uninhibited recognition of the indisoluble link between the anticipated war of conquest and a campaign of anti-Jewish persecution which already contained implications of annihilation.

These stupid, terrifying and ultimately irrational visions were neither 'symbols' nor 'metaphors',[41] nor were they the quirks of a handful of leading ideologues, but the binding models of Nazi policy. They bound the faithful no less – perhaps even more – than rationally constructed and unquestionably ethically superior Marxist theories. Innumerable party functionaries and propagandists, drawing their intellectual inspiration largely from leading policy-makers such as Hitler and Jung, but partly too under the influence of the old band of racist ideologues, successfully proclaimed the faith in countless speeches and newspaper articles, swearing the movement to allegiance.

Leaving aside the group around Otto Strasser, exceptional in that among their rather confused notions the most common enemy was the West, while from time to time Russia might not be an object of attack so much as a potential ally, and racism was not quite as important, there were differences of emphasis depending on who was speaking or writing, whether it was Walter Darré, Alfred Rosenberg or the future leader of the SS, Heinrich Himmler, some functionary or other from the middle or lower ranks of *Gauleiter* or Kreisleiter, or Konstantin Hierl, future head of the Reich Labour Service. Even such a dry type as the future Interior Minister, Wilhelm Frick, by all appearances a sober civil servant, became on close inspection an ideologue of the purest kind. During the Weimar Republic, the Nazi party group in the Reichstag, whose activity was determined to a considerable extent by Frick, demonstrated precisely the exceptional ideological tension and rigid ideological objectives with which the Nazis worked: Frick laboured tirelessly to incorporate pseudo-biological racist principles into bills presented to parliament. In any event the Nazi movement proved frequently and persuasively that 'Hitler's *Weltanschauung*' was not the *Weltanschauung* of Hitler alone.

There is, of course, no doubt that a community of political faith and struggle such as the NSDAP needs constant and active engagement if it is not to disintegrate, and the Nazi party developed a style of activism which would not have been satisfied by the creation of a continental European empire and the extermination of the Jews living in the Reich. If Nazi policy makers and even the simpler party functionaries spoke of an overseas colonial empire even before 1933, of 'world dominion' and the ultimate struggle with the USA for that world dominion, they doubtless betrayed the instinctive certainty that after every battle, even those final battles demanded by the party programme, National Socialist would have to redouble their efforts if the Nazi movement was to remain capable of survival. Yet as long as the imperial dream remained unfulfilled, and as long as no decisive blow was struck against the enemy race, Nazi activism was at the disposal of the party programme. If the policy objectives had been abandoned, or had even merely lost their binding compulsion, the Nazi movement would have lost more than the mere disguise for a fundamentally vacuous and aimless activism, it would have lost the basis of the claim to power – which the Nazis themselves treated with bitter and deadly seriousness – and with that the reason for its existence. In that sense Nazi activisim was determined entirely by its objectives, on a fixed path from beginning to end, from which it could not deviate without abandoning the movement itself.

If this path enabled the NSDAP, unlike its predecessors, to become the strongest political party in Germany, and then actually to make a bid for state power, which was finally presented to it more or less on a plate by the old German nationalist ruling class, this was not simply because it championed the *Weltanschauung* of the Pan-Germans, of Chamberlain and of Dühring with a degree more crudity and crassness, and at the same time more forcefully, more urgently and more ambitiously. Nor would it have been enough for the party to have had since 1921 a leader who took to the field as a thoroughly convinced Nazi and with a truly fanatical determination to fight for the *Weltanschauung*, and who was at the same time a genius of mass manipulation. The ideological and organizational advantages and the person of Adolf Hitler were both important factors, but even the combination of these two elements would not have brought the Nazi Party any more success than its predecessors if the movement had not been operating in the feverish atmosphere of a Germany shaken and completely transformed by an unprecedented crisis.

The first condition was the dissolution of the authoritarian monarchy and its replacement by a republic with a parliamentary system of government. For the first time in modern German history a situation was created in which a political party, with the support of other forces in society at large, was able to compete for governmental power and for the authority to implement its own political ideology. Socialists, liberals and conservatives had their chance to do this just as much as their racist rivals. Yet, although it was by no means clear to begin with, a party which could carry the nationalism, the imperialism and the authoritarianism of the Pan-Germans started with a considerable advantage. For countless Germans the fall of the monarchy signified the collapse of an order which was not just ancient and honourable, but sacred and holy, a political 'home' which had given them a feeling of intellectual certainty and spriritual security.

After the expulsion of the emperor and the princes, not by a powerful popular republican movement, but in accordance with the supposed wishes of the victorious Allies, those Germans lived their political lives in a state of constant crisis, or at least permanent disorientation. The nationalist dictatorship which Class had demanded in 1912 now seemed doubly attractive as a substitute monarchy promising security. 'Parliamentariza-tion' seemed 'unnatural' too to a majority of the German bourgeoisie, which had made itself at home in the Wilhelmine Empire, an illiberal state, certainly, but a constitutional one based on the rule of law, and in possession of a fine and efficient administration. Oswald Spengler – the first volume of his work *The Decline of the West* had just come out a few months before – diagnosed the situation accurately in March 1919. Many Germans were frightened by the public resolution of differences of opinion and conflicts of interest – not always a happy sight – and saw the Reichstag as a 'talking shop'. A nationalist dictatorship seemed to be a potential refuge and a means of overcoming political chaos.

If such instincts had led to a nationalist coup, the Weimar Republic might well have been come to an end in 1920 or 1921. The putsch attempt of March 1920 by Wolfgang Kapp, a politician with Pan-German sympathies, and the Ehrhardt naval brigade (a *Freikorps* para-military formation which wore the swastika on its helmets), was a miserable failure; and talk of the establishment of a 'national dictatorship' continued uninterrupted on the right until 1923 without any concrete result, but it was already clear that the survival of the republic depended not on its own strength, but was preserved largely because the West guaranteed its continued existence. Although the resistance of the workers and the left during the general strike of March 1920 was impressive, Kapp's enterprise failed, and others were either abandoned or, like Hitler's Munich adventure failed because the organizers did not find sufficient support on the right; the moderate right and the more reasonable representatives *within* the more extreme groups knew only too well that victory in a civil war and the establishment of a national dictatorship would only have provoked a French invasion, which could not yet have been repelled. On the other hand it is quite conceivable that, given the chance to develop undisturbed, the Weimar Republic would have become capable of survival. But crisis followed crisis, and the worst consequence of all the upheavals was that a majority of Germans, and the overwhelming majority of the middle classes, failed to understand the causes or the wider context.

This began with defeat in the First World War. Defeat came as something of a surprise to a country which had been wretchedly ill-informed, and had believed the frequent reports of victories until the last minute, despite material hardship. Consequently neither Allied superiority nor the exhaustion of the German army was accepted as a reason for defeat. Rather, it seemed that instead of continuing the war until it was victorious or at least until an honourable stalemate had been reached, the army had been forced to agree to an armistice suspiciously resembling capitulation, and one which opened the way for a peace to be imposed by the enemy. Yet, since the army was still 'undefeated on the battlefield', as even Friedrich Ebert, the social democrat and first president of the Republic said, its collapse – which was difficult to dispute – must have been caused by a treacherous stab in the back – a myth which was bound to give rise to a paranoid search for the guilty.

That the 'stab in the back' had cheated the nation of the fruits of victory was bad enough in itself. After all, a considerable section of the German middle class had thought it had within its grasp the domination of Europe by the Reich, the rise of Germany to the status of world power, extensive territorial acquisitions, and massive reparations payments from the defeated enemies; many had also hoped that military success and the triumph of German foreign policy would bring with them important gains in domestic politics, namely a postwar extension of the internal consensus (Burgfrieden) agreed in 1914, keeping the socialist movement quiet for some time to come, and perhaps even taming it altogether. The defeat not only thwarted these expectations, it put them into reverse.

The Treaty of Versailles disarmed the German Reich and forced Germany into a position of far-reaching dependence. It forced the cession of territories, which had long been considered German, to new states such as Poland or victorious powers such as France, and in addition it created the basis for absurdly high reparations payments to the Allies. By forcing Germany on to the path of republicanism and parliamentarism, the defeat was held responsible for unpopular political innovations, which on top of everything else greatly increased the influence of the left, which seemed to be provoked into a flurry of activity, exploiting the opportunity for development and expansion. At times there seemed to be a real threat that Germany would be 'socialized', either through reform or by revolution, and the fear of socialism and communism increased further when the parliamentary republic in Russia was replaced by the Bolshevik revolution and the installation of a Marxist-orientated socialist dictatorship. In the eyes of countless middle-class Germans the frightening example of Leninist Russia, protector of the German communists and potential instigator of a socialist world revolution gave the socialist threat in Germany a new dimension.

At the same time the population of Germany was plunged into economic catastrophe. The origins of the inflation which annihilated the German currency between the war years and 1923 were in themselves not difficult to recognize; with hindsight we can identify several factors which served to fuel the inflation, and which account for the final upward surge during 1923, when by November one American dollar was worth 4.2 billion (million million) paper RM. First of all Wilhelmine Germany financed the war by continually increasing floating debt; after the war Weimar cabinets continued this rather lax practice of covering domestic deficits simply by increasing the circulation of money; then came a time when the state let inflation run its course as a means of helping to pay off its enormous internal debts; German governments wanted to exaggerate the weakness of the German economy in order to avoid paying reparations, or at least to put off payments for as long as possible; finally, in 1923, following the occupation of the Ruhr by French troops, the so-called passive resistance of the German population was paid for by the printing press.

Apart from their helpless desperation, their ignorance and their stupid denial of the hard realities, there were also valid reasons for the behaviour of German cabinets, both during the Empire and during the Weimar Republic. However, they revealed neither their sound nor their ill-founded motives to the citizens of Germany; on the contrary they did everything within their power to conceal their own part in this breathtaking process. And for this reason the German middle classes and petty bourgeoisie could only look on helplessly, unable to make rhyme or reason of the catastrophe which in the course of a few years destroyed the savings and financial reserves they had built up over generations. They had lost their intellectual and political certainties, and the loss of material security which now seemed to threaten their very existence remained unexplained.

Still more difficult to understand were the reasons for the world depression that rocked the German economy along with those of the other industrial states in 1928 and 1929. The new crisis differed from the earlier one in that its effect on the currency was deflationary: prices collapsed, and the production and sales of goods – and of services too, of course – contracted continually. This meant that agriculture and industry, peasants and workers, were hardest hit. However, sections of the middle and lower middle classes were also affected. Everywhere there was fear of bankruptcy or unemployment, and even those who were relatively safe began to fear that the unprecedented dimensions of the crisis would lead to social upheaval and might even precipitate a Bolshevik revolution. The devastating force of the crisis, and the increasing doubt that the dams built to contain the left would hold, created open hostility to the capitalist economy among those who had never felt particularly at ease with it anyway: the anti-modern elements in both the bourgeoisie and the landed class. This did not mean that either bourgeois or agrarian anti-capitalists turned to socialist conceptions of economy and society. They directed their resentment only against the major banks and big business. Action was felt to be necessary but was channelled primarily, and with great enthusiasm, into exposing imaginary scapegoats and making them pay for an otherwise inexplicable disaster.

'The Jews are to blame!' Developments in Germany since 1918 held no secrets for the Nazis. The defeat, along with its repercussions in domestic and international politics, the economic crises and their devastating effects on society – all this, the Nazis argued, was without doubt largely the work of the November criminals, who had stabbed the German army in the back in 1918: communists and socialists, liberals and democrats, ultra-montane Catholics, Freemasons and capitalists. The November criminals were only tools however. Behind these diverse groups was the guiding hand of Jewry. 'The Jews', wrote Dr Joseph Goebbels, the future Propaganda Minister, in 1930, 'are both the cause and the beneficiaries of our slavery.' These 'versatile demons of decay' had caused Germany's defeat, they were the 'begetters of theories of class conflict', the 'creators and supporters of international finance capitalism' and the 'greatest enemy of German freedom'.[42]

Thus the Nazis neatly managed to fit the military, political and economic catastrophes into the ideological framework of their racial Manichaeanism with conviction. The bitter experiences of the Germans since the war and the frightening prospects for Germany in the future were seen as striking proof of a conspiracy on the part of both German and international Jewry, aimed at the subjection of the German nation and Jewish world domination. Seen from this angle the Weimar Republic appeared as a 'Jewish Republic', as an instrument for the establishment, consolidation and exercise of Jewish power over the Germans, obviously an indispensable precondition for world domination. 'The Jews', said Goebbels 'have polluted our race, sapped our morale, undermined our morals, and broken our strength.' Now they had emerged from their hiding-places to carry out an inevitable and 'criminal ritual slaughter of other nations', which would begin in Germany.[43]

'The Jews are to be blame!' In countless speeches and newspaper articles the Nazis sought to brand their simplistic explanation on the national consciousness. Hermann Esser, one of Hitler's earliest comrades in Munich, wrote a pamphlet entitled 'The Jewish World Plague', which was published with a massive print run; a certain Dr Kofler held forth on 'The Catholic Church and the Jews', and in his passionate polemic 'The Congress of the World Jewish Conspiracy in Basle' Alfred Rosenberg 'proved' the authenticity of the 'Protocols of the Elders of Zion'. Goebbels also spread the racist and antisemitic message in pamphlets with titles like 'The Nazi-Sozi. Questions and Answers for the National Socialist', 'Die verfluchten Hakenkreuzler' ('The Dammned Nazis') and 'The National Socialist's Little ABC', which sold in hundreds of thousands between 1929 and 1933.

The same views were echoed by others, such as Erich Ludendorff. Under the nominal command of the Kaiser and his chief of staff, Field Marshal von Hindenburg, Ludendorff had managed to exert considerable influence on both the domestic and foreign policy of the Reich between August 1916 and October 1918, creating in the process a rough prototype for nationalist dictatorship. From 5 May 1929 a journal entitled *Ludendorffs Volkswarte* ('People's Watchtower') was published by a group called the Tannenberg League, founded in 1926, and from August of the same year this was accompanied by a supplement, *Am Heiligen Quell* ('At the Holy Source'). Both publications were read by former officers and members of the educated middle classes, and were used by the general, who was still respected, and his wife Mathilde, who taught 'German religion', to conduct a hysterical campaign against Freemasons, Jesuits and Marxists, against the 'forces above the state' which were directed by 'world Jewry', and it was a campaign which was not to be underestimated, despite its largely ridiculous argumentation.

In many old upper-class families, among the bourgeoisie, the petty bourgeoisie and the peasantry, where racist and antisemitic attitudes were long established, the Nazi explanation of Germany's crisis immediately found a receptive audience. Millions of others, who had hitherto had no time for such a primitive and irrational view of the world, now listened attentively in their desperation and helplessness to the Nazi message, accepting it either fully or in part, not with their own Jewish neighbours in mind, but 'the Jews' in general. The radical racist antisemitism which Hitler and his followers preached exercised such a strong appeal for both peasants and petty-bourgeois that they were attracted to the Nazis by policies directed against the assimilation and the emancipation of German Jews.

Between 1929 and 1933 the NSDAP gained millions of extra voters who hoped that Hitler and his party would fulfil both their economic expectations and their social aspirations, but paid little attention to the central points of the Nazi programme. The NSDAP survived this growth in support without any real change in its ideological complexion. The party attracted such new adherents and sympathizers more easily than the other parties basically because it promised to do more than merely serve sectional interests, namely to provide a solution to all the turmoil, crises and conflicts of the present in a 'healthy' future. During its rise to power the Nazi movement was forced, in view of the real and urgent problems of Germany's economic and political crisis, to deal with subjects and address issues which were not directly, and often not even indirectly, related to the party programme. Yet Nazi agitation, which never underplayed the party's expansionist foreign policy (Raumpolitik), always made clear that behind every ill which afflicted Germany Jews were at work, and that therefore every cure must contain antisemitic policies as well, even if these only amounted to the reversal of Jewish emancipation and assimilation.

Whether in 1929 or in 1932, and without the least reduction of intensity or pressure, the NSDAP demanded: 'The rigorous weeding out of all alien elements from all areas of public life. A clear division between German and non-German, according to race alone and regardless of any counterfeit nationality or even religion . . . the destruction of the dung-heap of Jewish immorality and racial degeneration.'[44] Even those who did not vote for the Nazis primarily on account of their antisemitic policies, and those who voted for the party without being antisemites themselves, had all been clearly warned by Hitler and the hordes of other Nazi propagandists that the movement's racist gospel would be translated into actual policy as soon as political power had been won.

3

The Reversal of Emancipation

After Hitler's appointement as chancellor the Nazis quickly discovered that translating their racist message into political action was anything but simple. It was not that the Nazi movement had suddenly lost its enthusiastic antisemitic convictions. During the first months of the Third Reich the NSDAP had little need to assert its identity and preserve its solidarity with aggressive attacks on a purely ideological enemy; its paramilitary force, the SA, was by no means short of things to do. In the period immediately after 30 January 1933 the main task was to win for the new Nazi-led government some freedom of manoeuvre in domestic politics, to achieve one-party rule by the NSDAP, to transfer the party's leader principle to the state through the person of Adolf Hitler, and to 'co-ordinate' as many social institutions as possible, whatever their political significance, and prepare them to accept the will of the leadership without resistance.

These concrete goals gave the NSDAP and the SA a sufficient number of real opponents: socialists of all kinds, from communists to Social Democrats; members and functionaries of the middle-class parties, which had also been dissolved by July 1933; representatives of trade unions and 'political Catholicism'; defenders of a still genuinely Christian Protestantism. While the SA erected countless 'unofficial' prisons for all the actual, potential and alleged opponents of the new regime, the first concentration camp was established near Dachau on 20 March 1933 by Heinrich Himmler. At that time Himmler was still chief of police in Munich, but by 1934, he was already head of the Reich's political police, now called the 'secret state police' (Geheime Staatspolizei, Gestapo), and by 1936 head of the entire German police. In Dachau and in similar camps such as

Oranienburg, Papenburg and Esterwegen almost 30,000 people were taken into 'protective custody' during the summer of 1933. But even this occasionally hectic activity, aimed at seizing and consolidating power, was not enough to make any of the Nazis forget the Jews.

On the contrary, even before the Reichstag elections of 5 March, in which the NSDAP and its German National partners won a narrow parliamentary majority, and even more so after the elections were over, the party's raiding parties and stormtroopers launched a merciless campaign against German Jews. Throughout the country detachments of stormtroopers smashed the windows of Jewish businesses, brutally beat up individual Jews, and used naked terror to force the dismissal or suspension of Jewish office workers and civil servants. Since it was the curious aim of these preachers and practitioners of violence to present the assumption of power as legal, and to cultivate the impression of a non-violent amd bloodless 'revolution' for the benefit of both the German public and foreign observers, party leaders attempted – albeit inconsistently – to censor press reports of the mistreatment of Jews. Antisemitic incidents were not to appear as the work of Nazi organizations but as the result of 'popular anger', and sometimes there were even attempts to blame antisemitic terror on political opponents: on 11 March 1933, for example, Friedrich Alpers, the leader of the SS in Brunswick, a lawyer by profession who was later promoted to the post of Justice Minister in Brunswick, visited two Jewish department stores accompanied by a number of his subordinates. At a signal from this 'upholder of the law' the stores were devastated; shortly afterwards Alpers condemned the incident in a public speech, and blamed it on communist hooligans.[1]

Such cover-up attempts were obviously incredible to the point of being ridiculous, especially given the frequent occurrence during those weeks of Nazi attacks on department stores, which had been singled out in the 1920 party programme as instruments of the exploitation of Germany by the Jews. Hermann Goering – much-decorated fighter pilot of the First World War, last commander of the Richthofen Squadron, and already Hitler's second-in-command in the Nazi movement – was forced, in his new post as Interior Minister of Prussia to give way to demands for an explanation of what he meant by his remark, made in Essen on 11 March, that he would always and without hesitation deploy the police to protect the German people, but would refuse to use them to guard Jewish department stores.

The police were not always content to be passive onlookers, however; nor were they always withdrawn before prospective antisemitic activity, as had happened in Brunswick. In Breslau, for example, also on 11 March, the police acted against stormtroopers on the rampage in a department store, whereupon the SA occupied the entrance to the local court in Breslau on 13 March, demanding the expulsion of Jewish judges and lawyers. This time the police failed to intervene, and the chief of police himself demanded that the justice department acquiesce to the demands of the 'national population' and 'take action to stem Jewish influence in the administration of justice'.[2] Then, on 16 March, the number of Jewish lawyers practising in Breslau courts was in fact reduced to seventeen, and they were issued with special identity cards by the police. In other places stormtroopers blocked the entrances to Jewish shops, and here and there their destructive fury was even directed at synagogues. In addition the SA, which had been declared an 'auxiliary police force' on 22 February, did not hesitate to arrest individual Jews and give them a hard time in their unofficial concentration camps. Inmates of such camps were released only on condition that they sign a declaration stating that they had not been mistreated; occasionally they also had to pay a ransom.

However, one of the Nazi leaders' first problems was their uncertainty as to where to channel the appetite for aggressive antisemitic activity which was so obviously widespread in the ranks of both the party and the SA. As in other important areas of policy the Nazi movement had a furious urge to act on the 'Jewish question' but lacked concrete plans to harness this enthusiasm. What did 'regulating' or 'solving' the Jewish question mean either to individual Nazis or to the Nazi state? Before the assumption of power nobody had bothered to define or elaborate such propositions. Everyone knew who the enemy was, and was prepared to fight to the better end, yet it remained unclear exactly what fate awaited the enemy *at* the bitter end. There was still no answer even to the most basic question: was it a matter of establishing rules governing long-term relations with a Jewish community in Germany, or was it a question of driving the German Jews out of Germany? Since there was no clarity over this point, there could obviously be no detailed plan of individual measures to be taken, still less any decisive undertaking regarding the timing of the action.

It now proved to be a very difficult undertaking to make up for the opportunities missed after the assumption of power and to translate into a realizable plan slogans such as 'Jews perish!' or battle cries such as 'Strike the Jews down wherever you find them.' Every discussion of the aims and methods of antisemitism was now directly influenced by the frictions which had emerged from the early conflict between the antisemitic radicalism of the Nazi rank and file and the domestic and foreign policy realities of 1933. Hitler and his followers were to discover that in the 'Jewish question' they were still a long way from anything like freedom of action, in fact that since the assumption of power they no longer enjoyed the same 'freedom of discussion' (i.e. freedom of

uninhibited antisemitic agitation) which they had practised without embarrassment in the 'time of struggle'.

The brutal and open antisemitic agitation practised by the Nazi party –
and above all by the SA – in February and March 1933 failed to make any
positive impression at all on the majority of the population, and this was
an observation party officials made repeatedly and with increasing unease.
The workers, who were socialist-orientated, had long remained virtually
untouched by antisemitism. In the middle of the worst economic crisis in
living memory, they were more interested in wages and labour policies,
and reacted either with indifference or hostility to the antisemitic activities
of the SA thugs, especially as the same thugs were responsible for smashing
the workers' own trade unions and political organizations.

In the countryside Jewish cattle and grain dealers proved to be
indispensable at first, and even later when the regime increasingly provided
its own alternative institutions for buying up cattle and grain, it was still
far from easy to dissolve the relationship between the farmer and the
Jewish dealer, because many farmers began to recognize that they got a
better deal from the Jews they had cursed for so long than from the 'Aryan'
agents of the new co-operatives; even in 1935 many farmers, as the party
and the Gestapo both complained, were 'shameless' enough to put
financial gain before the arguments of racial politics and continue to sell to
Jews. Very often such acts were even prompted by Christian and humane
sentiments in view of the open persecution of the Jews.[3] Among the
middle classes there were even more determined groups who fundamentally rejected antisemitism on Christian, humanist or liberal grounds, and
even among the majority, who had gradually been won over to antisemitism and certainly demanded the 'suppression of Jewish influence', there
were expressions of disapproval: at least they found the crude terror of the
stormtroopers embarrassing and wanted it replaced by 'orderly' and
unobtrusive action.

These reactions, which were irritating, and to many Nazis surprising,
acquired political importance only through a further factor. On 30 January
Hitler had not become the head of a cabinet composed entirely of Nazis,
but chancellor in a coalition government in which the German National
People's Party (DNVP), although a less important force, was nevertheless
able to guarantee the government's all- important parliamentary majority,
and for that reason its opinions counted. In addition, everyone was aware
of the fact – and it became clear from June and July 1933 when the
DNVP, like the other political parties, disappeared – that the alliance
between the Nazis and the German Nationalists did not rest mainly, not
even primarily, on the party's political importance in the Reichstag, but
that the Nazis' most important German Nationalist allies were

much more likely to be found in the leadership of the Reichswehr and in the higher echelons of the civil service, along with a number of industrialists and bankers such as Hjalmar Schacht. At the head of this faction was Reich President von Hindenburg, who enjoyed widespread admiration among the middle clases. According to the constitution, he also continued to exercise supreme command over the armed forces, which were still referred to as the Reichswehr at that time, and to which the Imperial field marshal still felt stronger ties than to the Nazi-led government. Such hard realities demanded caution even from a man such as Hitler, and even from a 'community of struggle' such as the Nazi movement.

The Nazis' German National partners themselves espoused a type of antisemitism which could scarcely be called moderate. They demanded the closing of Germany's borders against further Jewish immigration from eastern Europe, the expulsion of Jews from political and public life, and the promotion of Jewish emigration. But they would not go any further. If the Nazis took the assimilation of the Jews as proof of how far the tumour had eaten into the body of the nation, and of how urgent the need for an operation had become, their allies hesitated to ignore the fact that the assimilation process had made the great majority of German Jews into German citizens. They demanded that certain limits be observed – above all that 'business' should not be included in the persecution of the Jews – and that even within these limits the well-earned rights of state officials or the merits of war service should be observed. They also insisted that at least the appearance of legal action should be preserved, and consequently one could only work through the law.

On 4 April 1933 President von Hindenburg pointed out to Hitler which points must be observed. In his letter the Field Marshal noted first of all that in the course of the previous few days, according to reports he had received, even 'war-disabled judges, lawyers and legal civil servants with spotless records had been suspended, and subsequently dismissed from office because they were of Jewish extraction'. He found such treatment of war-disabled Jewish officials 'personally quite intolerable'. He requested the Reich Chancellor 'most sincerely and most urgently' to 'deal with this question personally and to arrange for a consistent regulation of the matter in all branches of the public service throughout the Reich'. 'Civil servants, Judges, teachers and lawyers', Hindenburg pointed out, 'who are war-disabled themselves, or who served at the front, or are sons of men killed in action, or who themselves lost sons in action' should 'be allowed to remain in their posts: if they were good enough to fight and give their blood for Germany, then they should certainly be seen as worthy enough to continue serving the Fatherland in their professions.'[4] Hitler was left with no other alternative than to assure the Reich President that he would endeavour to do 'all possible justice' to these 'noble sentiments'. He himself 'suffered often from a harsh fate, which compels one to decisions which one would wish to avoid a thousand times over, for humane reasons.'[5]

An even greater obstacle was presented by Nazi Germany's international relations. Many people in the European liberal democracies and in the United States, and not least journalists and politicians, reacted with anxiety and horror to the events in Germany, to the destruction of parliamentary government and the rule of law, and to the wave of unashamed cultural barbarism in a country so important to the political and intellectual constitution of Europe and the world. The *Völkischer Beobachter* reported that the philosopher Martin Heidegger, as Rector of the University of Freiburg, had publicly welcomed, indeed celebrated, the abolition of 'academic freedom', and had argued that 'the whole of student existence should be understood as military service'.[6] The writer Rudolf G. Binding, anything but SA thug, wrote in a letter to the French writer Romain Rolland, one of the admirers of a Germany which was now disappearing, that he could 'conceal nothing' that had happened during the 'bloody upheavals' in Germany, and that the whole process must be recognized as a 'sovereign life utterance of the nation'.[7]

With shock and increasing anxiety meanwhile, all the Reich's neighbours, and all those who felt their interests to be affected by German policy, noted that the revolutionary upheaval in Germany had not – unlike the western revolutions or the October Revolution in Russia – taken place in the name of great principles or at least with some utopian blueprint in mind, but under the banner of an expansionist nationalism. The sense and purpose of the nationalist dictatorship which had been established in Germany amounted to little more than a psychological, industrial and military mobilization. So what was to be expected from the new Nazi Germany? Presumably nothing more than expansionist foreign policy and war.

Consequently a great part of the European and American press coverage of events in Germany was both nervous and critical. In a particularly threatened state such as Poland the government even began to toy with the idea of preventative action against the Nazi regime. Hitler himself, whose judgements were coloured by his own brutal Social Darwinist understanding of politics, was convinced that his regime was in extreme danger until it had attained a certain position of strength. In this period, he told the Reichswehr leaders on 3 February 1933, 'the French would demonstrate whether they had any statesmen; if they do they will not give us time, but will invade (presumably with their eastern satellites).'[8] So Hitler considered caution a necessity at first, and not only in foreign policy, but in acting against the German Jews as well. Since, like all Nazis, he believed in the existence of a politically organized 'international Jewry' acting together on the instructions of a secret leadership, Hitler considered it self-evident that every anti-Jewish act in Germany would provoke anti-German acts on the part of Jews in France, Great Britain or the United States, and since - again influenced by his ideology - he grotesquely overestimated the influence of French, British or American Jews on the foreign policies of their respective governments, he was also of the opinion that if the persecution of the Jews was too frequent and too harsh, 'world Jewry' might force the implementation of an active French intervention policy.

Theoretically Hitler could have taken ideological prejudice as far as the attempt to use the German Jews as hostages. Either use your power to influence foreign states in favour of a pro-Nazi, pro-German policy, the leaders of world Jewry would have been told, or we'll take it out on your racial comrades here in Germany, and show them what real antisemitism is like. In fact this obvious solution, while it was often discussed, was never seriously entertained by Hitler and the Nazi movement, either than or later, and for a quite simple reason: the Nazis would have had to honour the success of their blackmail by forgoing any further antisemitic activity, and the Führer and his followers would never have been prepared to do that or even have been capable of fulfilling such a promise. In reality the exact opposite was the case. The Weak position of the Reich in international affairs afforded the German Jews a degree of protection, while after every foreign policy success and every increase in Germany's power there followed an increase in antisemitic terror. Even in the first months of 1933 Hitler appreciated that he could not overdo things. This realization came all the swifter as a result of the immediate difficulties: after the numerous, and in most cases accurate, press reports about the persecution of the Jews and other acts of violence in Germany, many western European and American firms, most of them Jewish-owned, ended their business connections with German customers or suppliers; if this continued there might well be currency difficulties or shortages of raw materials, which had to be avoided at all costs, not least in view of the rearmament programme.

Both domestic and international pressures were reflected in the arguments of the Nazis' German Nationalist coalition partners, who supported their own opposition to the Nazis' radical racism with the claim that a certain caution was necessary in view of the importance of foreign opinion for economic, political and military reasons. In their dilemma, Hitler and his advisers hit on the idea of raising the illegal antisemitic practices of the Nazi party, the stormtroopers and the SS to the level of official policy, and quickly concentrated their energies in a nationwide demonstration of National Socialist antisemitism. In this way the basic political tendencies of the regime could be strengthened with a dramatic gesture, and the thirst for action on the part of both the Nazi leadership and the rank and file stormtroopers was satisfied; on the other hand the movement could be taken in hand afterwards and ordered to refrain from anti-Jewish activity which was too crude and too obtrusive. On 25 and 26 March Hitler and Goebbels got together and hatched out a decree which was finally formulated on 28 March and published on 30 March. Its first paragraph read: 'In every local group (Ortsgruppe) and organizational affiliation of the NSDAP action committees are to be set up immediately to organize the practical, planned boycott of Jewish shops, Jewish products, Jewish doctors and Jewish lawyers.' While the committees would have to 'popularize' the motto 'No Germans are still buying from Jews!' The SA and the SS would have the task of 'placing sentries who would warn the population not to enter Jewish shops'.

It was also the task of the committees to organize mass rallies throughout the Reich, the purpose of which was to announce 'a demand for the introduction of quotas governing the employment of Jews in all businesses, corresponding to the proportion of Jews in the German population. To increase the impact of the exercise this demand was restricted at first to three areas: a) enrolment in German secondary schools and universities; b) the medical profession; c) the legal profession.'[9] As

SA men standing outside a Jewish-owned property to enforce a boycott of Jewish-owned shops and businesses.
(Imperial War Museum, London)

head of a 'Central Committee for Defence against Jewish Propaganda and Boycott', which was to direct and co-ordinate the activities of the action committees, Hitler appointed Julius Streicher, editor of *Der Stürmer* and *Gauleiter* of Franconia. In this own boycott appeal of 30 March Streicher decreed: 'On Saturday 1 April, at ten in the morning, the German people's defensive reaction against Jewish world criminals begins.' The *Frankenführer* (leader of the Franconians), as he liked to call himself, added 'A defensive struggle is under way which is without historical precedent. Panjudaism wanted the fight, it shall have it! Panjudaism shall have the fight until victory is ours! National Socialists! Strike down the World Enemy! Even if the world were full of devils, we must succeed!'[10]

The boycott was indeed presented both to the domestic and to the international public as a reaction to foreign criticism – immediately declared the work of 'Panjudaism' – of events in Germany, so that effectively the hostage principle came into play. To the German National members of his cabinet on the other hand Hitler offered the explanation - and with it a little more of the truth – that he had to give the wild hordes an opportunity to let off steam now and again. In reality, however, the event was a gesture to disguise a certain tightening of discipline in anti-Jewish activities, and this was clear from the fact that the nationwide, united action was restricted largely to a few Saturday shopping hours, and that on Monday 3 April – after a Sunday when there had been nothing to boycott anyway - the exercise was only half-heartedly continued, and then on 4 April it was abandoned altogether. The official reason given for abandoning the boycott was the rather bold assertion that the boycott had had the effect of ending Jewish propaganda and had therefore become 'superfluous';[11] but of course the very reports of the boycott, illustrated with pictures of stormtroopers standing guard in front of Jewish shops, had unleashed another wave of foreign criticism, which had by no means receded by 4 and 5 April.

Besides, the policy of boycotting Jewish businesses had by no means been given up altogether. Members of the party and its affiliations remained sworn not to shop in Jewish shops themselves, regardless of the behaviour of Jews either at home or abroad, and they were instructed to persuade their fellow citizens to keep away from Jewish shops and department stores through persistent 'educational work'. It was understandable, then that under such circumstances visible tensions should arise between the party and the organs of the state, which took more seriously and implemented more rigorously the change to a disciplining of antisemitic activity. The Gestapo found itself in a remarkable position between the fronts. Its members, the majority of whom came from the SS or other Nazi organizations, and were no less antisemitic than the party functionaries or the stormtroopers, were hardly likely to object to the 'educational work' of the NSDAP or to want to impede its effects. However, as they became more accustomed to the habits of state officials they came to prefer quieter and more bureaucratic forms of persecution. This conflict produced bizarre contradictions. The Gestapo fulminated against the 'shamelessness' of the many Germans who continued to shop in Jewish shops, some of them even in the uniform of some Nazi association, and would arrest a senior state official, who was also a party member, because he had been caught out shopping in a Jewish shop. On the other hand members of the SA or Hitler Youth were also arrested because they had prevented other '*Volksgenossen*' (fellow countrymen) from entering a Jewish shop.

Furthermore, 'disciplining' persecution of the Jews meant above all a move away from the terror of the stormtroopers to formal antisemitic legislation which, although it was still to be kept within certain bounds would actually cause the Jewish population of Germany greater damage than the violence of SA thugs, which naturally affected only a small number. In this respect the organizers of the boycott of 1 April doubtless had a second objective in mind, to prepare the population and the bourgeois-national Establishment psychologically for the planned legislation, and – conversely – to give the laws the appearance of reflecting the will of the people.

It was not even so much a matter of introducing consciously *Völkisch* laws such as the (German Nationalist) State Secretary in the Reich Economics Ministry, Paul Bang, had suggested. On 6 March Bang, an eager disciple of Heinrich Class, had approached the Reich chancellery with the following suggestions: a) a ban on the further immigration of 'eastern Jews' (Ostjuden); b) the repeal of certain name changes which had taken place since November 1918; c) the expulsion of a number of 'eastern Jews' who did not yet have citizenship. On 9 March, on instruction from Hitler, Hans Heinrich Lammers, the head of the Reich chancellery, forwarded Bang's thoughts, with approval, to Reich Interior Minister Frick, adding: 'I am permitted by the Reich chancellor to leave to your discretion, most esteemed Herr Reichsminister whether other measures are necessary in the field of *völkisch* legislation.'[12] Bang's proposals had not been realized by the end of the summer of 1933, but had been significantly expanded with the Law for the Repeal of Naturalization and Recognition of German Citizenship, which was published on 14 July and made possible the repeal of all acts of naturalization effected between 9 November 1918 and 30 January 1933 'if the naturalization is thought to be undesirable.' An order of the Reich Interior Ministry of 26 July made it clear that the law was in fact directed against 'eastern Jews' in the first instance.[13] Ideas similar to those presented by Bang had already been

THE REVERSAL OF EMANCIPATION

voiced in the Interior Ministry in 1932, when it had been run by a German Nationalist, Freiherr von Gayl, and similar proposals had come through Frick from the Reich leadership of the NSDAP, where they had been formulated by Dr Helmut Nicolai, again during 1931 and 1932, for implementation after the assumption of power.

When Hitler asked him to review the possibility of further *völkisch* legislation on 9 March, Frick did actually consider for a long time a question which left far behind the problem of the 'eastern Jews', namely the issue of whether, despite all domestic and foreign resistance, the first task should not be to repeal the emancipation of the German Jews altogether, and again restrict them essentially to business activity. In the course of March and the beginning of April he discussed with Hitler and interested departments the pathbreaking first measure: the expulsion of Jews from the public service. Even here Frick could rely on prepared material; after all he himself had already presented to the Reichstag on 17 July 1925 a law for the dismissal of 'November criminals' in the state service and 'members of the Jewish race' holding official positions. Quite how precisely his plans also corresponded with the wishes of the rest of the Nazi movement is clear from the decisive actions of eager functionaries: on 25 March, for example, the Bavarian Justice Ministry ordered that no more Jewish judges should be allowed to officiate, and no Jews should be employed as public prosecutors in criminal or disciplinary cases. In Prussia Hanns Kerrl, the Nazi Reich Commissar who was responsible for the judicial authorities, even instructed that 'it should be suggested to all officiating Jewish judges that they immediately put in requests for leave of absence', otherwise 'they should be forbidden to enter the premises of the court'; Jewish public prosecutors too should all be suspended, and Jewish lawyers should be admitted only in numbers which corresponded to the 'proportion of the Jewish population'.[14] Yet Kerrl was still not satisfied. On 1 April he prohibited all Jewish notaries from practising, and on 4 April there followed the prohibition of all Jewish lawyers in Prussia.

In the debates of those weeks it also became clear that, provided Hindenburg's exemptions were allowed, the intentions of Frick and Hitler met with the approval of their German Nationalist coalition partners. So it was a piece of Nazi–German Nationalist coalition politics when on 7 April 1933 Frick's plans from the 1920s were realized and a Law for the Restoration of a Professional Civil Service was announced, whose main objective was to provide the legal basis for the dismissal of unwelcome state officials, and whose second aim was formulated in the following way in paragraph 3: 'Civil servants, who are not of Aryan extraction are to be pensioned off.'[15] An order of implementation of 4 May provided for the dismissal of 'non-Aryan' workers and white-collar workers employed by the authorities, and a further order of 6 May regulated the sacking of Jewish honorary professors, private tutors and notaries. In this way the antisemitic legislation went far beyond the public service – and extended to the judicial system and administration both of the Reich and its constituent federal states. On 7 April not only was the Civil Service Law promulgated, prohibiting Jewish lawyers from practising their profession, but there was a further law forbidding German Jews to act as jurors or commercial judges.

On 22 April it was the turn of Jewish patent lawyers and general practitioners, on 6 May Jewish tax accountants, on 2 June Jewish dentists and dental technicians. The Law against the Overcrowding of German Schools and Universities of 25 April limited new registrations of German schoolchildren and students (to 1.5 per cent of the 'Aryans'. as a further decree of the same day made clear), and the Reich Entailed Farm Law of 29 September also excluded Jews, as did the Editors' Law of 4 October. New regulations for doctors and dentists, which excluded Jewish students from the appropriate examinations, came on 5 February 1934, and law faculties followed this example on 22 July, pharmacy departments on 8 December. These developments culminated in 1935, when the 'Defence Law' of 21 May declared an 'Aryan' background to be the essential prerequisite for army service, and an absolute condition for an officer's career. A decree of 25 July then summarized the legislation by saying that no 'non-Aryans' were to be admitted to service in the armed forces under any circumstances.

Since Hindenburg's exemptions – including the stipulation that anyone who had practised a profession on 1 August 1914 would not be affected – were built into the legislation, many German Jews were of course not affected. This rather took the Nazis aback since the claim that Jews had avoided military service during the war was one of the standard lies in the repertoire of antisemitic propaganda, and had been widely believed. Now, however, it became clear that these exemptions were the rule rather than the exception. Almost 70 per cent of 'non-Aryan' lawyers – 3,167 out of a total of 4,585 – retained the right to practise. Of course, the discovery of this mistake by no means served to soften the approach of the persecutors. On the contrary, they set about fiddling the conditions of exemption by introducing ever more stringent conditions into the relevant paragraphs of the law. Already in the decree of 22 April, which forbade Jewish GPs to practise, proof of service at the front was not sufficient for any doctor who wanted to retain his practice. He had to prove that he had been a practising GP for at least a year before his enlistment.

On 26 September 1933 the 'Patent Lawyer Law' established that even 'non-Aryan' patent lawyers with a record of service at the front could be refused or dismissed, and on 17 May 1934 a further decree stated that in future a 'non-Aryan' would be allowed to practise as a GP only if he had served at the front for at least a year, or had suffered disablement; so a German Jew who had joined a front unit at the age of seventeen or eighteen at the beginning of 1918 lost his right to practise as a GP, even if he had been decorated or wounded in the last ten or eleven months of the war, so long as he had not been seriously disabled. Such chicanery testified to the fundamental meanness of the Nazis' treatment of the Jews, and to their dissatisfaction with Hindenburg's exceptions; and it was a promise of more terror in the future. The quantitative results of the legislation were small, and brought no real satisfaction to their inventors, who resented the high number of exemptions.

On the other hand the antisemitic legislation of the years 1933 and 1934 claimed many victims who had long since forgotten that there was any connection between themselves and the Jewish community. It quickly became clear that racial antisemitism, unlike the religious persecution of earlier centuries, not only demanded additional forms of persecution, but applied to a considerably wider constituency. The first Decree on the Implementation of the Law for the Restoration of a Professional Civil Service, which entered the statute book on 11 April, gave the following definition: 'Anyone who is descended from non-Aryan parents or grand-parents, and particularly from Jews, counts as non-Aryan. It is sufficient if one parent or grandparent is not Aryan.' The stipulation that 'non-Aryan descent' would be 'assumed in particular if one parent or grandparent has belonged to the Jewish religion' was an admission on the part of those who drafted the law that they had no objective racial criteria for distinguishing between 'non-Aryan' and those 'of German blood' and were therefore compelled to use religion as a defining characteristic, but such unconscious irony did not alter the fact that this definition provided them with an instrument to drive back into the Jewish fold all those who had left it through the conversion of their grandparents to a Christian confession, or through the marriage of grandparents or parents to a non-Jewish partner: people who had not only come to feel at home with German culture, but had become completely integrated into their German environment. The Reich entailed Farm Law even demanded proof of 'Aryan' descent dating back to the year 1800. The number of those affected has never been exactly established and there are widely differing estimates, but it can be assumed that obligatory re-judaization through this legislation brought at least a further hundred thousand into the sights of their persecutors in addition to the 500,000 practising Jews who lived in Germany in 1933.

It is not surprising that the war against the Jews, whether it took the form of acts of violence or whether it was waged with laws and decrees, created around all Jews in Germany, even those who were initially declared exceptions, an atmosphere of animosity and risk, which increasingly had the effect of deterring the average German from cultivating personal contacts with them. This was clear from the countless associations and clubs which followed the example of the Law for the Restoration of a Professional Civil Service, and swiftly adopted the 'Aryan clause', excluding members who belonged to the Jewish religion or who were of Jewish descent. The boards of large business or employers' associations, including the Reich Association of German Industry, and the veterans' associations of famous regiments and even simple Skat clubs also frequently adopted such clauses. On 8 October 1933 the General Association of Catholic Student Clubs (CV) adopted a rule, Article 3 of which was completely incompatible with Catholic doctrine: 'The CV is made up of associations, which are established in the universities of the German area of settlement. Only men of German descent, whose mother tongue is German may be members of these associations. Marriage to a non-Aryan woman entails exclusion from the association.'[16]

That German society found itself drifting so far towards antisemitism rarely had anything to do with individual hostility towards the Jews. A process of accommodation to the new regime was under way, and this often meant that the Nazi government's ideology and policies, although alien to the nature of many Germans or secretly disapproved of, were accepted and even welcomed and supported, when it seemed necessary from a tactical or political point of view to square one's position with the regime. Once the Nazi movement was in power, even the churches had avoided a conflict with the unchristian doctrine and behaviour of the Nazis. They sought to accommodate themselves as well as possible to the new situation, and opposed the regime only when they were directly attacked as institutions. So – apart from individual priests – they avoided fundamental and open opposition on the issue of the persecution of the Jews; they did not bother themselves at all with practising Jews, and their support of Protestants or Catholics of Jewish descent was restricted to measures which formed part of a church social policy, albeit one which was every welcome to those who were affected. Weaker groups and individuals were influenced much more by anxiety, and generally by an anxiety which was not so much determined by fear of the SA or the Gestapo, but by fear of some form of economic discrimination or professional difficulty or disadvantage.

In any event, by the end of 1933 German Jews had been driven both from the public service and the important free professions, their unimpeded participation in the cultural life of the nation was virtually a thing of the past, and they found themselves in the first stages of a general isolation, which meant at best the beginnings of re-ghettoization both individually and collectively. Under such circumstances economic activity was already beginning to suffer severe disturbances, and the persistent antisemitic rabble-rousing of the Nazified press – Streicher's *Stürmer*, with its concentration on antisemitism and the most primitive obscenity was the worst of the lot – together with the hostility of local Nazi functionaries, expressed in every possible type of cheap trick, pointed irresistibly to the conclusion that even those privileges which Jews had earned through their service to the nation could be understood only as a temporary reprieve.

Those Jewish children who were still able to attend German schools and institutions of higher education did so in an atmosphere which at least officially, and often also in practice, was dominated by a growing animosity. Mixed school attendance took on grotesque features as all types of school began to make the ramblings of racists a compulsory subject with examinations, as was the case in Prussia, for example, following a circular of 13 September 1933 from the Ministry for Science, Art and Education. 'Aryans' and 'non-Aryans' sitting side by side on the same benches now learnt that the former were noble almost to the point of divinity while the latter were innately inferior and dangerous. Following the public declaration by the *Deutsche Studentenschaft* (German Student Corporation) on 13 April 1933 that 'our most dangerous adversary is the Jew, and all those in his thrall',[17] the climate in German universities must have made the situation for Jewish students even more difficult. The conclusion is clear: the new regime in Germany had in effect virtually reversed the emancipation of the Jews in little more than a year, and now applied itself to the task of rooting out the consequences of assimilation.

Many German Jews were unable to understand the sudden change in their fortunes, and not a few of them at first refused to accept the dangerous implications of the course of events. As a result, very few sought asylum abroad as an escape from violence and legislative persecution initially. Of course, emigration was a very difficult undertaking at that time for a number of practical reasons. All of the states to which they might have migrated, both in Europe and overseas, were still in the grip of the world depression and massive unemployment. In western Europe it was relatively easy to get a residence permit, either for a short stay or for an unlimited time, but it was much more difficult to get a work permit. Overseas countries such as the United States, Canada, Brazil, Argentina or South Africa, in so far as they still accepted immigrants at all, demanded a surety from one of their own citizens, proof of financial assets, or qualifications for employment in jobs where there were labour shortages.

Other than in exceptional cases German Jews were prevented from providing proof of private assets by draconian currency laws which expropriated emigrants, leaving them with only a little pocket money;

furthermore the professional skills they had to offer were inappropriate: agricultural labourers, skilled workers and artisans were needed rather than businessmen and graduates. Finally, German Jews had to compete with the hundreds of thousands of other Jews who were trying to leave the Baltic states, Poland, Romania and Hungary in the 1930s in order to escape terrible economic hardship and growing antisemitism in eastern Europe.

Yet if only 37,000 Jews left Germany in the first year of Nazi persecution, the main reason was that the majority of the largely assimilated Jewish community were unwilling to believe what they saw happening around them, and even what they had suffered themselves. Their long-standing attachment to German culture and the German nation was too deep-rooted and too powerful. The predominant Jewish reaction to the intensifying Nazi terror was a tendency to keep one's head down and wait for the nightmare to pass, in the conviction that it must end soon. This meant that Jewish institutions and organizations orientated their policy towards three types of tactic: the right to live and work in Germany must be defended on the one hand, while on the other a greater tolerance on the part of the new rulers must be encouraged by their own good behaviour; and at the same time their own people must be encouraged to weather the storm. This was the strategy employed by the 'Reich Representation of German Jews', the new umbrella organization directed by Leo Baeck, which brought together all Jewish associations. Nevertheless the organization was soon compelled to consider the promotion of more Jewish emigration, but it was above all such German-minded associations as the Centralverein der Deutschen Staatsbürger jüdischen Glaubens (Central Association of German Citizens of the Jewish Faith), the Verband Nationaldeutscher Juden (League of National German Jews) and the Reichsbund Jüdischer Frontsoldaten (Reich Union of Jewish Veterans) who adopted such policies.

In March 1933, before the boycott of 1 April, such German Jewish organizations went to great pains to play down events in Germany, and to trivialize the vehement antisemitism in all their communications with both Jewish and non-Jewish organizations abroad. In a telegram to the 'American Jewish Committee' of 30 March The presidium of the Jewish community (Gemeinde) in Berlin spoke of foreign 'atrocity propaganda' against which 'as Germans and Jews we must enter a decisive protest';[18] in a letter to the American embassy in Berlin of 24 March the Reichsbund Jüdischer Frontsoldaten used the formulation, very moving in retrospect, 'alleged atrocities against the Jews in Germany'.[19] On the other had Dr Curt Elsbach, one of the leaders of the Reichsbund, speaking at a reunion evening in the East Prussian town of Königsberg in 1935, continued to maintain that the only possible response to the question of whether it was possible for Jews to continue living Germany, in a national community which rejects, or at best tolerates us' was the answer: 'We know only one fatherland and one homeland (Heimat), and that is Germany'.[20]

SS *Gruppenführer* Erich von dem Bach-Zelewski, director of the State Police Office in Königsberg and head of the SS North-east Region noted Elsbach's remark with the same astonishment which must also have greeted a similar declaration of 23 March 1935. Dr Löwenstein, a captain of the reserve, took up the subject of the reintroduction of general conscription in the name of the Reichsbund, 'in order to demonstrate our continuing loyalty to the German fatherland' and referred to armed service in the emergent army of the Third Reich as the 'inalienable right' of Geman Jews.[21]

Given the situation, it was inevitable that such a policy would occasionally lead to absurd and embarrassing aberrations, such as the case of Dr Naumann, secretary of the Verband Nationaldeutscher Juden, who wrote a letter to Hitler on 20 March 1935, also in connection with the reintroduction of general conscription, in which he spoke of the 'most determined struggle against all non-German delinquents (Volksscchädlinge) . . . particularly the eastern Jews and those politicians and writers who sympathize with them', as a good thing which the 'national Jews' were happy to support. At the end of his letter Dr Naumann wrote,

> Therefore, most respected Herr Führer, I would request of you, in the name of the national German Jews I represent, that we be permitted to fulfil our duty to serve in the army. In the matter of organizational details, particularly the necessary distinction between the national German Jews who are to be admitted, and the foreign Jews who are not, I am in a position to make certain suggestions. I would very much welcome an opportunity to put forward my views in this matter personally.[22]

Even in 1942 Curt Bleichröder, a grandson of old Gerson Bleichröder, begged to be allowed to serve as an officer in the army, pointing out that in the First World War he had been wounded three times, and that a brother of his had been killed.[23]

Yet even worse than such individual aberrations was the inevitable lack of success of the policy of the Jewish community as a whole. Despite the assistance that was given to Goebbels's propaganda machine, it was still impossible either to prevent the boycott of 1 April 1933 or to soften the blow of the unstoppable anti-Jewish legislation which followed. Perhaps least successful of all were the attempts to exploit the armed forces' transition from Reichswehr to Wehrmacht in order to improve the position of the Jews. Month by month it became clearer that the behaviour of the Jews themselves, whether inside Germany or abroad, had only a very modest place among the factors which determined the character, pace and severity of Nazi antisemitism. In relation to the scale of Nazi antisemitism the impact of their behaviour was insignificant. Yet the tendency of Jewish organizations to hang on grimly, asserting their membership of the German nation, had the unintentional effect of saving many Jews from a worse fate.

The reaction of the organs of Nazi Germany, those of the Nazi movement as well as those of the state and of the intermediate areas where the Gestapo had wheedled its way in, was to reject with the utmost vehemence such attempts at rapprochement on the part of their mortal enemy. However the ultimate objective of Nazi 'Jewish policy' might be defined, there was one thing of which every representative of the regime was certain: the Jews must be cut out of the German nation once and for all, and there was nothing more intolerable than this Jewish 'assimilationism'. The Gestapo, which was responsible for the surveillance of Jewish organizations, began to take measures against 'assimilationist' tendencies in Jewish associational life and the Jewish press. Finally, on 10 February 1935, Reinhard Heydrich issued the following instruction to all Gestapo offices: 'There has recently been an increase in lectures to Jewish organizations arguing the case for the Jews' remaining in Germany. Since such Jewish organizations are in any case so active that proper surveillance cannot be guaranteed, I am ordering the immediate prohibition until further notice of all Jewish organizations in which such propaganda is employed.'[24]

It was unavoidable, however, that discrimination against 'assimilationism' strengthened the position of those Jewish groups which considered the most comprehensive emigration of German Jews either inevitable or desirable, and were working on plans to implement it; this meant above all the Zionists, who had hitherto been a relatively insignificant force in Germany. As a result of this unintended preferential treatment, the state authorities – especially the Gestapo, whose interest in a more rational antisemitic policy was determined by its institutional character – developed a sort of political 'general line' which necessarily made Jewish emigration from Germany the goal of Nazi 'Jewish policy'.

Of course, there could be no immediate results of practical significance. The German authorities were unable to exercise the least authority on foreign labour markets or on the immigration policy of foreign states, while on the other hand they were totally unwilling to promote Jewish emigration by tolerating the export of Jewish assets or even making it easier. Besides, the Nazi attitude to Zionist aspirations remained ambiguous, to say the least. On the one hand Palestine was at first one of the few regions, which accepted rather larger contingents of emigrants from Germany, since German Jews were given a relatively high priority within the framework of the internationally directed migration to that country. On the other hand there was nothing to gain, from the Nazi pont of view, from the creation of a 'world centre of Jewry' in Palestine which might eventually become an independent state; on the contrary, it was a rather disturbing possibility.

Nevertheless, in order to give a certain degree of concrete form to the 'general line' of Nazi Jewish policy, the Reich Economics Ministry came to an agreement with Zionist representatives in September 1933 that permitted a number of German Jews to go to Palestine, combining the promotion of Jewish emigration with concern for the needs of German business for exports and foreign currency. To this end, Jewish emigrants were able to contribute in cash to a 'Palestine Advisory Trust Company for German Jews' ('Paltreu'). About half of the cost of German exports to Palestine could be paid for out of the fund built up by such contributions, while the remaining proportion had to be raised in hard currency in Palestine, although this proportion varied according to the type of goods and the Reich's foreign currency needs. In Palestine the Jewish organization Haavara, after which the agreement was named, dealt with the sale of German goods and paid back the investments of those who had emigrated through the agency of the Paltreu. The Paltreu and the Haavara agreed between themselves that the more affluent emigrants to Palestine would not be repaid in full, but would have to give up part of their investment to those Jews who were otherwise without financial means, and the rule of thumb was that a wealthy emigrant should support two who were poorer. Nevertheless the effect of the Haavara agreement was necessarily limited; in the end German exports to Palestine could not be increased above a relatively low level. By 1936 some 34,000 German Jews had taken advantage of the scheme.

Anyone who sought refuge in other states during 1933 generally had little chance of a reasonable existence without relying on the assistance of helpful relatives or friends, or on accumulated financial assets. This led to consequences which with hindsight seem not only regrettable but peculiar. The antisemitic legislation of 1933 – containing the first measure of racial policy affecting those 'of German blood', the Law for the Prevention of Hereditary Diseases of 14 July 1933, which provided for sterilization in certain cases – was not stepped up by further measures in 1934, but merely refined, and a not inconsiderable number of Jewish refugees returned to Germany. Clearly the new misery which characterized the lives of Jews still seemed much more bearable at home than abroad.

4

Isolation

There were three reasons for the brief respite from both stormtroopers and legislators which was granted to German Jews in 1934. Conflicts between different organizations within the Nazi movement, which had festered since 1933, broke out openly in the first six months of the year, and they absorbed a great deal of the party's attention and energy. The SA was increasingly distracted as it made powerful enemies from the Nazi party leadership to the Reich Ministry of Defence with its call for a 'second revolution', and with the demand that stormtrooper units be transformed into the popular militia of the Third Reich.

Firstly, Hitler's freedom to take radical measures was restricted in many different aspects of domestic policy by the political situation which the SA created, and he was not even able to act freely in the solution to the SA problem itself, which formed gradually and culminated in the bloodbath of 30 June. Foreign policy dictated the second reason. On 14 October 1933 Hitler had declared the withdrawal from the League of Nations of a German Reich which was still virtually defenceless in military terms, and instructed the German delegation at the Disarmament Conference in Geneva to pack their bags and come back to Berlin. Such an abrupt break with the prevailing order of international relations, and such a brutal challenge to the system of collective security – inevitably dramatic first moves in a radical policy of rearmament and expansion – provoked no small degree of international tension, and with it the isolation of Germany. Although the non-aggression pact with Poland signed on 26 January 1934 brought some relief, both these developments forced a temporary relaxation in both foreign and domestic policies which were not yet classified as urgent.

In addition, Hitler realized, when he began to work towards an alliance with fascist Italy, that the Italians, and not least the *Duce* (Leader), Benito Mussolini, considered the German worship of the 'Aryan' race not only a fatuous aberration, but one which was insulting to the Italian nation. In view of the tough beginnings of this German initiative – the two dictators met in person for the first time only on 14 and 15 June 1934, in Venice, without making any progress in either their political or their personal relationship – greater sensitivity to Mediterranean sensibilities seemed to be in order. Furthermore, the precariousness of Germany's international position, and Italian reservations about Nazi racist policy, were highlighted in the wake of the assassination of the Austrian chancellor Engelbert Dollfuss by Austrian Nazis in the course of an unsuccessful coup which Hitler himself had backed. Although the coup failed, the support which the German Nazis had afforded their Austrian friends, and their complicity in the preceding wave of Nazi terror, could not be disguised.

In any event international reaction was both sharp and extremely sceptical. Italian *raison d'état* ensured that Mussolini was even more interested in an independent Austria than the West, and he went so far as to order troops to the Brenner. When he met Dollfuss's successor, Kurt von Schuschnigg, in Florence on 21 August, the *Duce* emphasised his role as Austria's protector, and on 6 September he said in a public speech: 'Three thousand years of history permit us to look down with pity on certain ideas from across the Alps, ideas promoted by a breed whose illiteracy prevented them from leaving behind any trace of their existence at a time when Rome had Caesar, Virgil and Augustus.'[1]

During the summer of 1934 Hitler had managed to sort out his internal problems. By murdering the most important leaders of the SA on 30 June 1934 he had tamed the last significant political force in the Nazi state which still showed any sign of independence. Although he had exploited an opportunity to make a simultaneous strike against conservative and monarchist circles, and particularly the circle around vice-chancellor Franz von Papen, the action against the SA had so bound the army to Hitler that, as Field Marshal Hindenburg lay dying, there was no opposition to his Law on the Head of the German State, by which he became Reich President on Hindenburg's death; and there was also no opposition when on 2 August, after Hindenburg had actually died, he instructed the armed forces to swear an oath of allegiance to him personally. In the course of a few weeks Hitler's personal position had become unassailable, and the way was open to the consolidation of a 'Führer dictatorship' free of obstacles; at the same time, and despite the defeat of the SA, the balance of power between the Nazi movement and its German National partners had shifted decisively in favour of the former. In the autumn, as Germany conspicuously made an effort to make up for its bad behaviour over Austria, international tensions began to relax, and there was an improvement in relations with Italy.

Meanwhile, neither the consolidation of Nazi power in Germany, nor the relaxation in international relations gave the antisemitic activists an immediate free hand, because a third factor emerged which dictated good behaviour. The Treaty of Versailles had placed the Saarland under League of Nations administration for fifteen years. After this period the ultimate fate of the territory was to be decided by a plebiscite, in which the options were: a return to Germany, the maintenance of the status quo, or incorporation into France. The date of the plebiscite was 13 January 1935. Naturally, the Nazi government had a great interest in ensuring that the confidently expected majority in favour of a return to Germany be so impressively overwhelming – at least around 90 per cent – that it would lead to a much firmer political consensus at home, and bring greater security abroad. Such a high percentage could only be achieved, however, if those sections of the Saar's population which were less sympathetic to Nazism were not frightened off. During the last months before the plebiscite, at least, it was necessary to present an image which emphasized Germany's stability.

This did not mean that there were no attempts to step up anti-Jewish activity, and to increase the severity of antisemitic legislation, even during 1934. Although less frequent than in the spring of 1933, harassment of all kinds persisted. There had already been such massive pressure on Jews either to close down their businesses, or to sell them to an 'Aryan' at a fraction of their real value, that even Reich Interior Minister Frick, who doubtless looked forward to a time more favourable for the extension of antisemitic legislation, was forced to intervene: 'Germany's Aryan legislation is necessary both for reasons of state and as a consequence of its *Volkspolitik* ("national" policy). On the other hand the Reich government has set certain limits, which must be observed. The legislation would be more correctly assessed both at home and abroad if these limits were always respected'; activities not covered by laws or supplementary orders were to cease, and 'particularly unauthorized pressure on businesses'.[2] In addition there were increasingly vociferous demands in the course of that year strengthened by the developments of the previous year, for the Nazis to go beyond measures which merely reduced German Jews to the status of aliens.

In his programmatic work 'The Myth of the Twentieth Century', which had appeared in 1930, Alfred Rosenberg had already summed up one of the oldest objectives of racist antisemitism in the following way: 'Marriages between Germans and Jews are to be forbidden . . . Sexual intercourse, rape etc. between Germans and Jews is to be punished according to the severity of the offence with confiscation of property, deportation, imprisonment or death.'[3] On 13 March 1930 Frick had put before the Reichstag in the name of the NSDAP the draft for a Law for the Protection of the German Nation according to which 'anybody who contributes to the deterioration or destruction of the German people by mixing with those of Jewish blood or coloured race' should be punished by imprisonment and permanent loss of civil rights 'for their treason to the race; and Frick, like Rosenberg, also provided for the death penalty for serious cases.[4]

After the Nazis came to power, the new Prussian Justice Minister Kerrl, and his State Secretary Roland Freisler had worked out proposals for a reform of the criminal law in the spirit of the Third Reich, which was published in 1933 as 'National Socialist Criminal Law' and included 'racial treason' as a punishable offence; the two jurists, who wanted to make 'malicious' opposition to state enlightenment about the race question a punishable offence as well, also came up with the idea of an 'offence against racial honour', by which was understood 'consorting shamelessly in public' with 'members of a coloured race'.[5]

When this commission, which was later officially required to advise on the drafting of a National Socialist criminal law, addressed the question of 'racial treason' on 5 June 1934, Freisler, who was a member of the commission, forcefully argued for the adoption of his and Kerrl's views. In doing so he started an intense debate both within the Criminal Law Commission, and between the interested Reich authorities, namely between the Interior Ministry and the Justice Ministry, during which the future President of the People's Court was supported by hysterical propaganda in the party press. Streicher's *Stürmer* was by far the shrillest, and repeatedly reported on the 'shaming' of German girls by Jews. Streicher himself complained to the Reich Interior Ministry in an attempt to win a 'comradely pronouncement' from Frick in favour of a legal prohibition of 'racial treason'; 'Even if a Jew slept with an Aryan woman once', he argued, following Dühring and Dinter, 'the membranes of her vagina would be so impregnated with alien semen' that the woman would never again be able to bear 'pure-blooded Aryans'.[6]

At the beginning of December 1934 a medical conference on 'Racial Hygiene and Topical Questions of Biological Heredity' was held in Nuremberg, where Streicher lived. The conference, which Streicher attended, developed into a 'powerful demonstration' against any further 'poisoning or infestation of German blood by the Jewish race'. On 2 December the participants sent Frick a telegram, demanding that the Heredity Law of July 1933 should be supplemented by 'provisions clearly necessary for reasons arising from natural law and for the protection of the "nation", requiring that every attempted physical intercourse between a German woman and a Jew receive just as severe a punishment as a successful act'.[7]

By the end of 1934 the case for a Blood Protection Law had foundered repeatedly on the resistance of those Nazi leaders who, while no less antisemitic, had a broader perspective, and consequently always forcefully brought up those considerations of domestic and foreign policy which seemed to speak for a breathing space. The opposition was able to assert itself all the more easily as its arguments were repeatedly confirmed by the facts. The publication of the memorandum for a reform of the criminal law drawn up by Kerrl and Freisler, for example, had brought Germany more trouble than the Reich could cope with at the time: in particular, the ingeniously constructed offence of 'violation of racial honour' – a truly classic combination of blinkered ideology and arrogant insensitivity – provoked a torrent of press commentary in India, Japan and South America which ranged from the contemptuous to the furious, and many businesses in those countries had unceremoniously broken off their relations with German export and import companies, failing to see why they should continue with a partnership in which they were confronted with officially ordained and openly expressed contempt; the German Foreign Office had its hands full attempting, by means of discreet efforts and appropriate official declarations, to prevent things getting out of control.

Consequently everyone knew that it was not simply timid apprehension that prompted the rather wordy intervention of Vice-President Grau of the Prussian Interior Ministry during the Criminal Law Commission debate. He argued that although of course 'it was necessary to bring within the criminal law every kind of sexual miscegenation between Jews and those of German blood', it was nevertheless also the case that 'our international position does not permit us to introduce legislation, and particularly criminal legislation, which would lead to the complete implementation of these proposals.'[8] The Foreign Office made clear the necessity of bearing in mind foreign policy considerations to those members of the Nazi movement given to such declarations, and they did so by means which although often perhaps rather crude, were by no means without effect. For example, those passages of the minutes from the meeting of 5 June 1934 which referred to the discussion by the Criminal Law Commission of 'racial treason' were not even printed for internal use, because the Foreign Office had instructed that every precaution must be taken to prevent 'the deliberations of the Criminal Law Commission on this matter from reaching the public'.[9]

Interior Minister Frick, who was doubtless inclined to take the antisemitic legislation a step further, nevertheless kept things sufficiently in perspective to know that certain limits had to be observed at the moment. Franz Gürtner, the German Nationalist (although not racist) Minister of Justice even managed to let it be known that behind his emphatic rejection of the new racial laws there lay a more fundamental opposition to the obsession with race. Gürtner was not at all satisfied with the proposal, significant in itself, to abandon legislation and rely on more party propaganda. In the commission's sessions he managed to get the experts present to admit that – apart from the differentiation of the major racial groups by skin colour – there were no reliable objective criteria for establishing an individual's race, and on one occasion managed to make the point that a value-laden racial differentiation was the least useful of all. It bred popular discontent at home where 'one always hears that "the noblest race is the Nordic" and feels depressed because one knows that nine tenths of the German people don't even belong to this noble race.' He was even provocative enough to repeat before the apostles of racism the currently popular observation that 'one should look at the heads of the Nazi leaders, and see whether any of them has Nordic features.'[10] During a phase of primarily legislative antisemitism, in which the Interior and Justice Ministries were responsible and could not be circumvented, attempts to force the pace of 'Jewish policy' were bound to founder against the combined opposition and passivity of Frick and Gürtner. Only Hitler could have cleared the way and undammed the wave of antisemitism that had built up, and the Führer was still in favour of caution. Hitler, although himself the most radical and unscrupulous antisemite in the movement, was unable, as chancellor, and subsequently as head of state, to ignore Nazi Germany's internal politics and international position as easily as his *Gauleiter* in Franconia: it was above all his appraisal of the situation, and his instinct for danger which convinced him of the need for caution.

In 1935, however, the dams broke. On 13 January no less than 90.8 per cent of the population in the Saarland declared themselves in favour of reincorporation into the German Reich, and this triumphant success brought the Nazi regime an enormous gain in prestige which was immediately transformed into a real increase in domestic stability and greater international standing. A little later, on 16 March, Hitler announced the reintroduction of general military service, and by doing so officially revealed both to the Germans themselves and to the outside world Germany's intensive secret rearmament, and opened up the way for the rearmament to move into a higher gear. When Hitler found himself confronted with paper protests and ineffectual diplomatic gestures rather than more severe reactions from the other European powers, it was clear that this act – which, apart from the territorial provisions, finally consigned the Treaty of Versailles to the dustbin of history – had brought Nazi Germany a considerable increase in power, freedom of movement in international relations, and not least self-confidence.

This self-confidence and freedom of action in foreign relations was increased further when Great Britain provided to some extent an international pardon for German rearmament by concluding a naval agreement on 18 June. Hitler misunderstood this as the first step towards an Anglo-German alliance, which would give him a free hand in continental Europe. Throughout the summer of 1935 the talk of Europe was the apparently imminent invasion of Ethiopia by the Italian forces massed in Eritrea and Somaliland (actually launched on 3 October), and it was clear that this old-fashioned imperialist adventure would bring Mussolini and fascist Italy into conflict both with the League of Nations (of which Ethiopia was a member), and with the Western powers. This was a situation from which Germany could only profit. In parallel with this improvement in Germany's international position, the redistribution of internal political forces of 1934 began to make itself felt. The simultaneity of these two developments led to a more clearly Nazi emphasis in German policy-making, both foreign and domestic.

After the Saar plebiscite, and above all after the reintroduction of military service, the anti-Jewish activities of local and regional state and party officials increased dramatically throughout the Reich. In many places the conditions which had prevailed in February and March 1933 returned. Again the scale of violence ranged from attacks on Jewish shops, houses and synagogues to the physical abuse of individual Jews. It was noticeable, too, that this enthusiatic antisemitic activity was no longer fuelled entirely by ideological determination. The stormtroopers, who had had no real function since the elimination of all open opposition in Germany, and no political clout since 30 June 1934, were frustrated.

At the same time many Nazi party members were discontented. The maxim of 'party over state' was clearly realized at the top, where it was embodied in the dictatorship of the Führer, but their own experience was of daily competition for influence with older institutions, particularly with the state apparatus, and in many areas they competed without any substantial success. In addition, there was a stifling feeling, both in the party and in the SA, that the Nazi 'revolution' ought to have wrought more fundamental changes in Germany than it had. The most unambiguous and embarrassing failure was in the field of cultural aspirations, where the intellectual and political barrenness of the Nazi movement was obvious. The Nazis had concentrated all their energies on attaining power and mobilizing the nation and it now seemed reasonable to seek compensation and to take out their frustrated and incoherent 'will to act' on the

Jews, the arch-enemies of both Nazis and Germans, who seemed to have
been made specifically for this purpose.

A final and important factor was that the Nazis felt themselves
particularly provoked by their arch-enemy in the spring of 1935. They
perceived the 'assimilationist' efforts of Jewish organizations to extend the
recently reintroduced military service to the Jewish community as 'typically
Jewish insolence'. This reaction was only logical, given the way their
Weltanschauung worked, and their response to the affront was renewed
persecution. During the campaign against Jewish 'infiltrationism' the
central organ of the SS, *Das Schwarze Korps* ('The Black Corps'), founded
in March 1935, ran the headline 'No Room for Jews in the Army' on 15
May and followed it with words which clearly revealed the crude
vindictiveness of Nazi thinking. Rejecting any discussion of military service
for Jews, the paper argued on 29 May: 'Jews, too, must now come to terms
with restrictions on their rights, and accept them. Germans, however, have
never been accustomed to dealing with their inferiors in a comradely way,
but have always treated them according to the dictates of our race's healthy
sensitivity.'

It was ideological antisemitism, however, which was the most important
impulse. It was a force which now had free rein in the changed political
situation, and functioned as a prime mover for all the other influences. The
protagonists themselves did not see their actions as some sort of surrogate
activism, but as an offensive in an arena of Nazi policy which was second
in importance only to rearmament. Activity in this arena was considered
the holiest of obligations, inaction a sin. The momentum of racist
motivation was also evident in the activists' own attitude to the 1935
campaign, which they saw quite simply as a continuation, a resumption
under more favourable conditions, of the pressure of the previous year. The
anti-Jewish activity of May 1935 came to be dominated by boycotts along
the lines of 1 April 1933, and individual appeals for boycotts or actual
blockades of Jewish shops were increasingly accompanied (and ultimately
justified) by the demand that the legislative framework for the punishment
of 'racial treason' must now finally be provided. In the end the movement
developed into a forceful attempt to 'reopen the Jewish question from
below', and presented itself, in the terms of its originators and participants,
as a means of pressure to which 'the government would then have to
respond.'[11]

The regime did not respond to this pressure immediately, however,
and in the meantime an atmosphere developed which was characterized
by confusingly contradictory behaviour on the part of the institutions of
the Nazi state. While some authorities considered the law binding and
sought to prevent the illegal activity of the antisemitic activists, others

sided with the lawbreakers, behaved indeed as if a 'Blood Protection Law' already existed, and in doing so themselves moved into the terrain of illegality. The accumulation of such cases between May and September 1935 is remarkable testimony to the depth and corrosiveness of antisemitism. For example, it was by no means rare in the early summer of 1935, against the background of the campaign against 'racial treason', for registrars to refuse to marry 'Aryans' and 'non-Aryans', and when couples appealed to the appropriate district court, in an attempt to force the registrar to fulfil duties which, after all, were prescribed by law, they were by no means always successful. The district court at Bad Sülze, for example, rejected such an appeal on the grounds that 'from the *völkisch* point of view, a racially mixed marriage' would make the 'Aryan blood . . . useless for ever', and that although it was not 'formally' forbidden by law, it nevertheless conflicted with 'the most important laws of the state, which consisted in the preservation of the blood-purity of the German people. Such a marriage is therefore thoroughly immoral.' Therefore a civil servant could not be expected to 'participate in such an act'.[12] In the same way the district court in Wetzlar considered it no more than its duty to co-operate in preventing 'the degeneration of the German *Volk*' through 'racial miscegenation' and to secure its 'racial resurrection'.[13] No less widespread and equally illegal was the practice of local authorities of placing signs inscribed 'Entry forbidden to Jews' or 'Jews not welcome' on municipal amenities such as parks, theatres and swimming baths, and in some cases at the ends of access roads.

There were critics of this antisemitic 'advance guard' in the leadership of the party, in the Gestapo and in the government but, unlike in 1934, the criticism was too muted to tame those it addressed, and as a consequence the latter got the impression that they were not being discouraged, and that the 'people's will' would succeed in forcing through legislation that had in any case already been planned. This impression was undoubtedly correct. Although they repeatedly fulminated against the indiscipline and illegal pratices of both the party and the SA, the Gestapo and SS alike joined the lobby for a 'Blood Protection Law' while at the same time unscrupulously operating outside the existing law themselves. On 12 February 1935 the Gestapo forbade Jews to raise the Reich flag, thus confronting them with their exclusion from the 'German national community', and the SS position was made clear to the public in an article in *Das Schwarze Korps* on 10 April. Under the headline 'Is the Law against Racial Treason Imminent?' Dr Kurt Plischke demanded the punishment of sexual intercourse between 'Aryans' and 'non-Aryans' by imprisonent, loss of civil rights and confiscation of property. Between then and September every

Banner reading 'Jews Not Wanted Here' hangs over the entrance to the village of
Rosenheim in Bavaria.
(Imperial War Museum, London)

issue of the paper carried a similar commentary on the theme of 'racial
dishonour'.

Since Heydrich kept the official organ of the SS under strict control, the
article was not only a clear reflection of his own and Himmler's opinions,
but also constituted a clear warning to the government. At the same time
regional police offices tirelessly fed reports of 'racial scandal', described in
the most indignant terms, to all readers of their 'situation reports'. The
Jewish partners in such cases were named, and not infrequently arrested
and imprisoned in concentration camps. In some places the Gestapo had
the local registry office report intended 'mixed marriages', so that they
could 'enlighten' the 'Aryan' partner. On 28 May Gestapo head office
suggested to the Reich Interior Ministry that all registry offices be required
to report such marriages, and appealed to the Reich Justice Ministry to
clarify the situation as soon as possible by removing the current difficulties
with 'prompt legal regulation'. On 31 July Heydrich approached the
Justice Ministry again and demanded that 'in view of the popular unrest

Crude antisemitic cartoon from a school book for children purporting to show the
immorality of Jews compared to Aryans
(Imperial War Museum, London)

caused by the "racially dishonourable" behaviour of German women, not
only must mixed marriages be prohibited by law, but extramarital sexual
intercourse between Aryans and Jews must also be made punishable.'[14]

From the party leadership on the other hand Deputy Führer Rudolf
Hess, in his function as a sort of Nazi party business manager, reacted on
11 April 1935 to the wave of antisemitic violence (including the lynching
of Jews with 'Aryan' lovers or fiancées) with a memorandum circulated to
party offices warning against 'terror against individual Jews'. But the
warning was combined with an emphasis on the duty of party members to
preserve a strictly anti-Jewish attitude within the bounds of the law as it
stood, and of course any prohibition of individual initiatives lost all
meaning within such a context.[15] The recipients of the order interpreted
the memorandum as approval, and as an indication that while senior party
leaders were obliged to produce such a prohibition – above all for the sake
of foreign relations — they nevertheless wanted the antisemitic activity to
continue.

At a meeting with Frick, Schacht (Economics Minister and President of the Reichsbank), and Lutz Count Schwerin von Krosigk (the Finance Minister), Justice Minister Gürtner pointed out angrily that legal norms and instructions naturally had no effect so long as people were 'encouraged to believe that the highest authorities were not displeased to see the limits they set overstepped, because only political considerations prevented them from acting as they would otherwise like'.[16] Indeed nobody seriously doubted that the party leadership agreed with the antisemitic activists, at least in their objectives, or that it, too, was pressing for a Blood Protection Law. In August Ludwig Fischer, head of the Reich Legal Office wrote in the journal of the German Law Academy that 'the widespread dishonouring of German girls by Jews which has recently come to light' had 'provoked immeasurable popular resentment' and that this demanded 'firm intervention on the part of the state to protect the national community by introducing clauses into the criminal law making racial treason and racial dishonour subject to the severest punishment'.

Even in the state apparatus there was only one serious opponent of a Blood Protection Law, namely Gürtner, the Reich Minister of Justice; and in the context of the wave of terror even he could not prevent the new race experts in his ministry from competing with the Reich Interior Ministry by making preparations to draft a Blood Protection Law by the early summer. The Interior Ministry had already started work. The dominant influence here was Frick himself, who now obviously considered the time right to push seriously for a law against 'racial treason' of the kind which he himself had brought before the Reichstag in March 1930, and which would now be justified by reference to the ostensibly murderous 'popular will'. He even ensured that pressure built up within his own administrative apparatus. Local government chiefs had been reporting cases of 'racial dishonour' since the early spring, just as frequently and in the same spirit as the Gestapo, and stereotypical reporting of this kind presupposed some sign from above.

By 20 August, when Gürtner hit out at the tacit complicity between antisemitic terrorists and sections of party and state leadership at the meeting in the Reich Ministry of Economics, and when Schacht once more protested against the damage caused to Germany's foreign trade by antisemitic violence, everything had long been decided. Five weeks previously, on 16 July, Frick had instructed registrars to stop performing 'racially mixed marriages', and had indicated in his circular that the Reich government intended to 'regulate the question of marriages between Aryans and non-Aryans by law very shortly'.[17] The wave of violence had completely achieved its aims. The few who still preserved any shred of reason or political decency, such as Gürtner and Schacht, were now prepared to accept a Blood Protection Law: the choice was between legislation and the continuation of the terror, and legislation seemed to be the lesser evil – unless, of course, one were prepared to take what was surely the only correct step in such a situation, and resign.

By September, however, the planned legislation had failed to appear; nor was there was any adequate draft for a law for the definitive removal of political rights from Jews (an equally persistent demand). This was no longer due to conflicts over the principle, but the result of conflicts over a detail, albeit a detail which had considerable significance. In the debates between the institutions involved, the representatives of the Nazi party leadership, including (in this matter) the 'Reich Doctors' Leader', Dr Wagner, argued that in addition to those 'Jews' forbidden sexual relations with 'Aryans' under a Blood Protection Law, another category, of mixed descent ('Judenstämmlinge') should be counted, as had been the case with the Law for the Restoration of a Professional Civil Service. This category, they argued, should include all those with one Jewish parent or grandparent. In addition, existing mixed marriages should either be dissolved, or the 'Aryan' partner should be reduced to the status of a Jew. The ministerial bureaucracy opposed these proposals, arguing that the legislation should be restricted to 'full Jews', that is those whose parents were both Jewish. The civil servants considered their solution a more humane alternative as it would reduce the number of people affected, but they were also concerned with practicalities: by protecting German families related to Jews the whole operation would be more painless for the nation, and would not provoke as much protest against the state.

It was Hitler himself who finally brought the argument to an end. At the end of the Reich 'party conference' which took place every year at Nuremberg, the Reichstag was convened to pass a 'Reich Flag Law', which would make the swastika flag the official Reich and military flag. On the day before this session, however, while the party conference was still going on, Hitler unexpectedly ordered experts from the Reich Interior Ministry to come to Nuremberg and told them to work out the drafts for a new citizenship law which would discriminate against Jews, and for a law to punish 'racial treason'. He had suddenly decided that the assembled Reichstag should take this opportunity to pass these two long-discussed laws against the Jews. And that is what happened. The experts, who had already had plenty of time to familiarize themselves with the relevant material, quickly formulated various relatively presentable drafts – although in their haste they were unable to agree on a definition of the word 'Jew' – and Hitler himself introduced his preferred version of each law to the Reichstag, supporting each one with an uncharacteristically short speech.

On the evening of 15 September, therefore, the Reich Citizenship Law was passed, recognizing as a Reich citizen any subject of the state of German or kindred blood, and restricting the status of German Jews to an unambiguously inferior status, although one which was not clearly defined.[18] The Law for the Protection of German Blood and German Honour was also passed, criminalizing both marriage and extra-marital sexual intercourse between 'Jews and citizens of German or kindred blood', prohibiting the employment in Jewish households of 'female citizens of German or related blood under the age of 45 years', and finally legalizing the prohibition of the raising of the 'Reich and national flag' by Jews, a measure which had long since been imposed by the Gestapo. The Blood Protection Law provided for the imprisonment of those concluding 'mixed marriages', and of the male partner in extramarital sexual intercourse, whether Jewish or 'Aryan'.[19] Hitler persisted dogmatically in his belief that women were passive – above all in sexual relationships – and could not be held responsible for their actions.[20]

It is difficult to say why Hitler chose this particular moment, and the context of the party conference to intervene in the debate on the Reich Citizenship and Blood Protection Laws. It must have occurred to him in Nuremberg that to end the rally with the rather unimpressive Reich Flag Law as the crowning glory was not a particularly inspired piece of theatrical direction. One can also assume that he came under pressure from his Nuremberg satrap Julius Streicher and other antisemitic activists to nudge the ministerial bureaucrats into action – and this was after all a favourable opportunity. Such explanations, however, are by no means adequate. Obviously Hitler also felt much more secure in his foreign policy; his major conference speech was accompanied by the slogan 'The Reich is secured'. It is not improbable that in such a mood Hitler himself, no less than Streicher, was keen to introduce the Blood Protection Law and it may have occurred to him during the discussions in Nuremberg that he would have to wait a whole year if he did not act now.

On 6 February 1936 the Winter Olympics began in Garmisch-Partenkirchen, followed by the Summer Olympics in Berlin on 1 August; with the possibility of foreign boycotts in mind, it was inadvisable to announce antisemitic legislation either too close to 6 February, or between the winter and summer games. In addition Hitler had the opportunity in Nuremberg of killing two birds with one stone. Introducing the two anti-Jewish laws in such a dramatic and spectacular way would gratify his own antisemitism and that of his followers, at least for the time being. At the same time the laws had a positive effect which was urgently necessary. Despite vociferous declarations of intended boycotts from abroad, foreign opinion was calmed by the legislation, because it created the impression that a legal separation of 'Aryans' and 'non-Aryans' would at least bring an end to the illegal and violent persecution of the Jews in Germany.

In one respect the Nuremberg Laws, as they quickly came to be called, did actually bring some moderation. Simply by announcing the laws Hitler had made it necessary to agree on a definition of the term 'Jew'. At the same time he had let it be known in Nuremberg that although he did not accept the limited definition proposed by the civil service, he also found the comprehensive definition demanded by the party activists unacceptable. In the draft presented to him by Frick's civil servants and Justice Minister Gürtner he had personally deleted the clause which made the law applicable only to 'full Jews', but nevertheless ordered that the same clause be included in the reporting of the laws by the Deutsches Nachrichten-Büro (German News Service). In doing this the Führer himself had personally emphasized the need for a compromise, and such a compromise was found in the course of the following weeks. On 14 November 1935 the First Supplementary Decree on the Reich Citizenship Law was enacted, and paragraph 5 determined that

> A Jew is anyone who is descended from at least three grandparents who are racially full Jews . . . A Jew is also any half-caste Jewish subject of the state who is descended from two full Jewish grandparents who (a) belonged to the Jewish religious community at the time this law was passed, or have joined it since; (b) was married to a Jew at the time the law was passed, or has married one since; (c) is the offspring of a marriage with a Jew in the sense of section 1, which was concluded after the Law for the Protection of German Blood and German Honour came into force; (d) is the offspring of extra-marital intercourse with a Jew in the sense of section 1, and will be born outside wedlock after 31 July 1936.[21]

Those whom these definitions covered counted merely as a 'subject of the state' (Staatsangehöriger). All other 'Jewish half-castes' (Mischlinge) who were 'descended from one or two full Jewish grandparents' were awarded 'provisional citizenship' in accordance with paragraph 2 of the decree. Even those 'of German blood' were only 'provisional' citizens until the issue of a Reich patent of citizenship, and they remained so since neither the patent of citizenship nor the corresponding regulations were forthcoming before the end of the Nazi dictatorship.

The civil servants could look on the compromise as a success. It excluded a considerable number of the so-called 'Jewish half-castes', including the mixed marriages into which they were born, from much of the anti-Jewish legislation and other measures which were to follow. The Reich Ministry of the Interior had already ordered some time previously that the term 'mixed marriage' should not be used for marriages between partners of different religions, but exlusively for marriages between partners of different 'races'. Much more unambiguously than in the rabble-rousing of publications like the *Stürmer*, it was clear from this small gesture on the part of the administration that racism was to be the official religion of the Nazi state. In subsequent years there was a certain black farce as first-class jurists repeatedly gathered in the sober offices of Reich ministries to debate with dreadful seriousness and pedantic exactitude, with the hair-splitting precision of scholastic theologians, in an attempt to establish whether this or that anti-Jewish law could be applied to 'half-castes' and 'mixed marriages' or not.

'Half-castes of the first degree' (two Jewish grandparents) were accorded a status between that of Jews and 'Aryans' (initially somewhat closer to the status of 'Aryans'). This meant that for the time being they were allowed to attend both the senior schools (middle, higher and technical schools) and the universities; they were also eligible for military service. In connection with the latter privilege in particular, exemptions were also extended to the parents of 'half-castes of the first degree'; in contrast with 'legal Jews' (Geltungsjuden) whose marriages were now classified as 'simple mixed marriages', the special category of 'privileged mixed marriages' was created for them. The Nazis, however, made it clear from the outset that in the light of the 1935 legislation 'half-castes of the first degree' were already seriously and irreversibly tainted, and the interpreters and administrators of the racist religion gave them the right to cross freely into the Jewish community, either by marrying a 'legal Jew' or a 'full Jew', or by attending a Jewish school (which was considered a sign of commitment to Jewry), and even promoted such options, while they virtually barred the way to acceptance into the German nation.

Although the First Supplementary Decree to the Blood Protection Law (also on 14 November 1935) permitted marriages between 'half-castes of the first degree' and 'Aryans' or 'half-castes of the second degree' by 'special dispensation of the Reich Interior Minister and Deputy Führer',[22] such a dispensation was hardly ever given, so that 'half-castes of the first degree' were effectively forced to marry into the Jewish community if they wanted to marry at all. In addition they were barred not only from posts in the public service, but also from any number of other jobs where 'Aryan' descent was stipulated, and where 'Aryan' continued to be interpreted in the sense of the Law for the Restoration of a Professional Civil Service.

Furthermore, after the end of 1938 one privilege after another was lost. From 1939 'half-castes of the first degree' were generally no longer allowed to take degrees; a ministerial decree of 2 July 1940 excluded them from senior schools; and a secret order of the Armed Forces High Command

(OKW) expelled them from the army on 20 April 1940. Instead, on 13 October 1943, there was an order, ostensibly from Goering, as Commissioner for the Four-Year Plan, but prompted by Hitler, which introduced compulsory labour service within the framework of the Todt Organization from 1944 onwards. In practice this rarely differed from imprisonment in a concentration camp. Both Goering's order and that of the OKW were valid for the male partners in 'privileged mixed marriages', a category which also included childless mixed marriages if the husband was 'of German blood'.

On the other hand a childless mixed marriage between a Jewish man and a woman 'of German blood' counted as a 'simple mixed marriage', and the 'Aryan' wife generally had to share the fate of her Jewish husband. Of course, exceptions were possible. In exceptional circumstances a 'legal Jew' could be given status equal to a 'half-caste of the first degree', while the latter could be granted the status of a 'half-caste of the second degree' or an 'Aryan'. Only the Führer personally could decide in such cases. By the autumn of 1942, according to the notes of a racial expert in the Reich Ministry of the Interior, Hitler had declared 'legal Jews' 'half-castes of the first degree' in 339 cases, and permitted 'half-castes of the first degree' to join the armed forces and be employed as officers in 258 cases; 'half-castes of the first degree' had been given equal status with 'Aryans' in 394 cases.

'Half-castes of the second degree' on the other hand found themselves collectively and categorically placed with 'Aryans'. According to the commentary on the race legislation they possessed 'two-thirds German or kindred blood' and this 'valuable component' must be preserved by 'nordification' (Aufnordung). Meanwhile they were not given the option of joining the Jewish community, i.e. they were allowed to marry neither Jews nor 'half-castes', not even other 'quarter-Jews', and when they married 'Aryan' partners (for which no special dispensation was necessary in their case), Jews were not even allowed as witnesses. They were allowed to attend both senior schools and universities, and since they were 'capable of bearing arms', they had to complete both military and civilian labour service. During the war they could even be promoted in the army.

However, full equality of status was denied them. They were not allowed to become civil servants or to marry them, and there were several other professions along with the SS and other Nazi organizations, which demanded proof of pure 'Aryan' descent from 1800 onwards. Closed professions included those of journalist, farmer and vet, and consequently 'half-castes of the first degree' were also excluded from taking degrees either in agronomy or veterinary medicine. During the war there then followed a general restriction on entrance to university degree courses. For the Gestapo the privileges of 'half-castes of the second degree' were always an irritation in any case, and it undertook several attempts to have them removed. The reason for the exclusion of 'half-castes of the second degree' from the final solution was a counter-order of Hitler's, accepted only with gritted teeth by Heydrich and other senior personnel in the Reich Security Head Office (RSHA), and was no doubt based on a fear of irritating too many 'Aryan' families.

If one leaves aside the treatment of various categories of 'half-caste' and 'mixed marriage', the Nuremberg Laws brought a serious deterioration in the position of most Jews. At first the laws were often greeted with some relief, because the legal removal of political rights and the prohibition of sexual relations with 'Aryans' clarified the situation, and it was thought that this constituted the Nazis' final solution to the 'Jewish question'. Many German Jews thought that they had now survived the worst. After the wave of terror had ended one simply had to abide by the restrictions imposed by the new regulations, and at least one would be left in peace to work in those trades and professions which were still permitted. Such expectations were soon to be bitterly disappointed, as decree after decree was enacted, and it gradually became clearer that the detailed extensions of the Nuremberg Laws restricted the lives and livelihoods of German Jews in a dangerous manner.

It was clear, for example, within two weeks of its promulgation that the Reich Citizenship Law signalled the end of the agreement on Jewish policy concluded in 1933 between the Nazis and their German Nationalist coalition partners. Since the intervening redistribution of political power in German politics the Nazis no longer needed to respect the compromise which had then been forced on them by Reich President Hindenburg. An Interior Ministry decree dated 30 September, whose publication in official bulletins and in the press was forbidden, suspended from 1 October all Jewish civil servants whose positions had hitherto been protected on grounds of military or other national merit; the First Supplementary Decree to the Reich Citizenship Law of 14 November then subsequently provided for their compulsory retirement from 31 December, and provided them with a pension in the meantime.

The decree, which of course also disenfranchised the Jews, unleashed a flood of further professional disqualifications, excluding Jews not only from the civil service, but from any other 'public office' as well. By 13 December the Nazi interpretation of 'public office' led to all Jewish doctors being struck off, from 19 December Jews were no longer allowed to practise as 'poor lawyers' (i.e. unpaid lawyers representing the poor) or estate managers. Two days later the Second Supplementary Decree to the Reich Citizenship Law determined that Jews practising as company doctors or hospital doctors must be laid off by 31 March 1936, and on 21

December a decree from the Reich Ministry of the Interior confirmed the dismissal from their positions of Jews who were distributors of stamps, meat inspectors in abattoirs and members of arbitration boards. On 11 January 1936 Jewish tax assistants were hit, on 26 March Jewish pharmacists were informed that they must lease their businesses to 'Aryans', and on 27 July 1936 permission to run a restaurant or public house was made conditional on proof of one's ancestry. On 23 December 1936 it was the turn of Jewish auditors, that of dieticians and dietetic assistants on 5 April 1937, land surveyors on 20 January 1938, and auctioneers on 5 February 1938. On 25 July 1938 the Fourth Supplementary Decree to the Reich Citizenship Law put an end to any kind of medical practice by Jewish doctors, and on 27 September 1938 the Fifth Supplementary Decree to the Reich Citizenship Law liquidated all Jewish law practices; a limited number might still be allowed to work as medical orderlies or legal consultants, but only in Jewish clinics or for Jewish clients.

Parallel to this elaboration of the Reich Citizenship Law the bureaucrats themselves managed to come up with even more chicanery. From 24 March 1936 family allowances were stopped for large Jewish families; from 15 October 1936 Jewish teachers were forbidden to give private tuition to 'Aryan' pupils – and those already driven out of the teaching profession proper were further reduced from poverty to abject misery; and after 5 February 1937 Jews could no longer get a hunting licence. A decree of the Reich Minister for Education of 15 April 1937 made it impossible for Jews to be awarded doctorates, and there followed a further decree on 2 July, which drastically reduced the number of Jewish children in primary schools.

Hard hit as German Jews were by the loss of political rights and the professional disqualifications which followed in the wake of the Reich Citizenship Law in those superficially quiet years of undramatic persecution, and painful as the chicanery was which was practised by assiduous bureaucrats, the Blood Protection Law was worse. The tenderest, strongest and at the same time socially most important attraction which can exist between unrelated human beings was now declared a crime punishable by imprisonment if it drew together a Jew and an 'Aryan'. A minority which is seen to be so despised becomes literally, as well as metaphorically, untouchable. Even when they live among the majority, those who belong to the untouchables live in a personal ghetto from which there is no escape. Normal neighbourly relations are no longer possible and even the briefest and most sober professional or business contact has a feel of the forbidden, and even of the fundamentally sinful.

Although only a modest and increasingly small minority dared to maintain contact with the Jewish community, it is quite remarkable that under these circumstances German Jews did not immediately sink into total isolation, and that there were such frequent infringements of the Blood Protection Law. The first trials came in 1935, and by the end of 1940 German courts, which prosecuted the new offence with no discernible unease, had sentenced no fewer than 1,911 persons for miscegenation (1935: 11; 1936: 358; 1937: 512; 1938: 434; 1939: 365; 1940: 231). The reason for this was no doubt that the courts – following decisions of the Reich court of 9 December 1936 and 9 February 1937 – interpreted as 'sexual intercourse' any sexual activity, including 'actions . . . as a result of which either party seeks to satisfy his sexual urge by means other than intercourse'.[23]

In addition judges, who were frequently maliciously antisemitic themselves, often declared otherwise quite harmless words or gestures to be attempts – equally punishable – at 'racially dishonourable' sexual intercourse. For example, on 5 September 1938 the Reich Court decided that a man who accompanied a Jewish woman to her room and said, 'Well, let's take our coats off and make ourselves at home', should be considered guilty of attempting to commit a crime according to section 2 of the Blood Protection Law.[24] Furthermore, although the woman in question should ostensibly have been free to go, regardless of whether she was Jewish or 'Aryan', she was not allowed to get away scot free either, and at the latest after a decree from Heydrich of 12 June 1937 could be sent to a concentration camp without being sentenced in court. It must be said, however, that despite the Nuremberg Laws and even in the face of extremely unfair practice on the part of the judiciary and police, the number of sexual relationships between Jews and Aryans remained astonishingly high, even bearing in mind that the official figures were only the tip of the iceberg, and despite the enthusiasm for denunciation – which was particularly widespread among the 'Aryan' population, and more often than not arose from private rather than ideological motives.

5

Expropriation

Nevertheless the Blood Protection Law could be only a matter of dealing with individual cases. It was followed on 18 October 1935 by a further measure for the 'improvement' (Höherzüchtung) of the 'Aryan' race, the Law for the Protection of the Hereditary Health of the German People, prohibiting marriage in the case of certain illnesses. Such legislation inevitably meant that most Jews were increasingly cut off from their non-Jewish environment, and increasingly isolated. It also quickly became evident that even this isolation was not the end of the purge. It was now quite clear that racial antisemitism was founded on convictions so radical that its ambitions could not be satisfied with a solution to its self-created 'Jewish question' based on regulations and legal limitations. This much was clear from any close examination of antisemitic theory over the decades, and had been confirmed by the Nazi regime's behaviour during its first two years in power.

Now there was further confirmation of the unlimited ambitions of Nazi antisemitism: in the wake of the Nuremberg Laws a clear pattern of behaviour was beginning to emerge. The Nazis would present a series of definitive measures as the 'final solution' to the Jewish question, and promote them as such before they were implemented. Even some sections of the Nazi movement itself would perceive such measures to be 'final'. Once they were implemented, however, they would immediately be revealed as merely intermediate goals, to be superceded by even more 'final' solutions, which then, in turn, would again be revealed as simply the next stage. Even as the first stage of the persecution of the Jews was nearing completion – i.e. the exclusion of the Jews from politics, the public service, and some of the free professions – calls were already being heard for the complete removal of the civil rights of all Jews and the isolation of German Jewry. Even as he announced the fulfilment of such wishes with the promulgation of the Nuremberg Laws, Hitler himself gave notice of the next round. The Reich Citizenship Law and Blood Protection Law were to be seen as the ultimate solution to the 'Jewish question', he announced at Nuremberg, but, he continued menacingly, if this 'unique secular solution' should fail, responsibility for the problem would have to be removed from the state's jurisdiction, and passed over to the Nazi movement itself for a definitive solution.

During the year following the 1935 party conference the behaviour of the Nazis gave many observers, both at home and abroad, the impression that the Reich Citizenship Law and the Blood Protection Law – or their implementation and execution – would be followed by a period of calm which would allow the Jews, or at least those in skilled crafts, commerce and banking, to earn their living, or to live quietly off their property and assets. Thus, for example, Jewish sports clubs and their members were given more freedom, and in many places the forests of antisemitic signs ('No Entry For Jews!' – 'Jews Not Welcome!') which had burgeoned before the autumn of 1935 were now cut down; at the same time anti-Jewish propaganda receded, at least in volume. Yet this sudden outbreak of peace by no means indicated a preparedness on the part of the Nazis to establish a *modus vivendi* on the basis of the Nuremberg Laws; it had the purely tactical function of creating the appearance of such a mood in order to establish the smoothest conditions possible for the Olympic Games. The games had been given top priority by the Nazi leadership and with good reason, as events were to prove: no other single event brought the regime so great an increase in internal stability and international prestige; both the Winter and the Summer Olympic Games of 1936 were brilliantly organized and brought Germany considerable sporting success.

It was obviously difficult for Hitler and other antisemites to accommodate themselves to such tactical manoeuvres, to take into account foreign opinion, and to refrain from going beyond the Nuremberg Laws for the time being (internally, the need for such caution was only ever mentioned with regret), particularly since the events of 1936 reinforced their feelings of self-confidence and foreign policy security, and this in turn inevitably stimulated their drive for antisemitic action. On 7 March Hitler ordered German troops to reoccupy the Rhineland, a demilitarized zone guaranteed by Britain and Italy in the 1926 Locarno Treaty concluded by Gustav Stresemann. By cleverly exploiting Italy's involvement in North Africa and the resulting conflict between Mussolini and the West, Hitler succeeded in freeing Germany from the last multinational treaty system to which it was a signatory, and at the same time denied France its last possibility of relatively simple sanctions against Germany.

The German–Italian *rapprochement*, which had begun gradually in the wake of Mussolini's invasion of Abyssinia, and found its first public expression with Mussolini's approval of the German invasion of the Rhineland in March 1936, now gained a new quality, and began to resemble an alliance. From July 1936 both states intevened in the Spanish Civil War in support of the rebel generals. On 1 November 1936 Mussolini coined the term 'Rome–Berlin Axis' for the political co-operation agreed between Nazi Germany and fascist Italy on 25 October. On 25 November the Anti-Comintern Pact brought the first 'geopolitical' agreement between Germany and Japan. A few months previously, on 11 July, in the shadow of the German–Italian understanding, Hitler had been able to conclude a treaty with Austria, which committed the Schuschnigg regime to support of Germany; Mussolini, meanwhile, forced to seek German support for his imperialist adventure in Africa, had finally given up his role as guarantor of Austrian independence, and expressly approved the agreement of 11 July.

It is significant that immediately after the Olympic Games – the fanfares of the closing ceremony had hardly died away – representatives of the NSDAP publicly declared that the Nuremberg Laws were to be seen as no more than a stage in Nazi 'Jewish policy', and that there must be an immediate start on the implementation of the next stage. In September 1936 Julius Streicher wrote in *Der Stürmer* that the Nuremberg Laws could have been understood as a 'solution to the Jewish question' only by those 'who are acquainted only with the superficialities of what the Jewish question means to the knowledgeable', whereas it was now more essential than ever before that 'every last German should with hand and heart join those who have made it their goal to crush the head of the serpent of Panjudaism. Those who contribute to achieving this goal are helping to get rid of the devil. And this devil is the Jew.'[1] Many Nazi movement officials and even more civil servants often sneered at Streicher in those years. Such sneers were directed not at Streicher's antisemitism *per se*, but at his enthusiastic combination of antisemitic theory or propaganda with pornography.

The unease and embarrassment which the *Gauleiter* of Franconia often aroused did not alter the fact that by 1940, when his involvement in major corruption cases could no longer be ignored and he was forced to give up his *Gau* and retire to his estate, he had exercised a greater influence on the course of the Nazis' persecution of the Jews (and always knew the prevailing party line better) than any of the other leading party function-aries, such as Goebbels, and even Himmler. Even in an article of

September 1936 he could rightly claim that his eagerness for the antisemitic onslaught, and his call to go beyond the Nuremberg Laws, was not a cry from the wilderness. At the 1936 party conference he triumphantly declared that National Socialism 'had declared a war on the Jews which [would] end in their annihilation', and with equally satisfied approval he quoted the following from a speech given by Reich Doctors' leader, Dr Wagner in Nuremberg on 12 September 1936: 'To those who believe that the Jewish question has been regulated and settled by the Nuremberg Laws we say: The struggle continues . . . and we will be victorious in this struggle only when every one of the German people knows that it is a struggle for existence.'

Even more significant, of course, is the fact that at the time of Streicher's and Wagner's rhetoric concrete plans were already being forged for the next stage in the persecution of the Jews. On 29 September 1936 State Secretaries from the Interior and Economics Ministries met to discuss Frick's suggestion for the exclusion of Jews from further professions from the beginning of June, and the introduction of signs to identify Jewish businesses. Hitler himself now resolved to take up a suggestion made by Heinrich Class in his pamphlet 'If I were the Kaiser' of 1912, namely to bleed the Jews financially, by taxing them at a considerably higher rate than 'Aryans'. Frick's State Secretary Wilhelm Stuckart informed the Reich Economics Ministry on 18 December 1936 that Hitler had 'approved in principle the raising of an extra tax for Jews'.[2] The justification for this was to be the murder some time previously, in Davos on 4 February 1936, of Wilhelm Gustloff, the Nazi *Landesgruppenleiter* in Switzerland, by David Frankfurter, an émigré Yugoslav student, and according to Stuckart Hitler had ordered work on such a law to be accelerated, so that it could be announced to coincide with the end of Frankfurter's trial. In fact the Reich Economics Ministry presented a draft in June 1937, but after some to-ing and fro-ing it was postponed; Goering, responsible for all raw materials and currency matters since April 1936, and Commissioner for the Four-Year Plan since October 1936, decided in December 1937, that in view of foreign reactions 'the announcement of such a law would at present constitute a danger to the Reich's raw materials and currency situation.'[3]

It was clear, however, in the light of the activities of the ministries and Hitler's own considerations, that now – following the elimination of the Jews from the public service and the free professions, and the removal of all their political rights, and in parallel with the isolation brought about by the Blood Protection Law – that the 'solution of the Jewish question in the economy' had been selected as the next stage in the persecution of the Jews. Yet again, then, the Nazis had set themselves an objective which went far beyond anything that could be called 'legislation governing aliens', especially since it was clear from the outset that the 'solution of the Jewish question in the economy' meant the 'exclusion of the Jews from the economy': the process could end only with the prohibition of all Jewish employment and the expropriation of all Jewish property. In this way the greatest number of Jews possible would be driven to emigrate, and the existence of those Jews who continued to live in Germany would not merely be miserable but above all entirely dependent on the mercy of the regime. As Hitler said privately shortly before the 1935 party conference, 'Out with them, from every profession, Ghetto, have them locked up in one place where they can live in their own way, while the German nation looks on, in the way one watches wild animals.'

That the confiscated property of individual Jews could be used to relieve difficulties in financing rearmament and in the related forced production of substitutes and raw materials (initiated in the middle of 1936) was no doubt an important consideration for Nazi leaders, and not least for Hitler and Goering. Many party members were also quick to see that the 'Aryanization' of the economy presented them with an opportunity to enrich themselves personally, i.e. to buy up Jewish factories, shops and workshops at bargain prices. Houses and land were also attractive booty. Indeed the plundering of Jewish property was to assume the worst forms. On 16 April 1938 a 'National Socialist, SA man and admirer of Adolf Hitler' wrote a letter to the Chamber of Trade and Industry in Munich, in which he, a Munich businessman and hitherto employed as an expert in the 'Aryanization' of Jewish enterprises gave notice of his resignation: although he would lose 'a good income' by doing so, he could no longer, as 'an honest and upright businessman, look on as so many "Aryan" business-men, entrepreneurs etc. shamelessly attempt to accumulate Jewish shops, factories etc. for next to nothing. These people are like vultures who dive on Jewish corpses with their eyes watering and their tongues hanging out.'[14]

This was not the only way in which 'Aryanization' worked to the advantage of gentiles. Often Jewish businesses were simply liquidated rather than taken over – as in the case of the exclusion of Jewish doctors and lawyers – and this meant that competition was eliminated. For this very reason organizations in the Nazi movement which represented small business interests pressed the leadership of both party and state to intensify the campaign against the 'Jewish position in the economy'.

Yet public and private covetousness was neither the reason nor the dominant motive in the course of the process. Naïve in matters of business and economic policy, complete dilettantes, even, in some respects, Hitler and Goering were certainly inclined to see the expropriation of German

Jews as a source of state revenue, and to overestimate the potential profits. They were aware, however, of certain obvious facts. The transfer of Jewish property, industrial and domestic, to 'Aryans' meant a gain not for the exchequeur, but rather for countless 'Aryan' individuals, and what was more, after buying up a Jewish business or apartment block they would pay not a penny more in taxes than their Jewish predecessors, who were now impoverished or forced to emigrate. In any case the process of the 'exclusion of Jews from the economy' was to a considerable extent clearly irrelevant to the financing of the preparations for war. It was equally clear that the fundamental economic problems of rearmament would not be solved with confiscated Jewish banknotes and share certificates. Direct expenditure on the Wehrmacht alone between the beginning of 1935 and the end of 1938 ran to 40.5 billion (million million) RM; as a proportion of public investment it rose from 56 per cent in 1935 to 74 per cent in 1938. In view of such immense sums it was clear from the outset that the two or three thousand million RM which were squeezed from German Jews into the coffers of the state were a drop in the ocean; the sums involved could do nothing to alter the fact that the military and econonic costs of preparation for war had to be covered primarily by credit and the irresponsible printing of paper money.

It was not through the expropriation of the Jews that Nazi leaders expected to be saved from this dilemma, but by a successful policy of expansion. Acute financial problems which severely hindered rearmament did not arise from a shortage of Reichsmarks, but above all from a lack of foreign currency reserves, which in turn led to difficulties in obtaining raw materials. The fleecing of Germany' s Jews brought even less relief in this area, while on the other hand the loss of both Jewish and non-Jewish customers and suppliers abroad led inevitably to further disruptions of Germany's foreign trade, and this in turn exacerbated the shortage of currency. Goering clearly demonstrated his awareness that at least the more dramatic and more drastic acts of Nazi 'Jewish policy' would be more harmful than beneficial to Germany's economic and political interests when he justified his rejection of an extra tax for Jews in December 1937.

Even the pressure of party members drooling over the opportunities for effortless personal enrichment or the removal of competition did not really have much influence on the course of events. Although such factors may well have contributed to the tempo of persecution, especially since the material interests of leading Nazi functionaries – including Julius Streicher – along with those of their relatives and friends were at stake, 'Jewish policy' was always formulated independently of such considerations. In the course of a speech which Hitler gave to Nazi *Kreisleiter* on 29 April 1937, he came to speak about an article in a provincial newspaper which demanded a symbol of identification for Jewish shops.

> From whom does he demand it? [asked the Führer indignantly] Who can order something like that? Only I personally. So, in the name of his readers, the editor is demanding that I do it. First of all, long before the editor in question had any idea of the Jewish question, I had studied it very thoroughly; secondly this problem of an identification sign has been considered for the last two or three years and one day will be implemented quite naturally. For the ultimate objective of our policy is of course quite clear to all of us. My only concern is not to take any measures which I might then have to withdraw, and to take no step which might cause us harm. You know, I go as far as I dare, but no further. Even in the struggle with an enemy one has to have a nose for such things: 'What can I do now, what can I not do?' I will not immediately challenge my opponent to a fight, I will not say 'Fight!' because I want to fight but [screaming louder and louder] 'I want to annihilate you! And now, clever one, help me to manoeuvre you into a corner, so that you can't move a further step, and then I'll stab you in the heart.'[5]

These words expressed Hitler's justified conviction that he alone was in control on the Nazis' tactics in their persecution of the Jews, but also his resolve not to have his position challenged, particularly at a time when tactical caution seemed necessary; on the other hand his words betrayed an unquenchable thirst for battle and a fanatical will to destroy, neither of which needed 'pressure from below' – desirable as it occasionally was to provide pseudo-democratic legitimation. Although he felt a fundamental affinity with his followers, the demand for activity and satisfaction sprang from Hitler's own radical ideology and mentality.

Hitler's feeling that his motives and objectives as Führer were always in harmony with those of the movement was, of course, completely justified. Even among the majority of the profiteers from 'Aryanization', hostility to the Jews was basically motivated by racist antisemitism, and their actions were backed up by the not uncommon opinion that personal gain could easily be combined with the fulfilment of ideological imperatives. The prevalence of this conviction, which very much reflected Hitler's own thinking, was to be found above all among those functionaries of the Nazi party and the state who, in framing laws, decrees and instructions, were responsible for implementing policy, and were therefore not without influence on events. If they now decided on the 'exclusion of Jews from the economy' it was not because they, any more than the Führer, had given in to the pressure from 'Aryanizers' greedy for profit; in any case, the depth and extent of such greed became clearer only after the 'Aryanization' process had started. Rather, the expropriation of the Jews seemed to Hitler and his executive quite simply the logical and inevitable restoration – at the earliest possible opportunity – of existing policy, namely the resumption of the boycott campaign of 1935. What had then been passed off as a terroristic tactic, and indeed had functioned as such, in order to help promote the Blood Protection Law, now became an objective in its own right, in keeping with its true character.

Furthermore, once they had embarked on this new stage, party functionaries and state officials alike acted independently of 'Aryanization' squabbles. They threw themselves into their work with all the seriousness and enthusiasm of crusaders; they neither had nor sought personal gain, and for the most part they looked down with grim disdain on the vultures (both within and outside the party) who hovered over the property of the Jews. It is very significant that by 'exclusion of Jews from the economy' they by no means meant only the 'Aryanization' of relatively prosperous Jewish businesses, and the expropriation of those Jews blessed with earthly goods; with equal meticulousness and with equally battle-hardened mercilessness these ideological warriors persecuted even Jewish hawkers as dangerous enemies, although they could expect to get nothing from them, and although their 'Aryan' competitors were in no position to influence the policies of either the Nazi party or the state bureaucracy.

Moved by political and ideological passion and fuelled by public and private greed, the attack on the 'position of the Jews in the economy' quickly brought results. In January 1933 there had been around 100,000 Jewish businesses, including warehouses, private banks and factories, medical and legal practices, and retail outlets, artisans' workshops and independent businessmen. Following the losses which had already taken place in the years from 1933 to 1936, and in the wake of the campaign itself which was repeatedly stepped up from the beginning of 1937, only 39,532 Jewish businesses remained by April 1938: more than 60 per cent had been 'liquidated' or 'Aryanized'. In addition many of those businesses which survived were already in the throes of death, according to the reports of the party's regional economic advisers, who had opened a file on every Jewish business at the begining of 1937 and since then – in close co-operation with the Chambers of Trade and the Finance Offices – had carefully observed the turnover and development of the businesses which had not been 'Aryanized'. The situation was 'generally very bad', according to their reports; frequently they wrote: 'business has virtually ground to a halt' – 'only Jewish customers left' – 'generally closed'.[6] Since at the same time Jewish manual and clerical workers were laid off in all sectors of the economy, definitive Jewish unemployment rose to 60,000 by the spring of 1938.

Just as the German economy was beginning to suffer from a labour shortage, the proportion of Jews who were unemployed was now higher than the level of unemployment in Germany in the worst days of the slump. Yet Jews who had lost their own businesses, or had been laid off, and found temporary employment with a Jewish firm that had survived – positions which were in any case generally badly paid – were only postponing unemployment, and many former doctors, lawyers, business proprietors and senior white-collar workers, who now tried to survive as hawkers, found themselves squeezed down below the poverty line. Emigration, as always, was an option fraught with difficulties, particularly since the Nazi state, as ever, did little in financial terms to promote it. If no more than 25,000 Jews had been able to leave the Reich in 1936, only 23,000 were able to do so in 1937. The pauperization of Germany's Jews which was the predictable and intentional consequence of the programme for the 'Exclusion of Jews from the Economy' was combined with the psychological burden of despair.

Nevertheless the Nazis, eager for the total success of their campaign, found the tempo slow and the results unsatisfactory, especially since there was a further strong impetus to antisemitism in the spring of 1938. First of all the 'Fritsch crisis' considerably strengthened the Nazi movement. Following the dismissal on 4 February 1938 of War Minister Werner von Blomberg, who had married a woman of bad reputation, and Werner von Fritsch, supreme commander of the army, whom Goering and the SS had framed with false charges of homosexuality, Hitler personally took over as supreme commander of the armed forces; in future General Wilhelm Keitel functioned beneath him as head of the War Ministry, renamed Supreme Command of the Wehrmacht (OKW), and Fritsch's successor was General Walther von Brauchitsch.

At the same time Konstantin von Neurath, the Foreign Minister, was ousted and replaced by Joachim von Ribbentrop. The two last German Nationalist bastions of any significance in the German state after Schacht's retirement as Economics Minister in November 1937 had been stormed by the Nazi movement and were now under direct Nazi control (or at least they were headed by pliable military functionaries). Scarcely was this final co-ordination of the armed services and the Foreign Office completed than Hitler and the Nazi movement pulled off their greatest national and foreign policy success to date: the *Anschluss* (annexation) of Austria which began with the German invasion of 12 March 1938. Both at home and abroad this coup brought the Führer and his regime an enormous gain in prestige, while at the same time it brought about a tangible increase in

Germany's real political strength and a clear improvement in the strategic position of the Reich. The self-confidence of the Nazis, already well developed from the Führer to the stormtrooper in the street, was inflated into provocative arrogance.

The Jews of Austria were made to realize just how much the occupation of that country by the German army had swollen the heads of the Nazis. Here, in one of the breeding grounds of antisemitism (of both the German Nationalist and the racist varieties), March 1938 saw a wave of anti-Jewish terror sweep through town and country alike, resembling the atrocities in the *Altreich* (pre-1938 Germany) immediately after the Nazi assumption of power, except that in Austria the party, the SA and the SS now went to work on a much grander scale, with much greater malicious brutality. They were completely unabashed, and certainly did not stop to consider the opinions of foreign observers. At the same time the heirs of Schönerer took up the 'exclusion of the Jews from the economy' with considerable energy, i.e. in countless cases they simply threw out the proprietors of Jewish businesses and installed in their place commissars appointed by the party, who were to oversee the 'Aryanization' of the establishment. The expropriation was carried out without even a shadow of a legal basis, and on such soil greed and corruption flourished luxuriantly.

Austrian Jews scrubbing streets after the Anschluss, 1938
(Wiener Library, London)

Many Jews fled to neighbouring states or were driven over the border by Austrian Nazis. The latter, less a policy of emigration than one of expulsion, quickly came to acquire an organizational framework. Heydrich sent SS *Obersturmführer* Adolf Eichmann to Austria. (Eichmann's background was the Austrian SS, but he had emigrated to the Reich in 1934 after the ban on the Austrian Nazis, and had latterly been employed as an expert on Jewish matters in the head office of the SD.) In August 1938 Eichmann set up in Vienna a Central Office for Jewish Emigration, which developed a system that was to be very important in the future. The compulsory application of the principle that affluent Jews who wished to emigrate must not only pay their shilling to the state but must also give up a further sum to finance the emigration of poorer Jews was not in itself so revolutionary. After all the Haavara Agreement of 1933 functioned in a very similar way – albeit on a voluntary basis. The novelty was that Eichmann and the Nazi regime he represented delegated much of the responsibility for the running of the scheme to Jewish bodies, in Austria principally the Kultusgemeinde (Jewish community organization), while the Nazis themselves were content simply to provide the idea, to order its implementation, and to ensure – with the menacing presence of Nazi thugs – that the order was obeyed. That the 'Central Office' was set up and occupied by Heydrich's organization was an indication that the Security Police and the SD were beginning to take over both general responsibility for the 'Jewish question', and particular responsibility for the details of its implementation.

Parallel with events in Austria – now renamed the Ostmark – the persecution of the Jews in the *Altreich* continually increased in scope and in severity. While at the beginning of 1933 there had been more than 50,000 Jewish shops, there were only 9,000 left in July 1938 (of which 3,637 were in Berlin) and the majority disappeared between March and July 1938. Munich was typical. In February 1938 there were still 1690 Jewish traders, while in October of the same year the number had fallen to 666, two thirds of whom were foreign nationals. Even larger Jewish businesses, which had hitherto fared better than smaller and medium-sized establishments, fell victim in ever greater numbers to the increasing pressure. Between January and October 1938, for example, no fewer than 340 factories were 'Aryanized', 260 in the textiles and clothing sectors, thirty in the leather goods and shoe industries, and an additional 370 firms in the wholesale trade. The simultaneous 'Aryanization' of twenty-two Jewish banks, including such prestigious names, resonant of the emancipation and assimilation of the Jews, as Bleichröder, Warburg, Arnhold, Dreyfus and Hirschland was of a significance greater than the sum of the individual cases, since banking houses such as that of Max Warburg in

Hamburg had played a great part not only in supporting Jewish businesses and financing Jewish organizations, but also in promoting Jewish emigration, and there was now no one to take over their role.

In addition, the authorities introduced further professional exclusions to supplement the Reich Citizenship Law which had already put an end to any professional activity by Jewish doctors and lawyers in 1938. The Trading Regulations Amendment Act of 6 July 1938 prohibited Jews from: (a) employment as security guards; (b) provision of information on personal circumstances or financial status on a commercial basis; (c) dealing in land; (d) acting as commercial agents for letting and financing accommodation, or in the administration of sales of property or land; (e) acting as commercial marriage agents; (f) acting as travel agents. The most damaging clause, however, was the one which made it impossible for Jews to work in future as sales representatives or hawkers; even these final escape routes into a pre-emancipation existence which at least ensured a living, and which so many doctors and lawyers had had to take, were now cut off by the regime, which combined ideology, malice and infamy with thoroughness.

Furthermore 'Aryanization' and anti-Jewish legislation were accompanied, in the spring and summer of 1938, by countless acts of violence against Jews and their homes and businesses, in the *Altreich* as well as in Austria. On 9 June Munich's synagogue was destroyed, followed on 10 August by that of Nuremberg. On 22 June the American ambassador reported to Washington: 'The current campaign against the Jews exceeds . . . anything of its kind since the beginning of 1933.' Obviously remembering the connection between 'popular anger' and legislative activity in both 1933 and 1935, he added, 'It is expected that this will lead to further legislative measures.'[7]

In fact the leaders of Nazi Germany saw no reason to be satisfied with the results of their antisemitic campaign of the spring and summer of 1938. There were still almost 40,000 Jewish firms, not all of them in poor condition by any means; there were still Jews with a capital stake in German businesses, and there were still Jews who could live off their private assets, whether these were saved, inherited or otherwise acquired. It later became clear, of course, that since the beginning of 1933 capital assets held by Jews had declined from a total twelve thousand million RM – around three or four per cent of all capital assets in Germany at that time – by more than half, to 5.1 thousand million RM, proof enough of the pauperization process, especially since the Jewish population of Germany had shrunk by only about a third (to around 360,000) in the same period of time. Nevertheless this Jewish capital (with a total value of 5.1 thousand million RM) was still there in the spring of 1938, and with

Austrian capital its value was increased to 8.5 thousand million. Of course 'Aryanization' had made its mark to the extent that business assets amounted to only 119.5 billion RM in the spring of 1938, i.e. 14.5 per cent of total Jewish assets, and had declined further by the summer; the value of domestic property was estimated at some 2.5 thousand million, while 'other assets' – mainly stocks and shares – were worth 4.88 thousand million. In addition, the regime was forced to come to terms with the fact that, despite the 'Aryanization' campaign, despite exclusion from professions, and despite the increase in acts of violence reminiscent of pogroms, Jewish emigration had still not reached the expected levels, partly because there were real difficulties involved, partly because many Jews were persistent in their patriotism and resilient in the face of suffering. Although the number of Jewish emigrants rose to 40,000 in 1938, that was not so much due to an increase in the rate of emigration as to the annexation of Austria, and Eichmann's activities there.

The authorities estimated the scale of remaining Jewish assets in 1938 with some accuracy, following two decrees passed in April of that year, which made it clear that the leaders of the Third Reich, were no longer capable of keeping their impatience in check or satisfied by the measures hitherto employed in the attack on 'Jews in the economy', and had decided to solve the problem immediately with a radical and comprehensive set of laws governing 'Aryanization' and expropriation. On 22 April came the Law against Supporting the Concealment of Jewish Commercial Enterprises, which threatened with imprisonment any German citizen who 'conspires to disguise the Jewish character of a commercial enterprise in order to mislead the public or the authorities, and four days later this was followed by the Order Governing the Registration of Jewish Assets, which obliged all German Jews – and their non-Jewish spouses – to register the exact amount of their total assets both within Germany and abroad, if the total value exceeded 5,000 RM. Even Jews of foreign nationality had to register their assets in Germany.

The intention behind all this was expressed unambiguously in paragraph 7 of the order: 'The Commissioner for the Four-Year Plan may take any measure deemed necessary to secure such registered assets for deployment in the interests of the Germany economy.' On 14 June the Third Supplementary Order to the Reich Citizenship Law created the official term 'Jewish commercial enterprise', and required the registration of all such enterprises; at the same time it enabled the Reich Minister of Economics, along with the Interior Minister and the Deputy Führer, to introduce the long awaited identification symbol for Jewish businesses.

Other measures, too, contributed to the impression that a major onslaught against German Jews was soon to be expected. On 23 July 1938

Jews were compelled to have their own identity cards forcing the Jews not only to identify their businesses as Jewish, but also their persons, although of course an externally visible badge was not yet required. This measure had scarcely been announced before the Jews had to endure a further bureaucratic innovation: an order of 17 June restricted the number of forenames they were allowed to use, or compelled them to take an additional forename 'namely the forename Israel for men, and the forename Sara for women'; the adoption of these names had to be recorded at local registry offices, and the local police had to be notified in writing. Failure to include the names 'Israel' or 'Sara' in business transactions was punishable by imprisonment.

It must be clear that Hitler saw these orders and his approval of the preliminary measures as closely related to his foreign policy, which had brought Europe to the brink of the greatest crisis since the First World War. The total 'Aryanization' of Jewish businesses and confiscation of Jewish assets – 'the compulsory exclusion of the Jews by force', as Interior Minister Frick described the objective of the policy on 14 July 1938[8] – was to come during or immediately after the annexation of Czechoslovakia, planned for the autumn since the beginning of that year, a crowning glory which would end this chapter of persecution and coincide with a triumph of foreign policy. Significantly, on 19 August the Reich Ministry of Economics was already putting pressure on those offices concerned with the registration of Jewish assets to complete their work by 30 September. Since June, finance offices and the Security Police, supported by the Chambers of Trade and regional economic advisers, had been busily occupied with the compilation of lists of wealthy Jews. In addition new baracks were built in the concentration camps at Dachau, Buchenwald and Sachsenhausen by 1,500 Jewish prisoners arrested on 13 June during a major wave of arrests of allegedly 'asocial' elements.

Of course the Sudeten crisis of 1938 did not lead to the invasion and annexation of Czechoslovakia by Germany. In view of the preparedness of the West to make concessions, Mussolini's fear of a European war, and the military and political passivity of Czechoslovakia itself, Hitler had to be content for the time being with the Sudeten districts, which served to remove any excuse for greater plunder. Yet in spite of Hitler's disappointment the success of the Munich agreement of 29 September 1938, and the increase in power and authority which that success brought with it, were great enough to fuel a further boost in the Nazis' self-confidence. There were no changes, therefore, in the course of 'Jewish policy'. From 5 October German Jews were obliged by law to hand in their passports within fourteen days. Passes valid for foreign travel were returned only after they had been stamped with a 'J', marking out the holder as a Jew.

The civil service cheerfully continued to come up with more antisemitic chicanery, and at a meeting on 14 October Goering, the regime's second-in-command, declared: 'The Jewish question must now be tackled by every available means, because they must be driven out of the economy!' As one with not inconsiderable experience of corruption himself, he went on to add that care was needed only to ensure that the confiscation of Jewish assets by the state should take place in such a correct way that they were not squandered by 'incompetent party members'.[9]

Nevertheless Goering's words indicate that the unexpected course of events in foreign policy had upset the 'Jewish policy' agenda, and that the Nazi leaders were beginning to wonder how they would now bring about the 'exclusion of the Jews from the economy' without disrupting the calm which had descended throughout Germany and Europe in the wake of the sudden diplomatic detente brought about by the Munich agreement. Although 'only' Jews were to be affected, the operation nevertheless amounted to expropriation on the grand scale, and as such constituted a serious affront to the sanctity of private property, which would cause unwelcome, or at least unnecessary disquiet among the German public if it were not accompanied by an appropriate justification. So was there not a need for a specific, or even better a spectacular event, which would serve as a relatively plausible excuse and protective diversion in place of the postponed march into Prague?

It was at this moment of tense insecurity that Herschel Grünspan's shots were fired in the German embassy in Paris. The incident was doubtless a godsend to antisemitic activists in the Nazi leadership. Certainly, Hitler and Goebbels immediately recognized the unusual opportunity which the assassination attempt provided. Pogroms had already been acknowledged in January 1937 by the Jewish expert in the head office of the SD to be the 'most effective means' of speeding up 'Jewish policy'.[10] An opportunity had now been presented by a Jew to use that solution and stage such a pogrom: 'sudden', nationwide, and with an element of 'popular anger' correspondingly greater than in April 1933 or the summer of 1935, as befitted the occasion and the ulterior motives behind the operation. Hitler and Goebbels calculated that after a typical Nazi performance, with savage outbursts of rage in the press and on the radio and fires in the night, violent terror and squads of stormtroopers and party members masquerading as the 'offended public', the pseudo-legality of 'Aryanization' and expropriation legislation would seem to be a logical step to enforce the people's will, and a step which (thankfully!) would restore law and order.

Yet the assassination and the pogrom were probably welcomed by Hitler for a further reason as well. As his speech to the representatives of the German press on 10 November 1938[11] demonstrated, the evident lack of public ethusiasm for war at the time of the Munich conference had both disappointed and irritated the Führer as much as the relief which had characterized the response of the German public to the peaceful outcome of the Sudeten crisis. Hitler considered it urgently necessary to make every attempt to prepare the nation psychologically for future developments in his bellicose policy of expansion. The pogrom was an excellent opportunity to disabuse the German people of the growing illusion that the Munich agreement marked the end of crisis, and that the German ship of state was at last entering calmer waters. Goebbels was keen to use a display of enthusiastic antisemitism in order to win greater influence within the Nazi leadership. He was also eager to win back Hitler's favour after the intervention of the Führer had frustrated his attempt to marry a Czech actress, and his interpretation of the requirements of war propaganda certainly did not differ from that of Hitler. So Hitler and Goebbels set to work on the psychological preparations for the pogrom from 7 November, unleashed it on 9 November, and during its closing stages used it to announce and legitimize their intention of completing the plunder of Jewish property with a legislative *coup de main*.

Goering and Himmler thought along similar lines, although they spoke about the 'Night of Broken Glass' in rather different terms from those of Goebbels, who noted triumphantly in his diary: 'Radical opinion has prevailed . . . Now the slate can be wiped clean.'[12] As dictator over the economy, the 'Commissioner for the Four-Year Plan' ranted about the destruction of property, and the Reich Leader of the SS considered both the timing wrong and the disturbance which a pogrom entailed too obtrusive. To wipe the slate clean, however, was not Goebbels's business but that of Himmler and Goering, and although the Reich Propaganda Director's plan to pass the whole thing off as a popular demonstration failed completely, they did not hesistate for a moment to assume the success of the plan, and make use of the opportunity. When the British chargé d'affaires in Berlin wrote to the Foreign Office on 16 November that he had 'not met a single German, of whatever class, who in varying measure does not, to say the least, disapprove of what has occurred', he added: 'But I fear that even the outspoken condemnation of professed National Socialists or senior officers in the army will not have any influence over the insensate gang in present control of Nazi Germany.'[13] Indeed.

In the wake of the pogrom Himmler had around 30,000 affluent Jews arrested, in accordance with existing plans prepared with the original justification in mind. The same combination of blackmail and expulsion was used that Eichmann had tested in Vienna. Goering thoroughly approved of the pogrom in principle and chastised Goebbels only with the characteristic remark, 'I would rather you had killed a couple of hundred

Jews than destroyed all that property!'[14] He immediately set in motion the means of evaluating the political consequenes of the pogrom, not just in the sense intended by Hitler and Goebbels, but also with his own objectives in mind, as formulated on 14 October.

In his capacity as 'economic dictator' of Germany Goering was particularly responsible for this phase of the persecution of the Jews. (At the same time, of course, he was also Minister President of Prussia, Aviation Minister, Supreme Commander of the Air Force and even Reich Chief Forestry and Hunting Commissioner.) On 12 November he called a meeting at the Reich Aviation Ministry for the heads of relevant ministries or their representatives, including a representative of German insurance companies. At the end of a debate characterized both by ideological blindness and crude brutality, resolutions were passed which Goering had outlined in his introductory speech, thereby presenting them as the programme of the Führer. It was typical of the fundamental callousness of Nazi functionaries in their treatment of the Jewish enemy that the meeting resolved, under the influence of Goering's genial, boyish spite, to require the mistreated Jews, in accordance with a Decree for the Restitution of the Street Scene passed the same day, to repair immediately the damage caused by Nazi party members and stormtroopers, and to pay for the repairs themselves. Although the insurance companies' representative at the meeting had declared that in the interests of their national and international credibility the societies he represented must insist on fulfilling their duty to pay, Goering decided, after accepting the insurance companies' point, that the payments should go not to the Jewish claimants, but directly to the German Reich, and this was duly recorded in the Reich Statute Book and reported in the press.

This particular act of piracy brought the state's coffers 225 million RM. Of greater significance, however, was the resolution, which also became law on 12 November, to take up Hitler's idea of 1936 and actually impose an extra tax on the Jews, although in the form of a one-off levy rather than regular taxation: As 'compensation' for the Paris assassination attempt, the law decreed, 'a levy of one thousand million Reichsmarks is imposed collectively on the Jews of Germany.' In practice, and in accordance with conditions added later, this meant that all Jews living in Germany who still had assets of 5,000 RM or more were required to liquidate 20 per cent, to be paid to the Reich in four instalments by 15 August 1939. In October 1939 this amount was raised to 25 per cent, because the required sum had not been reached. In total the Reich made a profit of 112,700,000 RM.

The meeting of 12 November 1938 in the Reich Ministry of Aviation resolved on this form of taxation not least because, directed by Goering, it agreed on other measures which would have made impossible the sort of regular taxation foreseen in 1936. A Law for the Exclusion of Jews from German Economic Life was also passed on 12 November, forbidding Jews to undertake any form of independent business activity, from wholesale trade to corner shops, or to practise any form of craft. Senior white-collar workers of Jewish extraction were to be dismissed without compensation or pension rights. This law, and a number of supplementary decrees which followed swiftly on its tail – e.g. the Eighth Supplementary Decree to the Reich Citizenship Law of 17 January 1939, which prohibited Jewish dentists, vets and pharmacists from practising their professions – brought to an end any type of professional activity on the part of Jews which either required contact with the 'Aryan' world, or even made such contact possible. German Jews would have been sentenced to work only in a purely Jewish environment and therefore, with the help of what little private capital they had so far managed to save, to inhabit a sort of economic ghetto.

The Nazis did not let the matter rest there. As agreed at the conference of 12 November, the Law on the Use of Jewish Assets was enacted on 3 December 1938. On the one hand this provided for the compulsory closure or 'Aryanization' of surviving Jewsh businesses and the compulsory 'Aryanization' of land belonging to Jews, from agricultural land and woodlands to urban estates. On the other hand it ordered the depositing of cash, share certificates and other valuables in closed accounts. Depositories were arranged in the clearing banks, and the deposits could be used only with the permission of the Reich Ministry of Economics. This law made it impossible for Jews to deal freely in precious metals, jewellery or works of art, which could be disposed of only at state purchasing offices. On 21 February 1939 the Jews were ordered to deliver all precious metals, precious stones, jewellery and pearls to these purchasing offices within two weeks; only wedding rings could be retained. Even without these acts of state plunder it would have been clear that the German Jews were now much more than excluded from the economic life of the German nation; they were effectively already expropriated and reduced to the status of lodgers in the German Reich.

Furthermore the Nazi leaders of the Reich left no room for doubt that the Jews of Germany had to reckon with meagre fare and malicious treatment. In response to a demand from Goebbels the meeting in the Reich Ministry of Aviation had also agreed on a law, passed on 12 November, which strictly prohibited German Jews from visiting theatres, cinemas, concerts, exhibitions, music halls, cabarets, circuses, dance performances and other 'presentations of German culture'. On 28 November Himmler issued a decree which gave heads of local authorities the right, and thereby effectively instructed them, to 'impose on Jews of German nationality and stateless Jews restrictions of movement to the effect that there are certain districts which they are not allowed to enter or that they are not allowed to appear in public at certain times'. The restricted areas created by this law – which effectively placed Jews under martial law – were called 'Judenbann'. At the same time both state and municipal authorities reinforced a process which had long been under way. Increasingly this meant that certain blocks were inhabited exclusively by Jews, and minor ghettoes were created.

The Seventh Supplementary Decree to the Reich Citizenship Law reduced the pensions of Jewish civil servants dismissed in 1935, i.e. civil servants with 'national merit', from 5 December 1938, and regulations issued by Reich Education Minister Rust on 14 November and 8 December 1938 drove the last Jews from German schools and universities. A law of 29 November prohibited Jews from keeping homing pigeons, and on 3 December Himmler withdrew both their ordinary driving licences and goods vehicle licences; on the same day Jews learned that they were no longer to be allowed to use sports grounds, public or private swimming baths, or open air swimming pools. A law of 30 April 1939 'relaxed' rent protection provision for Jews. How did Goering put it, with deep conviction, towards the end of the conference of 12 November? 'I would not like to be a Jew in Germany.'[15]

6

Approach to Genocide

Yet the significance of the 'Night of Broken Glass' both in the development of Nazi antisemitism, and in the history of the persecution of the Jews by the Nazi movement and the Nazi state, was not that it marked the completion of a phase whose catchword from 1936 to 1938 had been 'Jews out of the economy', and which had now culminated in the complete expropriation and legal incapacitation of the Jews. As during and after the enactment of the Nuremberg Laws, many Nazis had the impression that this was merely a stage along the way. Of course the pogrom and the ensuing series of legislative acts did mark the high point and the end of one round of persecution. Yet the radical nature of the antisemitism which underpinned the Nazis' 'Jewish policy' was such that completion of one stage necessarily entailed the commencement of another, and one which was much more intensely malicious, whose objectives were of a completely different order. Goebbels, who had staged the 'Night of Broken Glass', had already noted on 12 November: 'The whole question has now been moved on a good deal.'[1]

It was also quite clear to Goering that the matter would not rest with the pauperization of the German Jews. At the end of the conference of 12 November 1938, during which he 'pulled no punches', as Goebbels (who got on with him 'splendidly') confirmed,[2] he said: 'Should the German Reich become involved in a diplomatic conflict in the foreseeable future, it is obvious that we in Germany will be thinking first and foremost of a great reckoning with the Jews.'[3] Since the regime's second-in-command could scarcely have doubted that Germany would be waging war in the near future, in whatever circumstances, this remark did not refer to the vague possibility of a future eventuality but to a situation which was to be expected with certainty.

But what sort of intensification of persecution could Goebbels and Göring actually have had in mind? Surely not the emigration of those Jews living in the German sphere of power. Compared with the existence to which the Jews of Germany and Austria were condemned, emigration would not mean they were worse off, but much better off. Certainly, in the months that followed the 'Night of Broken Glass' the regime had stressed that the emigration of the Jews, a policy touted since 1933 as a solution to the 'Jewish question', but implemented only half-heartedly and with inadequate resources, was now at last being pursued seriously. Goering, as Commissioner of the Four-Year Plan, charged by Hitler, in the wake of the pogrom, with full exceptional powers as supreme co-ordinator of anti-Jewish measures, issued a directive to Reich Interior Minister Frick on 24 January 1939, of which the first sentence was as follows: 'The emigration of Jews from Germany is to be encouraged by all possible means.'[4]

The directive made the ministry responsible for setting up a Central Office for Jewish Emigration, which in turn had the task of forcing all Jews living in Germany, whether German nationals or stateless, to join a 'Reich Union of German Jews' as a Jewish institution for the organization of emigration. Responsibility for Jewish education and social welfare was also transferred to the Reich Union, which came into being on 4 July 1939. This was effectively an attempt to apply throughout the Reich the methods of expulsion used by Eichmann and his Central Office for Jewish emigration in Vienna – and from March 1939 at a second, similar institution in Prague, and the Central Office's tasks, described in Goering's instructions, clearly reflected Eichmann's principles. This policy – already tried out on a large scale on the Jews arrested in the wake of the pogrom – coincided with an understandably greater willingness to emigrate on the part of the Jews themselves, and between the end of 1938 and the autumn of 1939 80,000 Jews had left German territory (even though this generally meant the loss of all their possessions) and escaped to Hungary, Italy or France, and a life of wretched poverty, rather than overseas to a life of relative material and political security.

At the same time the negotiations continued which had begun at the end of December 1938 between Schacht, President of the Reichsbank, and the director of the London-based International Committee for Political Refugees, an American called Rublee, in order to establish the conditions for the emigration of a further 400,000 Jews. Following Schacht's dismissal on 20 January 1939, the negotiations were conducted on the German side by *Ministerialdirektor* Helmuth Wohlthat, the civil service head of Goering's Four-Year Plan Office, with the participation of the ambassador, Eisenlohr, representing the Foreign Office, and Ribbentrop, who had initially been passed over. In the meantime the Foreign Ministry's special German Section (Sonderreferat Deutschland), recently set up by Ribbentrop, circulated a memorandum to all diplomatic missions and consulates in the Reich on 25 January 1939, in which emigration was again presented as 'the ultimate aim of German Jewish policy', although it was pointed out that there would be no support for a Jewish state in Palestine which might become a world centre for the Jews.[5]

In truth, however, the 'Night of Broken Glass' opened up an entirely new stage in which a completely different 'solution to the Jewish question' competed increasingly with the tendency to drive the Jews out of Germany. This alternative was not so much a radicalization of previous policy as its logical culmination. It was based on a conviction which was radical by its very nature but relied on the implementation of the preceding stages: only now, following the deprivation of the Jews' civil and political rights, and their isolation and expropriation, did the extermination of the Jews seem both possible and desirable. The pogrom itself made that much clear. The most significant feature of the pogrom, and the one which indicated most clearly the future direction of Nazi persecution was not the destruction of Jewish shops and homes, nor even the burning down of Jewish synagogues, but the fact that ninety-one Jews, some of them women, had been clubbed, kicked or beaten to death by Nazi murder units, and that the culprits had been tried neither for manslaughter nor for murder.

During the pogrom itself Goebbels had greeted such murders with cynical approval, but above all as acts which corresponded fully with the new approach to the persecution of the Jews.[6] As Goebbels recorded in his diary, Hitler spoke out 'very sharply against the Jews', and in this matter was of one mind with the Reich Director of Propaganda[7] – much to the latter's delight. When, on 24 November, the South African Minister of Defence and Economics, Oswald Pirow, wanted to discuss with the Führer generous international plans for the emigration of all Jews, the latter rejected such projects persistently and with the flimsiest of arguments.[8] Nor could Ribbentrop's success in stalling his sterile and fruitless negotiations with Rublee have happened without the knowledge and approval of the Führer.

Obviously Hitler was not in the least interested in getting as many Jews as possible – perhaps all of them – out of Germany. This could have been because he wanted to keep a certain number of hostages; Jews throughout the world, but most importantly in France, Britain and the United States, might be persuaded by the threat of intensified persecution to bring pressure to bear on their governments to tolerate the German territorial expansion presaged by the Munich agreement. Indeed, on 30 January 1939, while speaking in the Reichstag on the anniversary of the Nazi assumption of power, Hitler said:

> Throughout my life I have often made prophecies, which have generally been greeted with ridicule. During my struggle for power it was always the Jews who laughed loudest, when I prophesied that I would one day be head of the state, and leader of the entire German nation, and that among other things I would find the answer to the Jewish problem. I imagine that the Jews who laughed so loud then are now choking on their laughter. Today I will play the prophet again: if Jewish international financiers, both inside and outside Europe, succeed in forcing the peoples of the world into another war, the outcome will not be the Bolshevization of the world, and therefore a victory for the Jews; it will mean the annihilation of the Jewish race in Europe.[9]

However, this speech constituted only a fleeting and none too serious flirtation with the hostage principle. By the outbreak of war neither Hitler nor any other Nazi negotiator in international relations ever attempted to dissuade any western politician from supporting Poland, the next victim in Hitler's expansionist policy, by resorting to threats against the Jews. They would not have been successful in any case. In the first place the policy of Western governments towards Germany was determined by factors other than consideration either for the Jews in their own states, or for those living in Germany. Secondly, the Nazi leadership had consistently shown, most recently during the 'Night of Broken Glass', that protection for the Jews could not be bought by guaranteeing the success of Hitler's foreign policy. On the contrary, every success on the international stage was automatically followed by anti-Jewish activity. Rather, Hitler's reluctance to undertake more comprehensive emigration projects, and the bleak prophecy in his Reichstag speech, not to mention Goebbels's cynicism during the pogrom, and Goering's remark of 12 November, were obviously nothing other than the first symptoms of a growing will to destroy, now that all the more modest ways of satisfying the drive to persecute the Jews had been exhausted. On 21 January 1939 Hitler made this clear, and did so in a conversation with a foreign politician. According to the official German minutes, the Führer bluntly told the Czech Foreign Minister, Chvalkovsky that 'the Jews here would be destroyed. Not for nothing had the Jews acted on 9 November 1918. This day would be avenged.'[10]

Furthermore, the mood at the top thoroughly reflected the opinion in the institutions and organizations of the Nazi movement; this had been demonstrated clearly enough on the 'Night of Broken Glass', when numerous killers from the ranks of the party and the SA had murdered not as a result of clear orders, but had been prompted to commit their crimes on the strength of vague slogans such as 'Death to international Jewry'. The dominant tendencies in the SS were now particularly important in this context. After the pogrom the 'Jewish question' seemed to the Nazi leadership to be a police problem, and it was left to the police to deal with it on a practical level. In his decree of 24 January 1939 Goering nominated Heydrich as leader of the Reich Central Office for Jewish Emigration, and made him answerable, in this capacity, only to himself and, of course, Himmler, rather than to his formal superior, Interior Minister Frick. Heydrich in turn selected SS *Standartenführer* Heinrich Müller, head of Department II of the Secret Police Office (*Gestapa*) in Berlin as manager of the Reich Central Office, and he replaced Eichmann in October 1939.

Following the merger of the SD (the SS Security Head Office) with the Gestapo and the Criminal Police (Security Police Head Office) to form the Reich Security Head Office (Reichssicherheitshauptamt, RSHA) on 27 September 1939, Eichmann assumed responsibility anyway. Having returned to Berlin from Vienna and Prague, he took over Section IV D 4 (Emigration and Evacuation) in Office IV (Geheime Staatspolizei) of the Reich Security Head Office; this later became Section IV B 4 (Jewish Matters, Evacuation Matters). Those ministries which had been involved in the establishment and execution of Nazi anti-Jewish policy so far, i.e. above all the Interior and Justice Ministries found themselves increasingly demoted to auxiliaries to the police operation. Otherwise they remained quite free to continue to make life difficult for the Jews with legislation, although now, of course, such legislation had less and less to do with the real thrust of anti-Jewish policy. Thus on 18 December 1941, for example, the Reich Ministry of the Interior came up with the idea of taking passes away from Jews severely disabled in war.

In the meantime, however, the police had come within the domain of the SS. At the top Heinrich Himmler was 'Reich Leader of the SS and Chief of the German Police', and Reinhard Heydrich was Chief of the Security Police, and the middle and lower ranks of the SS and the police had merged. Nor did the SS leave any doubt as to how it would use this new stronghold against the Jews. On 24 November 1938 the *Schwarzes Korps* published an article which is remarkable not so much for its characteristically crude racism, but for the cynical clarity with which the expected consequences of current anti-Jewish measures were outlined, and for the perfidious single-mindedness with which these consequences were used in turn to justify the next stage of 'Jewish policy'. After the author had described how the isolated and pauperized German Jews would necessarily sink into a miserable parasitical existence and 'resort *en masse* to criminality', he drew the following conclusion: 'At such a stage in developments we would be confronted with the hard necessity of exterminating the Jewish underworld just as we exterminate criminals in our state of order: with fire and sword! The result would be the actual, final end of Jewry in Germany, its total destruction.'

Of course, it was impossible to translate such visions into reality for the time being. The 'Night of Broken Glass' had caused outrage outside the German Reich and completed the moral isolation of Nazi Germany. The incident also immediately gained political significance. Independently of the fate of the German Jews, which touched no vital French or British interest, and so would have had consequences of relatively little weight, the pogrom was nevertheless taken as proof in France and Britain that the Nazi regime was characterized by an inherent aggressiveness which could not be satiated, as most people had hoped, by the Munich agreement and the annexation of the Sudetenland, and which prompted expectations of further aggression. This above all necessitated resistance to Nazi Germany. Statesmen such as the British Prime Minister Chamberlain, who on his return from Munich had shown a piece of paper to the press containing an Anglo-German commitment to peaceful understanding, and declared to them that here he had 'peace in our time', were humiliated, and the appeasement policy they had followed towards Germany was discredited.

When Hitler invaded Czechoslovakia on 15 March 1939 and set up the 'Protectorate of Bohemia and Moravia', thereby confirming that in foreign policy, too, Nazi aggression was unstoppable, the West finally woke up to the fact – which would have been much less clear without the pogram – that Germany's next international act of violent aggression must be countered by military means. Ernst Woermann, director of the Political Section of the German Foreign Ministry, issued a memorandum on 20 November 1938 which, although phrased in the correct ideological terms, constituted a serious warning about the foreign policy effects of violence against the Jews. Concentrating on the impact on the United States, Woermann made it clear that the pogrom had made it considerably easier for President Roosevelt to popularize his anti-Nazi policies. The recall of the American ambassador in Berlin, Hugh Wilson, on 14 November, had met with universal approval and 'certainly for the time being the whole people' stood united behind Roosevelt. 'Our few friends have been silenced.'[11]

Although the Nazi leaders were unable to grasp the depth and extent of the Western reaction, they were nevertheless conscious of having upset the apple-cart, and knew that they would be well advised to observe some caution in the field of 'Jewish policy', at least for a while, and at least as long as attempts were being made to obtain from France and Britain a free hand in eastern Europe. It was also clear to the leadership of the regime that the majority of the German public had thoroughly condemned the brutal violence of the pogrom, and that this included many who had had nothing against the removal of the Jews' civil and political rights or their isolation, and were even prepared to accept the expropriation of the Jews without raising any serious objections. Of course, there was no real reason to fear that the indignation – often quite openly expressed in November – might crystallize into political opposition. After all, the mass unemployment of the slump had been replaced by full employment, and Hitler's foreign policy successes also had a calming effect on German consciences. Yet the transition to an openly violent persecution of the Jews could be achieved on a large-scale basis only if the German public received more education in antisemitism, if the moral sensitivity of the nation were further dulled, and if the public were distracted by other factors. Otherwise there was a serious threat that the relationship between the regime and the people would be seriously weakened, and that this would hinder Germany's expansionist plans.

Yet some outlet was needed for antisemitic urges, and the policy of expulsion provided just such an outlet. Indeed the process of piecemeal expulsion was conceived by Nazi leaders as just such an emergency measure, a policy of moderation dictated by circumstances. It is instructive enough that Jewish emigration was now ascribed an effect which even made it appear, in the long term, an instrument of annihilation. In his conversation with Pirow, Hitler had said that by expelling the Jews he hoped to export antisemitism, and in the above-mentioned Foreign Ministry memorandum the point was also made that the mass expulsion of Jews could be expected to lead to an increase in antisemitism in the countries which accepted them. The wishful thinking here was quite clear: that the whole earth would become uninhabitable for the Jews.[12] It was, of course, highly doubtful that such wishes could be fulfilled. The assumption that antisemitism could be exported by expelling the Jews, could only be a meagre consolation, and altered nothing of the emergency nature of the operation. What Heydrich said in retrospect several years later is entirely credible: that the emigration policy was a course whose disadvantages had to be 'accepted in view of the absence of other possible solutions'.[13]

The outbreak of war, and the first campaigns, which led to the conquest of Poland, Denmark, Norway, Belgium, Holland, Luxembourg and France between the beginning of September 1939 and July 1940, brought no fundamental change to this situation. In the wake of the military victories the Jews in the occupied territories – above all the Polish Jews – were immediately and unhesitatingly subjected to the usual Nazi treatment.

Himmler and Heydrich set up special Security Police units (Einsatzgruppen) for the attack on Poland, as they had done with the occupation of Austria and the invasion of Czechoslovakia. These followed immediately behind the regular army, dissolving Jewish organizations, confiscating their property, and making large-scale, if unsystematic, arrests. At the same time Jews lost their civil rights and suffered isolation and expropriation as the process which had taken place gradually over six years in Germany was now telescoped into a few days or weeks.

Dr Hans Frank became head of the administration which was formed in the so-called 'Government General' after the conquest of Poland, i.e. the administration of rump Poland without the districts ceded to the Soviet Union in the second half of September 1939, and without the western districts which were directly incorporated into the Reich as the *Gaue* of Danzig–West Prussia and Wartheland, and without the administrative districts of Kattowitz and Zichenau, which also became German. On 26 October and 12 December 1939 Frank ordered the introduction of compulsory labour service for the dispossessed Polish Jews. Following local trials, e.g. from 24 October in Wloclawec, an order was issued which made it compulsory not only for all Jewish shops to display the 'star of David', but also for individual Jews to wear it as a mark of identification. On 11 December there followed the effective removal of freedom of movement, and train journeys were formally prohibited in any case from 26 January 1940. In addition, the councils of Jewish elders which were set up in all Jewish communities, following the example of the Reich itself, were forced to co-operate – willingly or unwillingly – in this process as instruments of the German executive authorities.

In addition the Jews were outside the law in that they could be moved around according to the discretion of the police. On 21 September Heydrich had already ordered that all Jews, both in the Government General and in the areas incorporated into the Reich, should be concentrated in the larger towns, where a process of ghettoization should be commenced. Although this process was neither as swift nor as comprehensive as Heydrich wished, it nevertheless very quickly involved large movements of people. By April 1940 the major ghetto in Łodz – annexed to the Reich as Litzmannstadt – was 'sealed'; in October–November 1940 it was followed by Warsaw, in March 1941 by Cracow, in April of the same year by Lublin and then Radom. The competition between the Nazi viceroys to be the first to make their *Gau* or town 'free of Jews' now became much more intense, and was expressed in large scale operations, since the Government General was deemed an appropriate place for any group of people not wanted in the Reich. In December 1939, for example, 87,000 Jews and Poles were deported to the Government General from

A Jewish citizen of Warsaw, forced to wear the 'Star of David', employed turning a public park into a Jewish cemetery, winter 1940
(Imperial War Museum, London)

the *Reichsgau* Posen (Poznán) – as *Gau* Wartheland was called until 29 January 1940. On 13 February 1940 came the first mass deportations from the Reich, from Vienna, Mährisch-Ostrau, Teschen and Stettin. Occasionally the police referred to the creation of a 'Jewish reservation' somewhere in Poland as the ultimate objective of such deportations, both now and in the future, and this is what Heydrich himself told Walther von Brauchitsch, supreme commander of the army, in September 1939.

Such explanations did not, of course, reflect any serious intention. At any rate, any plans for reservations were quickly abandoned. In April 1940 Friedrich Wilhelm Krüger, a senior figure in the SS and police in the Government General said as much of the reservation ostensibly hitherto planned for the Lublin district, and Hitler himself, in a conversation with the Austrian travel writer Colin Ross, had stated that 'the construction of a Jewish state around Lublin could never constitute a solution.'[14] The prime consideration here, as in the opposition to large-scale emigration, was the will to total destruction, and the aversion of the police to reservations must have been based on similar reasoning. In the internal order of 21 September 1939, which marked the beginning of the drive to ghettoize the Polish Jews, Heydrich characterized the migratory movement he had ordered as merely the condition for an 'ultimate goal, which needs a rather longer time span', and he warned the recipients of his instructions, namely the commanders of SS special units (Einsatzgruppen) who had received oral instructions from him shortly before their written orders, that this ultimate goal must be kept 'strictly confidential'.[15] This can only be understood as an intention to exterminate the Jews which was to be realized in the near future. At this stage there was no form of persecution left for the Jews which would have required secrecy, or where secrecy would have been relevant, apart from mass murder, and certainly none which would have required of the regime's policemen so strict a confidentiality as Heydrich now demanded.

There were other signs that the dream of mass extermination was on the point of becoming reality. During the Polish campaign, and in the weeks immediately afterwards, many members of the SS special units and other Nazi formations behaved in such a way that it was clear they were working themselves up for a formal command ordering mass killings. Although the special units 'only' had an order to 'liquidate' the Polish intelligentsia, there were many shootings of individual Jews, and several more extensive massacres: an *Einsatzgruppe zur besonderen Verwendung* (unit designated for special purposes) under SS *Obergruppenführer* Udo von Woyrsch rampaged in Galicia, while in Wloclawec the leader of an SS Death's Head Unit, with 800 arrested Jews in his charge, had a considerable number shot 'in flight'.[16] Significantly, like the murderers of the 'Night of Broken Glass', the culprits again went unpunished. Although the army, under whose jurisdiction the SS units stood, instituted a series of cases before courts martial, Hitler himself issued an amnesty for such violent crimes on 4 October 1939, from which the *Obermusikmeister* (direct of music of the

Leibstandarte Adolf Hitler (Hitler's 'Bodyguard' Regiment) profited, having had fifty Jews shot in Blonie during the night of 18 and 19 November.

On 17 October 1939 the 'Führer' simply removed the SS and police units from any military or other normal jurisdiction. From now on 'exceptional' jurisdiction was exercised in criminal cases for senior members of the Reich Leadership of the SS, the SS *Verfügungstruppe* (later the *Waffen-SS*) and the SS Death's Head Units, for members of police units 'on special duties' etc. Such far-reaching interference in the administration of justice on behalf of the murderers naturally had anything but a restraining effect on the SS and police formations involved, and there were further executions in the autumn of 1939, during the winter, and in the spring of 1940. On 19 March 1941, following a visit to Posen, where the local Nazi potentates had sketched the history of the young *Reichsgau*, Goebbels wrote: 'Everything has been liquidated here, particularly the Jewish filth.'[17]

The leaders of the regime were readier than ever to issue the order for mass murder (much awaited by their underlings) since the liquidation of the Polish intelligentsia and the liquidation, since October 1939, of so-called 'unfit life', one with guns, the other with poison gas, actions which had in any case initiated the process of mass murder. For both murder programmes Hitler had fulfilled the most necessary condition in the Nazi system, by issuing the instructions personally, written instructions for the 'Euthanasia Programme', organized by his personal secretariat, the 'Führer chancellery' under Philipp Bouhler and Viktor Brack, and oral instructions for the murders in Poland. His impatience to give the signal for a new, final stage in his 'Jewish policy' as well was clearly demonstrated by the amnesty for the murders of the Jews in Poland.

At the same time there was a growing feeling among many Nazis that the imminent mass murder should be justified by reasoning similar to that of the '*Schwarzes Korps*' article of 24 November 1938, namely by pointing out with indignation and disgust the miserable squalor of the Polish ghettos (which, of course, had largely been created by measures undertaken by the Germans). After a visit to the ghetto in Łodz, Goebbels noted on 2 November 1939: 'These are no longer human beings, they are animals. So our task here is not a humanitarian one, but a surgical one. Incisions are necessary, and very radical ones at that. Otherwise all of Europe will perish with the Jewish disease.'[18] On the following day the Führer thoroughly agreed with him. He, too, was of the opinion that it was 'more of a clinical than a social matter'.[19] Furthermore, two films were made at this time which reflected very well the attitudes of Hitler and Goebbels, namely the feature film *Jew Süss* and the ghetto documentary *The Eternal Jew*. *Jew Süss*

A page from the medical register of the Hadamar 'sanatorium' in Austria, where the handicapped and insane were murdered as part of the Nazis' Euthanasia Programme, giving details of victim's name, age, nationality and the 'official' cause of death
(Imperial War Museum, London)

ends with the public hanging of the film's anti-hero, and in *The Eternal Jew* the Jewish migration from Poland to the west is compared with the migratory routes of rats. 'Wherever rats appear they carry plague and devastation across the land, and it is exactly the same with Jews in human society.' 'These Jews', Goebbels confided in his diary after preliminary showings of the Ghetto film, 'must be destroyed.'[20] In 1940 it was made obligatory for members of the Security Police and other Nazi formations to see the film.

And yet it was still impossible to translate these murderous intentions into an order to kill. As ever, there were important objections to such a command. Until the second half of 1940 Hitler hoped to be able to win British recognition of his continental German Empire. As long as this hope persisted the moral reputation of Germany in the British Commonwealth – or British Empire, as the Nazis, with characteristic lack of understanding, continued to call it – and in the United States must not be entirely ruined, and the opportunities for 'international Jewry' to put pressure on the British and American governments had especially to be taken into account. The German Reich was still open to foreign journalists, not least Americans, and the occupied territories were by no means sufficiently protected against the scrutiny of inquisitive outsiders. The declining importance of such factors in the eyes of Nazi leaders was, of course, already clear from the two murder campaigns of 1939: the 'Euthanasia Programme' was conceived as an internal process, which affected only the German population, and every effort was made to keep it secret from beginning to end. The murder programme in Poland must have given rise to less apprehension, since the fear of international attention and pressure on British and American politicans was not as great as it would have been had the operation been undertaken against the Jews.

In addition, the Nazi leaders were forced to recognize that the murders in Poland, both the authorized murders of members of the Polish intelligentsia and the spontaneous murders of Jews, did provoke criticism, and less so abroad than in Germany itself, where the extent of criticism took them by surprise. Even the evacuation of Jews met with resistance from the railway workers involved, and General Blaskowitz, Supreme Commander in the East, justified his condemnation of these operations, in a note for a paper to be presented to the Supreme Commander of the Army on 6 February 1940, with the following words:

> It is obvious that the starving population, in its struggle to survive, will look on the masses of totally bereft refugees, snatched overnight from their homes, and crawling naked and hungry among them, with the greatest concern. It is also understandable that these feelings will intensify to immeasurable hatred with the numerous children who have starved to death and the wagon-loads of frozen human beings.[21]

With similar horror the army registered cases in which a dreadful mixture of ideology and sadism was unleashed on the Jews. One such case was noted in an official report from Defence Area Command XXI (Posen) of 23 November 1939:

> In several towns operations have been carried out against the Jews which have degenerated into the worst excesses. In Turck three van-loads of SS men under the command of a senior SS leader drove through the streets on 30 October 1939 indiscriminately beating people around the head with bull-whips. The victims included German nationals. Finally a number of Jews were driven into the synagogue, where they had to crawl among the pews singing, while being whipped repeatedly by SS men. They were then forced to drop their trousers in order to be beaten on their naked behinds.[22]

Such incidents, commented the author of the report, were 'not without their impact on the troops, who . . . as a result, are coming to oppose the administration and the party'. Full of indignation, army officers went on to report that Himmler's special units were indulging in widespread plunder. General Blaskowitz reported, with astonished disbelief, that in a discussion with Governor General Frank on 23 January 1940, the Administrator of the Four-Year Plan, Major General Rührmann had boasted that the 'gifted' director of one of his branch offices, a cavalry officer by the name of Schuh, had managed 'to persuade the SS to give up large quantities of watches and gold'. Blaskowitz added the following remark: 'It is hardly surprising, in the light of such occurrences, that the individual takes every opportunity to enrich himself. He can do so without risk, for when theft is a universal practice, the individual thief need fear no punishment.'[23]

But of course it was the murders that had the greatest effect. Blaskowitz, who hoped to achieve something with his paper to the Supreme Commander of the Army, Brauchitsch, and through him, perhaps, to make an impression on Hitler, also used the argument of political damage in putting his case against the rampages of the SS.

> The devoutly religious Poles are not only filled with revulsion at the open acts of violence against the Jews, they are also very sympathetic towards them, whereas in the past their attitude was characterized to a greater or lesser extent by hostility. Before long our two arch-enemies in the east, the Poles and the Jews, supported in addition by the Catholic church, will be totally united against Germany in their hatred of their oppressors.[24]

For him and other officers such reprehensible murders constituted a greater danger than the possibility of fraternization. The Supreme Commander of the southern section of the border, Alexander Ulex, an infantry general, wrote on 2 February 1940 that 'the violence of the police units' demonstrated 'a totally inconceivable lack of human and moral feeling, so that one could almost speak of brutalization', and he added: 'The only way out of this demeaning situation, which tarnishes the honour of the entire German nation, is, as far as I can see, to disband and disperse all the police units, including all their senior leaders, and all the directors of administrative offices in the Government General, and replace them with sound and honourable units.'[25]

So for several weeks, and even months, the Security Police found itself involved in total conflict with the army, ranging from direct clashes between the leaders of roving murder units and local army commanders to indignant protests registered at the highest level. In some cases local army officers ordered their men to load their guns and, without any resistance from their own troops, forced the Security Police to withdraw under threat of armed conflict. Himmler, Heydrich and their police units were by no means in a strong position in this conflict. They could not justify the murder of Jews by reference to any 'Führer order', and had to resort to the explanation that heartfelt and active hostility to the Jews was the mark of a true National Socialist; nor could they appeal to any 'Führer order' permitting the murder of Poles; they could only argue that a perhaps somewhat harsh revenge for the murder of Germans by Poles in 1939 was as understandable as it was necessary. Obviously Hitler wanted to preserve a certain distance between himself, as a head of state who needed room to manoeuvre in international affairs, and these murderous activities, which is why Heydrich complained at the beginning of July 1940 that 'the activities of the police and the SS' had 'appeared as arbitrary and brutal high-handedness' because 'it had not been possible to inform the army command posts' of the 'order to liquidate numerous members of Poland's ruling classes'.[26] Most indiscreet of all was Himmler, who said, in the course of a speech to army commanders in Koblenz on 13 March 1940: 'I do nothing which the Führer does not know about.'[27]

Despite its promise, however, the wave of protest never attained the breadth and intensity necessary to change things; and then it soon died away again. First of all Hitler himself made it quite clear whose side he was on, and not only by issuing the amnesty of 4 October 1939 and establishing separate legal jurisdiction for the SS and the police. On 26 November 1939 he freed the army from virtually any role in the administration of Poland, thereby also freeing it, both in his own view and that of many officers, from any responsibility for what Himmler was doing there. On 7 October the Reich Leader of the SS had been appointed 'Reich Commissar for the Consolidation of German Nationhood' and expressly given the task of 'excluding the damaging influence of those foreign sections of the population which pose a danger for the Reich and the German national community'. Furthermore when, in the middle of November 1939, Hitler was presented with the first of two memoranda from Blaskowitz on the atrocities in Poland, he reacted with violent rages against his generals, who seemed to believe war could be waged by 'Salvation Army methods'.[28] In doing this he broke the back of the protest, because after Hitler had taken up such a clear position General von Brauchitsch no longer dared to relay any more criticism of the atrocities either in a mild form, or as spokesman of a movement pressing for the replacement and punishment of the guilty.

Brauchitsch's attitude was also significant, however, in that in an institution like the army most of the protesting officers considered their duty done once they had reported wrongful incidents to their immediate superior, and in the case of senior officers this was the Supreme Command of the Armed Forces (OKW). The OKW was indispensable to the critics if they were to achieve anything politically. Brauchitsch's behaviour, which by no means remained a secret, also provided a clear indication of Hitler's position, and since the Führer and Führer power had now become incontestable official sources of professional, political and moral decision-making, even for the vast majority of the officer corps, knowledge of the 'Führer's will' was sufficient for them to put aside any qualms of a professional, political or even moral nature.

Naturally there were some who were not prepared to accept the Führer as a substitute for their consciences, and many too who were not persuaded that with the removal of its administrative responsibilities on 26 October 1939, the army's moral responsibility for Poland had also come to an end. When such officers seriously began to take stock of their position, however, they almost immediately found themselves in a dilemma: basically they were faced with the choice between gritting their teeth and obeying orders or plotting a coup, and if some of them chose active resistance, or felt themselves strenghthened by it, most of them chose the way which was both psychologically and morally more straightforward, and kept to their oaths. Trivial factors also played a part, for example the rapid transfer of almost all active units to the western front, where they were able to recuperate with the preparations for the attack on France, Belgium and Holland. There were also personal political interventions. After his protests, for example, the troublemaker Blaskowitz was ousted from his position as Supreme Commander in the East, and was transferred to the west as Supreme Commander of the Ninth Army, where on 3 June 1940 he was relieved of his commission on Hitler's orders.

It cannot be denied, however, that the miliary faction against the Security Police suffered above all from a serious weakness. The basis of their criticism of the murder of Jews was very narrow: their protests were directed exclusively against open violence or murder, or against the worst effects of the 'resettlement' programme. They failed even to mention the other ways in which the Jews were persecuted and ultimately reduced to the level of slaves: the removal of civil rights, expropriation, compulsory ghettoization. This was not, for the most part, because they wished to concentrate on the worst excesses for tactical reasons; they had simply become accustomed to such things, and insensitive to them, and the routine torment of the Jews was already taken for granted and hardly even noticed any more. Seven years of living under a regime which made antisemitism the central tenet of a state religion of racism had not failed to have an effect on the majority of even the more morally sensitive officers.

For Hitler, of course, it was sufficient to sense the existence of a broad-based and critical opposition movement. He did not know that in the winter of 1939–40 some of those officers who had resolved on active resistance were campaigning for support for a coup in the Supreme Command of the Army, the Supreme Command of the Armed Forces, and among the chiefs of staff of the armies mobilized for an attack in the west, and that they were often using material on the atrocities of the Security Police in order to win support. He nevertheless realized that there were important political reasons for respecting a final limit to 'Jewish policy' for the time being – in the light of a mood in the army which caused Blaskowitz to write: 'The attitude of the troops towards the SS and the police fluctuates between revulsion and hatred. Every soldier feels nauseated and repelled by the crimes being perpetrated in Poland by men from the Reich representing the state authorities. The men fail to understand how such things – which happen, so to speak, under their aegis – can go unpunished.'[29]

It is not clear precisely when Hitler and the other leaders of the regime, including Goering, Himmler and Heydrich came to consider it possible after all to follow the murderous logic of their *Weltanschauung* to its conclusion, to cross the boundary to genocide in their war against the Jews, and actually to undertake the extermination of their opponents' race and the historical evil which – for them – it embodied. It is certain, however, that the military victories in Scandinavia, and above all in France, provided their murderous will with new impetus, and at the same time furnished the necessary conditions. The military and political self-confidence, but more than that the 'ideological' arrogance of the Nazi leaders, now reached such heights of hubris that nothing seemed impossible. The usual pattern of promptly following such victories with a new chapter in the persecution of the Jews combined with this inflated arrogance in an extraordinarily dangerous way.

Furthermore, the right to this sort of arrogance was granted to Hitler, and to other Nazi leaders, such as Goering and Goebbels, by the nation. In other words, the fact that the prestige of the Führer and some of his henchmen rose to an unassailable peak was not without political significance. So much so that for a time the terms 'the Führer's will' and 'the orders of the Führer' attained an almost magical force. Hitler was fully aware of this. Furthermore, in the wake of the defeat of the French army, reputedly not just the best in Europe but the best in the world, he considered himself the unchallengeable master of the continent of Europe. For some time after the fall of France he probably hoped Britain would come to terms with the situation, and seek an understanding with him. The new balance of power would be sufficient to force Britain to yield, especially if the German air force dealt a few sharp blows to the stubborn British, in an attempt to make them grasp the futility of continuing the war. In addition, he considered it increasingly unnecessary to take into account Germany's moral reputation in Britain and America.

On the other hand, ever since the invasion of Austria, those senior SS leaders directly responsible for the 'Jewish question' had repeatedly observed that with every extension of German power over foreign territory, a considerable number of Jews was added to those already under Nazi rule, and the increase always exceeded the reductions achieved by emigration. The political implications of this repeated observation could no longer be avoided. Following the invasion of Poland and the states of western Europe, which even returned some of the Jewish refugees to Nazi control, the leaders of the police were faced with a quantitatively new dimension to a problem they had created for themselves: emigration was no longer a possible solution to the 'Jewish question'. And the expansion of Nazi Germany was by no means at an end. On 24 June 1940 Heydrich wrote to Foreign Minister von Ribbentrop: 'The whole problem – there are now three and a quarter million Jews in the areas *presently* [Heydrich's emphasis] under German rule – can no longer be solved by emigration; a territorial final solution is therefore now becoming necessary.'[30]

In fact a plan emerged in the summer of 1940, which was a characteristic product of this transitional period. The 'German Section' of the Foreign Ministry now included a 'Jewish Section'. It was Franz Rademacher, a legation counsellor from this department, who in June, as the defeat of the French became a certainty, came up with the idea that the defeated French must be forced to part with the island of Madagascar in the peace treaty. The French inhabitants of the island would then be evacuated and a ghetto would be created for four million Jews, controlled by Heydrich's Security Police, and run by a police governor responsible to Himmler.[31] The leaders of the SS were thinking along similar lines. When Hitler committed to paper his ideas 'On the Treatment of Foreign Nationals in the East' in May, he wrote: 'I hope to see the term Jew extinguished, through the possibility of a large-scale Jewish emigration to Africa, or some other colony.'[32] So the RSHA took up Rademacher's idea 'enthusiastically', and within a few weeks a complete 'Madagascar plan' had been prepared, under the direction of Eichmann. Himmler approved the project, and at first Hitler, too, gave his approval. On 26 July 1940, following a conversation with the Führer, Goebbels noted in his diary that 'all the Jews of Europe are to be deported to Madagascar after the war',[33] and Hans Frank confirmed with satisfaction on 12 July that on the basis of a decision of Hitler's there would be no more transports of Jews to the

Government General, because the Jews still living in German-ruled territory 'must start a new life in Madagascar'.[34]

This intention reflected precisely the mood of the Nazi leadership after the victory over France. There were three very significant features. Firstly, the authors of the plan were clearly confident of having a free hand both among the states of continental Europe and in their overseas colonial empires; secondly, they betrayed their intention of using their territorial hegemony in Europe to extend their persecution of the Jews to the entire continent; and thirdly, they gave notice of their resolve to conclude the persecution of the Jews with a total solution, i.e. to make the whole of Europe entirely 'free of Jews'. Arising as it did from three such impulses, the Madagascar plan contained only a modest dose of the old policy of emigration and expulsion; it was much more a sign of the scarcely concealed intention to destroy the Jews completely, although of course there was no intention yet to achieve this by means of guns or poison gas, but rather with the forces of nature.

The plan was evidently inspired by the expectation that the Jews of Europe would perish miserably if they were torn from their homes and jobs, sent with 'little more than hand luggage' on their unwilling way, and then herded together, without any reasonable possibility of work, on one of the most inhospitable islands in the world for Europeans. Hitler speculated that the climate alone would have such an effect, and the planners in Berlin, with their collected experience of the Polish ghettos, could easily rely on all kinds of diseases to sweep through such a ghetto. The plans of Rademacher and the RSHA therefore had no more than the geographical destination and the name in common with the Madagascar projects which were occasionally suggested between the wars as a possibility for the emigration of a limited number of Polish Jews. The German Madagascar plan of 1940 had much more in common with the suggestion of Karl Paasch in 1892 that the Jews who could not be killed in a Germany which had become far too soft and tame should at least be deported to New Guinea, and left to rot there.

Genocide

The African schemes of the Security Police were never undertaken seriously. This had nothing to do with the course of the war, which would have put an end to such plans in any case; it was the result of the Nazis' decision to do the job themselves rather than leave it to the forces of nature. Yet this step was not just an intensification of the Madagascar plan. The idea that the 'Jewish problem' could, must and would be definitively 'solved' in Europe, and that it would be solved by murdering all the continent's Jewish inhabitants developed alongside the RSHA's work on its deportation project, and it evidently originated with Hitler alone. In May 1940 Himmler had still rejected the 'method of physical extermination of an entire people' as 'Bolshevist' and 'un-German'.[1] This remark referred to the Poles, who according to the SS and the party – and this was explicitly stated in their later plans for the future of eastern Europe[2] – would have to be treated better than the Jews.

Himmler himself, although quite unscrupulous in his readiness to implement large-scale murder programmes, nevertheless seems to have had such difficulty with the thought of actual genocide that he cannot have been the first to contemplate it, even for the Jews. When he told his Finnish masseur, Felix Kersten, that the Führer had ordered the step-by-step extermination of the European Jews in the summer of 1940, immediately after the French campaign, it was clear that the idea for this 'final solution' must have been Hitler's, even though Himmler detected the influence of Goebbels and Martin Bormann, the head of the Party Chancellery.[3] In addition, Kersten certainly misunderstood his patient. Hitler cannot have given such an 'order' in the summer of 1940, although it is quite possible that he told Himmler at this time of his intention to issue such an order, probably in the near future. Also in the summer of 1940, on 20 July, Hitler told Goebbels that 'short work' would have to be made of the Jews: 'Otherwise they always spread like bacteria.'[4]

It is not the date of these two remarks which is significant. They both occurred at about the same time that Hitler first mentioned his intention of invading the Soviet Union in the near future. Hitler's decision to attack Russia and his resolve to implement the murderous 'final solution to the Jewish question' were obviously connected from the outset. Once he had decided to commit mass murder, this connection must have seemed to Hitler both 'ideologically' consistent and appropriate to the situation. His decision to attack the Soviet Union no doubt arose from his interpretation of the military situation after the campaigns in northern and western Europe, and thus from Germany's inability to conquer the British Isles, and therefore from the supposed necessity of at least eliminating Britain's last potential continental ally. Yet he also resolved on his march to the east above all because, despite his failure to defeat Britain, he nevertheless now felt strong enough to wage the real war, the war to win *Lebensraum* and create the continental empire he had first set his sights on, the war for which the Nazi movement was founded, for which it had used its political power in the German Reich, the war for which the successes of Nazi Germany had prepared the way.

Given the breathtaking pace of events, someone of Hitler's mentality could only feel compelled to combine as closely as possible this one genuinely National Socialist war, with the other, the racist crusade against the Jews, and not only ideologically, but in every possible practical way, so that ultimate victory in the two campaigns would coincide. Putting aside plans for the unloved Operation Sea Lion, he postponed the attack on Britain and, at the same time, the Madagascar plan (which had been accepted with equal reluctance), presumably with feelings of both liberation and relief. Instead he began preparations for Operation Barbarossa, to be combined with a solution to the 'Jewish problem' such as he and other Nazis had wanted since the 'Night of Broken Glass', but had so far not dared to implement.

The goals of these campaigns would necessitate an immeasurable increase in suffering and an immense increase in the number of victims in comparison with previous Nazi operations. Plans for the *Lebensraum* war alone foresaw a reduction of some thirty or forty million in the Soviet population. Despite their recent gains in authority, the Nazi leaders recognized that the reaction of the German public would not be unproblematic, and particularly so since the disquiet provoked by events in Poland had been followed by opposition to the 'Euthanasia Programme' initiated in the autumn of 1939, and had in fact begun to make itself felt just as the first plans were being made for Operation Barbarossa. However, the attack on Russia could be presented as a holy war against Bolshevism. By insisting that completely different rules were necessary to wage this war of extermination against the mortal enemy of the bourgeois world, the Nazis felt they could expect both the army and the general public to accept a brutalization of war and politics such as had never been known before. It was also expected that in such a crusade the noise of battle and the fanfares of the victory celebrations would drown out the salvoes of execution squads hunting down the Jews. So Operation Barbarossa offered an opportunity for the 'final solution of the Jewish question' which might never be repeated.

While the regime's media, along with its institutions for 'ideological education' worked on public opinion, Hitler himself made much greater efforts than before the Polish campaign to win the support of Wehrmacht leaders. On 30 March 1941 he ordered the commanders of his shock troops, by now already in the east, back to Berlin, along with their chiefs of staff, and there, in the Reich Chancellery, sought to hammer home the idea of a 'struggle between two opposed ideologies'. As with the Supreme Command of the Armed Forces (OKW) and the Supreme Command of the Army (OKH) weeks before, he explained that the Bolshevik system must be exterminated root and branch, and that in concrete terms this meant the liquidation of all political functionaries, including all Red Army Commissars: in fact the destruction of the 'Communist intelligentsia', or as he put it the 'Jewish-Bolshevik intelligentsia'.[5]

The main burden of this destructive task, he told the assembled generals, was to be borne by special units (*Einsatzgruppen*) under the Reich Leader of the SS, who would have independent responsibility for their operations in the occupied areas. The participation of the army would be necessary too, however, in that they would have to be responsible for shooting the political commissars themselves, or if that was not possible, they would have to hand them over to the special units. Several weeks later, on 6 June 1941, the staff of the army in the east received a communication from the OKW in which Hitler's instructions, in so far as they affected the treatment of Red Army Commissars, were formulated as a command (the Commissar Order) which contained references to the existence and independence of the special units mentioned by Hitler. A Führer Decree of 13 May had already established that, 'in matters of martial law within Operation Barbarossa', acts of violence against the Soviet civilian population by German soldiers were not generally to be prosecuted in courts martial.

Neither in Hitler's speech of 30 March, nor in the commissar Order or the Führer Decree was there any mention of the fact that the special units had received orders to exterminate the Jews living in the Soviet Union. By 26 March 1941 negotiations between Heydrich and General Wagner, the Quartermaster General in the OKH had led to a written agreement concerning the relationship between the army and the special units. Again, there was no mention of such a commission. Yet the OKW, OKH and the generals in the east now knew that the campaign would involve a murder programme of unprecedented dimensions, on a much larger scale than anything that had happened in Poland, and in the light of their experiences in the Polish campaign, the army must have considered it highly probable, at the very least, that the Security Police, let loose with an unambiguous Führer Decree, would use their new powers to murder countless Jews.

Nevertheless, Hitler's instructions encountered no challenge, still less resistance, except perhaps a certain unease arising from the apparent threat posed by the Führer Decree to military discipline. Most soldiers accepted the announcement of mass murder passively and obediently precisely because it came from the Führer. As with the atrocities in Poland, the 'will of the Führer' silenced any objection on moral or religious grounds, or any protest based on a concern for international law. In this respect both the morally stunted and those who experienced a real conflict of loyalty between obedience to the Führer order and their consciences were assisted in their acquiescence by the conviction that Germany would be invulnerable after the swift defeat of the Soviet Union – whose inevitability no one doubted – and that there was therefore no punishment to be feared. Hitler's faith in the efficacy of his anti-Bolshevik rhetoric also proved correct: a considerable section of his audience was thoroughly convinced by the relevant parts of his speech of 30 March, and it struck a real chord with the others as well. Officers such as General Guderian, who played such an important part in preparing and leading the campaign in Russia, had learnt in the Baltic in 1919, when German troops took on Communist units, that Bolshevik commissars were to be shot, not taken prisoner.

In this spirit the army of Nazi Germany accepted the Commissar Order without demur, and initially, immediately after the invasion, they implemented it without protest – until it became clear that the order forced the commissars, along with the units they commanded, to fight to the last bullet. Nor did the Nazis have a monopoly of the term 'Jewish-Bolsehvik'. Guided by their own 'vulgar antisemitism' (to coin a phrase), many German Nationalists too now also automatically associated the terms Jewish and Bolshevik with each other, and it was a widely held belief among the German officer corps that Soviet Jews provided a disproportionate number of Stalin's political functionaries and Red Army Commissars.

There might have been greater opposition if the Führer had stated quite clearly before the invasion that the special units had been instructed to shoot all the Soviet Jews they encountered. The deliberate ambiguity regarding the full extent of the murder programme, and the clause in the written orders – itself unclear – which restricted the victims to various categories of Communist functionary, certainly contributed to the obedient acceptance of Hitler's instructions. Yet the decision to exterminate the Jews had in fact long been taken by the time the Commissar Order and the Führer Decree reached the eastern front. The extermination plan had been hatched months before, and finally agreed in March 1941, when Hitler, along with other 'political' aspects of the Barbarossa campaign, clarified the tasks of the special units, i.e. established, in discussion with Himmler and Heydrich, which categories of people were to be liquidated.

The role of the Führer as initiator and dominant actor is as clearly recognizable as it was in other matters connected with the war against Russia. Despite the universal agreement and compliance which Hitler encountered, and without which he would have been unable to act, no problem with implications or significance for the regime's principles could be solved in the Nazi state (which to a great extent had taken on the character of the Nazi movement itself) without the Führer's decision, and least of all in an area where he reserved for himself the right to make all the more important decisions. At that time the Gauleiters, such as Schirach in Vienna and Goebbels in Berlin, impatient as they were to make their cities 'free of Jews' (Judenfrei) were unable to deport a single Jew to the Government General without Hitler's permission; for want of Hitler's agreement, Goebbels was unable to introduce identification badges for Jews in the Reich itself, or even in Berlin, and a project such as the Madagascar plan obviously had to be presented to the Führer for inspection.

In such a situation it is absurd to think that men such as Himmler and Heydrich who, while not without power themselves, were ultimately second-rank, and had only second-rank authority, could have fundamentally changed the course of Nazi 'Jewish policy' of their own accord, and could have done so with an order which would have changed Germany's international position, determined the nature of German occupation policy in Russia, and would necessarily have given rise to friction between diverse offices and organizations within the Nazi state. An authority was needed which was above all the conflicting opinions, plans and interests; only this authority was able to raise Nazi 'Jewish policy' from the level of Madagascar plans to the level of genocide. That Hitler not only took this decision, but initiated the policy is clear from the fact that until orders were given in the spring of 1941 there was not the slightest trace of an initiative from the SS leadership or the RSHA. Neither claimed, even later, to have been the instigator of mass murder but rather consistently referred to a 'Führer order' whose existence nobody doubted – something they had not been authorized to do during the Polish campaign.

References to Hitler's will and the Führer's instructions began with the briefing of the leaders of the special units (Einsatzgruppen). Units 'of the Security Police and the SD', referred to as A, B, C and D, were set up between March and June 1941. These units, which ranged in size from five hundred to a thousand men, were composed overwhelmingly of more or less arbitrarily seconded members of the lower ranks of the SD, Gestapo, Criminal Police and *Waffen-SS*, while Department I of the RSHA, which was responsible for personnel, was careful to choose dyed-in-the-wool and tried and tested Nazis as leaders of such units. In June these leadership cadres had to take courses, including geographical studies, in preparation for their activity in the Soviet Union, and their actual duties were explained to them on two occasions:[6] once in Pretzsch (on the Elbe, north-east of Leipzig), apparently by Bruno Streckenbach, the head of Department I of the RSHA, and again, probably on 17 June in Berlin, by Heydrich himself, head of the RSHA. They learnt that four groups of persons were to be executed by their units: all functionaries of the Soviet system, 'inferiors', Asiatics, gypsies and Jews.

It is clear that the command was given to murder all Jews, whether men, women or children, even before the attack on the Soviet Union. Otto Ohledorf, chief of *Einsatzgruppe* A, testified as much after the war, as did several of the surviving leaders of the *Einsatzkommandos*, such as Dr Walter Blume (*Sonderkommando* 7a of *Einsatzgruppe* B) and Dr Alfred Filbert (*Einsatzkommando* 9). When SS Brigade Leader Dr Walter Stahlecker, chief of *Einsatzgruppe* A, which was to be sent to the Baltic, arrived at the Gestapo office in Tilsit on 23 June 1941 and there passed on Heydrich's orders of 17 June to the local functionaries, who had so far received none, he left no doubt that all Jews, including women and children, were to be shot, and within the next few days a Tilsit *Einsatzkommando* was formed and began to carry out the orders.

On 2 July 1941, when the border conflicts initiated on 22 June were already in full swing, Heydrich did in fact send a written instruction to the four senior SS and police leaders who would be going to the Soviet Union which only contained the instruction to execute 'Jews holding party or state offices'. However, this instruction was obviously intended only to serve the recipients as a means of calming army officers who might ask searching questions or criticize their operations, as had happened in Poland. There is no other explanation why the 'command' was never followed by any police unit in the east ('Ostraum'), and certainly not by the senior SS and police

officers to whom it was addressed; a little later their immediate subordinates undertook the most extensive massacres of Jews in their careers. The
testimony of the surviving members of the *Einsatzgruppen* is equally clear:
Heydrich had to present the murder command as a '*Führer* order' in order
to ensure that it was obeyed.

The leaders of the *Einsatzkommandos*, such as Dr Filbert in Treuburg,
East Prussia, repeated Heydrich's example, when informing their units of
their task, either shortly before or shortly after the crossing of the Soviet
border. Dr Otto Bradfisch, too, of *Einsatzkommando* 8, informed his
subordinates with similar 'military succinctness' that the whole of occupied
Russia must be rendered 'free of Jews' on the orders of the Führer, and that
'other racially inferior elements, too, such as Communist party functionaries' were to be 'liquidated'.[7] Himmler and Heydrich had, of course,
allowed group leaders and commando chiefs a certain measure of tactical
flexibility. In the Baltic states, for example, and in the other parts of the
Soviet Union, they were empowered to tolerate anti-Jewish pogroms on
the part of the indigenous population, and even to instigate them as long
as the Germans responsible were not compromised. This approach enabled
the setting up and affiliation of indigenous militias, and its purpose (as with
Heydrich's instructions of 2 July) was to make the mass murder of the
Jews more bearable for the German population. So when Stahlecker was
making an intermediate assessment of the situation in October 1941, he
wrote that it was 'not undesirable' if the Security Police, who were
'resolved, in accordance with their orders to solve the Jewish question
decisively, and with every means at their disposal; 'did not immediately
make an appearance', since 'the unusually severe measures . . . would
inevitably attract attention in Germany.'[8]

At first, too, the effect of the operation on the nerves of the members of
the execution squads was also taken into account. The commandos were
not entirely composed of antisemitic fanatics, and the order to murder all
Jews was rather different from the shooting of individual Jews or isolated
massacres. The masterminds of the operation in Berlin seem to have looked
on the shooting of children as a particularly unreasonable demand to make
on their marksmen. Not that the order to murder Jewish children was an
afterthought after the beginning of the campaign, a necessary measure for
the completion of a murder programme not intended as total until the first
phase of its implementation. Among others SS *Obersturmbannführer* Karl
Tschiersky, who collaborated closely with Stahlecker, testified that 'the
liquidation order applied to all Jews from the very beginning, including
women and children.'[9] Obviously, however, group leaders had permission
to break their subordinates in gradually, if necessary, and allow a process
of brutalization to take place. Arthur Nebe, leader of the Reich Criminal

Office before, during and after his activity as leader of *Einsatzgrupe* B, was able to report by 13 July 1941 that his commando units had already 'begun the liquidations, which are now taking place on a large scale every day'.[10] There proved to be no personal problems, however, least of all among the leadership cadres. Only one who was repelled by the business of murder, SS *Sturmbanführer* Ernst Ehlers, had resigned immediately after the orders had been given at Pretzsch, and he had experienced no difficulties as a result.

So the *Einsatzgruppen* entered the Baltic states, Byelorussia and the Ukraine, again following closely behind the regular troops, and sent reports regularly to the RSHA in Berlin, where they were summarized in comprehensive reports for a readership which was by no means small. The reports showed that within a short time the units had begun the 'comprehensive removal of the Jews' with terrifying conscientiousness. *Einsatzkommando* 3, for instance (to take but one example from the daily routine of these 'ideological warriors') reported that on 29 August 1941 alone 582 Jewish men, 1731 Jewish women and 1469 Jewish children had been shot in Utena and Moletei.[11] The reports further show that the 'solution of the Jewish question' in the Soviet Union became for the *Einsatzgruppen* an enterprise which quantitatively overshadowed any other execution commissions, including the executions of Communist functionaries.

The numbers of Jews murdered and buried in mass graves reported to Berlin, day by day, week by week, and month by month, gradually accumulated in total figures which must have taken away the breath of some readers even among the leaders of the SS and the police. *Einsatzkommando* 3, mentioned above, reported the following results by 25 November 1941: 1,064 communists, 56 partisans, 653 mentally ill, 44 Poles, 28 Russian prisoners of war, 5 gypsies, 1 Armenian, and 136,421 Jews.[12] *Einsatzgruppe* A, to which this commando unit belonged, reported the execution of 229,052 Jews over the same period of time. *Einsatzgruppe* B reported that 45,467 Jews had been shot by 14 November 1941, *Einsazgruppe* C (SS *Brigradeführer* Dr Otto Rasch) 95,000 by the beginning of December, and *Einsaztgruppe* D 92,000 by 8 April 1942. In addition there were the Jews murdered by the units of senior SS and police officers: for example in August 1941 around 23,600 carpatho-Ukrainian Jews in the area of Kamenez-Podolsk, on 13 October 1941 10,000 in Dniepropetrovsk, and at the beginning of November 1941 at least 15,000 in Rovno. At the massacre of Kiev (Babi Yar), in which several other units took part alongside *Einsatzgruppe* C, there were no less than 33,771 Jewish victims in the course of three September days in 1941. In addition there was no respite from the murder after the group leaders and commando leaders had become stationary as Security Police commanders and subordinate commanders respectively in the autumn of 1941. In the first nine months after 22 June 1941 this Nazi campaign of annihilation had already cost a total of 700,000 to 750,000 Jews their lives in the Soviet Union, and 1942 saw only an increase in this murderous insanity; for example, the Führer was informed by Himmler on 20 December 1942 that between August and November of that year 363,211 Jews had been shot in the Ukraine, southern Russia and in the district of Bialystok alone.[13]

The *Einsatzgruppen* and units of senior SS and police leaders did not in fact succeed in exterminating all the Jewish citizens of the Soviet Union. Many Jews escaped the murder units by fleeing the German armies in time. Others, who were fortunate to survive the first few months after the German invasion, managed to find jobs in the offices and factories of the Wehrmacht or the administration of the civilian occupation, as highly valued artisans and skilled workers. Such occupation offered only precarious protection, since the Security Police – on the orders of Hitler and Himmler[14] – repeatedly disregarded the interests of the Wehrmacht and above all the civilian administration, giving the extermination of the Jews priority over the contribution of Jewish slave labour to the war effort, and from time to time raiding the Jewish workforce; but many Jews were saved by this slavery. Many also joined the partisans or formed specifically Jewish partisan groups. Nevertheless, and even though the monstrous dimensions of the task simply exceeded the abilities of the Security police, Hitler's and Himmler's murder units managed to kill almost half of the Jews living in Soviet territory on 22 June 1941: no less than 2.2 million out of a total of some 4.7 million.[15]

In view of such figures it made no real sense for Himmler and Heydrich to instruct units reporting massacres of Jews to insert a clause stating that the executions had taken place as a 'reprisal' for some hostile action or other. Who would be convinced that the Jews had been shot not on account of their race, but on account of their behaviour? The *Einsatzgruppen* themselves did not seem to grasp the principles of this 'linguistic regulation'. Month after month such vague and stereotypical formulas were used that there was no possibility of their being believed, and when the authors of the reports went into detail they often lapsed into the ridiculously gruesome, as when it was reported that 996 male and female Jews had been shot in Marina Gorka because they had worked 'grudgingly'. *Einsatzgruppe* B on the other hand did not concern itself with the linguistic regulation at all throughout 1941, and reported the execution of Jews without giving any reason at all, until Nebe, the leader of the group, was obviously cautioned, and adapted his reporting style accordingly.

Three to six months later, admittedly, reports from all the groups ignored the rule, but by then it was because the racist campaign of annihilation against the Jews had been clearly separated from all other activities. The 'reprisal' formula was taken much less seriously than the ideology of racism in internal communications, and this is nowhere clearer than in an exchange between Ohlendorf and the RSHA. In the autumn of 1941 the head of *Einsatzgruppe* D was faced with the question of what to do with the Caraites and the Crimean Tatars. In response to enquiries in Berlin he learnt from the RSHA that the Caraites certainly belonged to the Jewish faith, but were not racial Jews, whereas the Crimean Tatars although they had abandoned the Jewish faith, were racially Jews; the group later reported the 'inclusion of the Crimean Tatars in the fate' of the 'actual' Jews.[16]

There could be no pretence for the *Wehrmacht* or the civilian administration that the mass murder of the Jews was in any sense either an act of war against the Soviet Union and the Soviet system, or even that it arose from the waging of that war. It was clear to everyone that the Russian campaign had made possible the murder of the Jews living there, but that it was not the cause. Even in the first weeks after the invasion of 22 June 1941, expectations based on experiences in Poland were confirmed: rather than risk hostile actions against German troops, the behaviour of the Jewish population was 'anxiously co-operative', as a representative of the Defence and Armaments Office in the Supreme Command of the Armed Forces wrote to his superior, General Georg Thomas,[17] and in the further course of events it was also established that this orgy of murder committed in the name of an abstruse *Weltanschauung*, which deprived both the Wehrmacht and the civil administration of valuable and often irreplaceable labour resources, was a gross impediment to the conduct of the war.

Yet even leaving aside questions of usefulness or damage to the war effort, a clear majority of soldiers and occupation officials who came to hear of the mass murder considered genocide a crime which lost none of its gruesome horror, even in the context of a war which, from the start, had been waged without mercy by both sides. And knowledge of such a gigantic murder programme quickly became widespread: it could not be implemented in secret, and with the backing of the 'Führer order' the Security Police were not inclined to bother with secrecy in any case. As a result a certain disquiet began to spread through the army.

On 9 December 1941 the signals officers (Ic) of Army Group Centre wrote in his service report after visiting the Divisions of the 4th Army:

In all my lengthier conversations with officers I was asked, without referring to it myself, about the shooting of Jews. I had the impression that the shooting of Jews, prisoners of war and even commissars was disapproved of in the officer corps . . . The question of responsibility for the action was raised with greater or lesser vehemence according to the temperament of the individual. It should be noted that the facts of the matter are fully known and that they are much more widely discussed among the officers at the front than was expected.[18]

On 31 December 1942 Ernst Jünger, who was then touring the southern front in Russia, mentioned a report of 'the monstrous crimes of the Security Service following the defeat of Kiev' in his diary as part of the 'general' conversation among the chiefs of staff of the German army in the east. Jünger, a conservative writer who had earned the 'Pour le mérite' as an infantry lieutenant during the First World War, then described in moving terms the revulsion which seized him later when faced with uniforms, medals or weapons.[19]

In 1941 talk among the army in the east reached such proportions that the leadership felt it necessary to intervene. Field Marshal General Walther von Reichenau, Commander-in-Chief of the Sixth Army, issued his men with an order on 10 October 1941 in which he declared that they were not only 'warriors according to the rules of the art of warfare, but bearers of a merciless racial (völkisch) idea, and must therefore 'fully understand the necessity of the severe but just punishment for the subhumanity of the Jews'. Field Marshal von Rundstedt, Commander-in-Chief of Army Group South, was so pleased with von Reichenau's words that he made them known to the other three armies in the Army Group, and called for the issue of similar instructions. After Hitler, too, had commented favourably, Brauchitsch circulated the text of Reichenau's instructions on 28 October 1941 to all Army Groups, armies, Panzer Groups and commanders of the rear army districts in the east, with the request that orders 'in a similar vein' should be issued. In order to comply with the wishes of the OKH, General Hermann Hoth, Commander-in-Chief of the Seventeeth Army, and General Erich von Manstein, Commander-in-Chief of the Eleventh Army, even issued orders which, in terms of ideological content, went beyond Reichenau's.[20]

Such interventions indicated that the generals were seeking to prevent the widespread criticism of the Security Police in the army from gaining political impetus. But the disapproval and horrified incomprehension which Reichenau, Hoth and Manstein denounced showed no sign of becoming political. With some exceptions, of course, generals and field marshals, no less than the other ranks, either felt instinctively, or were persuaded, that from the start of the Russian campaign they were engaged in a life-and-death struggle against the worst of all enemies of European culture and morality, and therefore felt tied to the regime in power, at least for the duration of the war, and this was a further factor which ensured their obedience to 'Führer orders'. As a result, the disquiet caused by the crimes of the police was quickly suppressed, and with it even the very knowledge of the events. Instead there was a resolve to concentrate on the requirements of the immediate situation, which were by no means unimportant.

Indignation, of course, was not the only response in the army to the extermination campaign of the Security Police. The army consistently provided the logistical and technical support which made the work of the *Einsatzgruppen* possible, and the OKW acquiesced in allowing the Security Police to take all Soviet prisoners with Jewish backgrounds out of the camps; in addition, there is the well-documented observation that such assistance was often rendered willingly. In several cases it was not only *Waffen-SS* units such as the First SS Cavalry Brigade, led by Hitler's future brother-in-law Hermann Fegelein, who took part in executions, but individual members and units of the Wehrmacht as well – sometimes on orders, sometimes without compulsion. The poison of Nazi ideology had already contaminated all the arteries of the German nation.

Hitler therefore caused no great unrest among his audience when on 30 January 1942 he announced in a public speech that his prophecy of 30 January 1939 – that the result of a war would be the 'extermination of Jewry' – was beginning to be fulfilled, 'eye by eye, tooth by tooth!'[21] Of course by this time the reference was not just to the activity of the *Einsatzgruppen*. The RSHA, the 'Führer chancellery' and several other of the regime's institutions had long since commenced the preliminary work for an additional murder programme, whose dimensions would far outstrip those of the extermination campaign in the Soviet Union, and whose methods would make the approach of the *Einsatzgruppen* appear old-fashioned. When Hitler, pondering the political conception of Barbarossa had given the Security Police their task, his order to murder all the Jews in the Soviet Union had been only the first part – to be implemented immediately after the invasion – of a much more far-reaching decision, namely to murder all the Jews in German-occupied territory, or within Germany's sphere of influence, to exterminate European Jewry in its entirety. In his eyes, and in accordance with the deathly logic of the Nazis' lunatic antisemitism, it would have been perverse to order a partial extermination of the Jews, i.e. one restricted to the Soviet Union. Not even in the sense of concentration on the 'eastern Jews' as the kernel of 'world Jewry' would Hitler have been able to contemplate or endure such a modest objective, and not only because the Nazis thought of the Polish Jews, rather than the Soviet Jews, as 'eastern Jews', nor because they considered the Jews in the west as at least equally pernicious, but because taking the decision to plan such a partial extermination was a sheer ideological and psychological impossibility.

The notion of extermination implies totality, and the intention to exterminate a particular group of people requires the will, and the intention, to achieve a total result. The idea can also be dismissed that Hitler and the inner circle of party leaders intended to murder the Soviet Jews and then settle the rest of the European Jews in their place, particularly since such a gigantic deportation programme would have stood in stark contrast to the policies of plunder and eradication which characterized the war in the east and would have also encountered objections. For example, it was estimated in Berlin that victory over the Soviet Union would not necessarily mean the end of all military conflict, and years of minor warfare were expected along an uncertain border with Asiatic Russia. In view of such a perspective there can have been no intention to accommodate millions of the 'Aryan' race's most dangerous enemy permanently beyond that border in vast regions which would be difficult to control. Such an idea would never have occurred either to Hitler, or to the security-conscious chiefs of the Gestapo, the SD and the Ordnungspolizei.

As far as we can see, Hitler betrayed for the first time that he had resolved to exterminate not just the Soviet Jews but all of European Jewry in March 1941, when the task of the *Einsatzgruppen* in the Soviet Union was also clarified. On 17 March the Führer conferred with Hans Frank in Berlin in order to discuss both the problems which had arisen in the Government General from the German invasion of Russia, and the political future of the territory, which would have to be reorientated following the success of Barbarossa. Quite apart from the fact that Hitler took this opportunity to make the vision of a long-term resettlement of the entire Polish population – over a period of fifteen or twenty years – a guideline of German policy, he also told his governor in Cracow that the Government General was to be the first German occupied territory to be made 'free of Jews', and that this would happen 'in the foreseeable future'.[22]

Since he had already shelved the Madagascar plan, and he cannot have entertained the idea of transporting the Polish Jews to the Soviet Union, his promise to Frank was obviously based on the decision to kill those Jews living to the west of the Soviet border as well, and furthermore to start doing so from the autumn of 1941, by which time he fully expected the major military conflict in Russia to be over. This interpretation is confirmed by the fact that the administration of the Government General left itself until July 1941 before it came back to Hitler's promise and started 'preparations for the removal of Jews from the GG, beginning with the Warsaw ghetto'.[23] The task of the *Einsatzgruppen* differed from the implementation of the extermination order, in that the former was to be carried out immediately, while the latter could be implemented only once there were places in the east where it could be executed without attracting attention, whether in the conquered Soviet territories, or in the Government General itself, after the departure of the troops which had been assembled for the attack on Russia.

A few weeks after his conversation with Frank, Hitler seems also to have given instructions to Alfred Rosenberg, whom he certainly never counted among the more important political or administrative figures in the regime, but nevertheless consistently respected as supreme guardian of the faith in all 'theological' questions touching on the Nazi *Weltanschauung*. He may therefore have considered Rosenberg as one of the first who should know of the plan to destroy the 'Jewish world plague'. In any event Rosenberg noted in his diary on 2 April 1941 that the Führer had disclosed intentions to him which 'I do not wish to record today'.[24] Finally, in June 1941, when he was presented with the draft of an Interior Ministry law concerning the legal status of Jews living in Germany, the Führer rejected not only this, but any attempt to fix the legal status of the Jews, because, as the head of the Reich Chancellery wrote to the head of the Party Chancellery, he was of the opinion that after the war 'there would be no more Jews left in Germany in any case.'[25]

In the spring of 1941, when Hitler informed the organizers of his 'Jewish policy', Goering, Himmler and Heydrich, of his order for the liquidation of the Soviet Jews, he obviously also indicated that a definitive change of course was soon to be expected, which would lead to a comprehensive final solution. There are certainly hints of such an expectation in police correspondence from this point. Although an order issued from the RSHA on 20 May 1941 to state police offices and the SD in Belgium and France still spoke of the encouragement of Jewish emigration from Germany – in any case scarcely possible during the war – this was followed by the prohibition of all emigration from France and Belgium 'in view of the doubtless imminent final solution to the Jewish question'.[26] The RSHA must have been able to assume, at least, what sort of 'final solution' this would be, given that it already had a clear idea of the fate of the Soviet Jews, and within a few weeks the regime's police chiefs no longer needed to rely on mere assumptions. Himmler and Heydrich must have learnt from Hitler at some time during the first half of June that the imminent 'final solution' meant the murder of all European Jews.

Of course Nazi linguistic usage eschewed the terminology of criminality, preferring terms with the ring of a historical and political mission, such as 'physical annihilation' and 'extermination', which were then circumscribed with the formula 'evacuation to the east'. In one of his speeches Himmler even used the words 'evacuation' and 'annihilation' as synonyms within the same sentence.[27] When Stahlecker, head of *Einsatzgruppe* A argued with the Reich Commissar for the 'Ostland' that it was wrong for the Jews in the east to enjoy the same treatment as they had hitherto experienced in the Government General, as was foreseen in the Reich Commissar's draft proposals, and that the Security Police had been ordered to liquidate the Jews, he linked that order with the 'the purging of the Jews from the whole of Europe', on which he shortly expected to receive a 'statement'.[28] So the leaders of the Security Police already knew, from the beginning of the invasion of the Soviet Union, that the mass murder of the Soviet Jews was only the first act in a comprehensive solution, similar in principle but on a European scale, and that the second act was close at hand. Stahlecker could only have been so confident, however, if Heydrich had at least made it clear to the leaders of the *Einsatzgruppen* on 17 June, when he gave them their instructions along with the leaders of the commando units, that the murder programme was not restricted to the Soviet Union, but was to be applied to the whole of European Jewry. That Heydrich was in a position to do this presupposes that Himmler, and perhaps even Hitler himself, had told him at some point in the previous few days that the Führer had come to such a decision.

Yet Hitler seems to have waited until July to issue an order to make preparations to carry out his decision. (Although this was a formal order, it was delivered orally, following the example of the instructions to the *Einsatzgruppen*.) We may suppose that before he issued a definitive order which would set the practical measures in train he first wanted to gain some military security. By the middle of July he was able to feel confident that he had the security he wanted. The German armies had successfully concluded the first frontier battles, and Army Group Centre had won the first battle of encirclement of the Russian war. Franz Halder, Chief of the General Staff, had already confided to his diary on 3 July his certainty 'that the campaign against Russia has been won in the first fortnight'.[29] Führer HQ reckoned that another successful campaign would have been completed by the onset of winter, and with it the Third Reich's politically most important campaign, which would ensure the fulfilment of the Nazi dream of *Lebensraum* and bring the continent of Europe under German control. On the brink of such a momentous triumph, and apparently free from all risks, Hitler now considered it time to mobilize for the second genuinely Nazi war. Waged initially in the USSR, it was now to be extended to many other parts of Europe. The storming of the last bastions of European Jewry could begin immediately after the victory in Russia.

The clearest sign that Hitler and Himmler had actually ordered the RSHA to prepare the way for a 'final solution' on a European scale was the creation of a new plenipotentiary office for Heydrich, who was now absolved of his duties as director of emigration and expulsion policy, which dated from January 1939. Goering, who occupied many offices, was chief co-ordinator of Nazi 'Jewish policy' (particularly in matters concerning the state authorities), and as such signed an instruction on 31 July, apparently drafted by Heydrich himself, commissioning the head of the RSHA 'to make all the necessary organizational and material preparations necessary for a comprehensive solution to the Jewish question in the German sphere of influence in Europe'. In the second paragraph Heydrich was instructed to present a draft of 'preliminary measures for the implementation of the desired final solution to the Jewish question'.[30]

Goering demonstrated a couple of weeks later that he was perfectly aware of the meaning of the term 'final solution', when he told a conference on armaments questions that the Jews would disappear from 'all the territory ruled by Germany'.[31] With his decree of 31 July he had appointed Heydrich director of the murder programme, and given him the instrument he needed to secure the co-operation of other state authorities and institutions, from the Reich Foreign Ministry to the railways.

Three spheres of activity were already clearly distinguishable in the (as yet unconfirmed) plans for July and the later summer of 1941, when Hitler's orders had scarcely begun to be transformed from intention and resolve to concrete planning and practical preparations, and they were to be reflected in both the implementation of the 'final solution' and the operations of the *Einsatzgruppen*. In practice of course such strict distinctions were neither permitted by the realities of the situation nor foreseen in the draft planning.

The first sphere of activity was the annihilation of the Polish Jews, i.e. the Jews in the Government General. On 20 and 21 July 1941 Himmler stayed in Lublin, where he must have discussed the plans with the man chosen as director of the operation, Odilo Globocnik, the local resident SS and Police Leader:[32] this was confirmed by the entry in the Governor General's service diary relating to the planned 'evacuation' of the Jews. (Globocnik belonged to the elite of the Austrian Nazi party, and had once been *Gauleiter* of Vienna.) At around the same time Himmler and Heydrich also made an agreement with Philip Bouhler, head of the 'Führer chancellery', that he would release some of the personnel hitherto involved in his 'Euthanasia Programme' (Operation T4) and place them at Globocnik's disposal. Between January 1940 and August 1941 Operation T4 claimed some 70,000 handicapped victims, who were gassed with carbon monoxide in institutions such as Grafeneck, Hartheim and Hadamar.

As a result of vehement protests by the public and the churches, however, the operation was in such severe difficulties, that it seemed advisable to abandon it for a while and redeploy the redundant workforce, with their appropriate experience, on other work. One of the organizers of T4, Christian Wirth, who came from a Criminal Police background and later held the rank of Police Major, had to report to Himmler with his commando unit in the late summer of 1941, and the latter sent him immediately to Lublin, explaining his next job, and adding that his task was at once 'superhuman and inhuman', but that it was an order from the Führer.[33] Wirth and his men arrived in Lublin at the beginning of September. Until the autumn of 1943, when their Polish activities came to an end, they were categorized by the bureaucracy as 'executors of an exceptional commission from the Führer', and were paid by Hitler's personal chancellery. Directly subordinate to Globocnik, they immediately started to build up an organization to meet the demands of Operation Reinhard (as the extermination of the Jews in the Government General soon came to be called by the SS bureaucracy); they themselves constituted a core unit, supported by local auxiliaries, and members of various SS and police formations. In September Globocnik and Wirth's scouts went out to look for a suitable place for mass murder. Having found one, in October one of these groups demanded workers from the Polish administration of Belzec to the south-east of Lublin. These workers would then begin to erect the necessary installations under the direction of the Germans. Work began on 1 November 1941. At the beginning of March 1942 the Belzec annihilation camp, fitted out, like the institutions of Operation T4, with facilities for the use of carbon monoxide gas, was ready for use.

Apart from the co-operation of the Security Police with Operation T4 from its inception, Himmler's tour of the eastern theatre of Nazi 'ideological warfare' also had a certain significance for the *Einsatzgruppen*. On 15 or 16 August 1941 Himmler observed shootings in Minsk, i.e. in the sphere of operations of *Einsatzgruppe* B. Still not convinced that the means of execution employed by Heydrich's commando units was technically the best, he seemed to be looking for a more suitable method. He formed the impression that the shooting did have serious effects on the nerves of his staff, and for this reason he ordered Group Chief Nebe to find a more 'humane' method.[34]

After Nebe had experimented unsuccessfully with dynamite in bunkers full of mentally handicapped Russians, he had SS *Obersturmführer* Dr Albert Widmann come to Minsk. Widmann was director of the 'Chemistry and Biology' Section in the Kriminaltechnisches Institut (KTI) of the Reich

Criminal Office (Department V of the RSHA). Under an SS *Sturmbann-führer*, Dr Walter Heess, the KTI had already afforded the 'Führer chancellery' resolute support in the gassing of the handicapped. Following successful experiments, and on the instructions of Himmler and Heydrich, who had immediately been informed of the results, Widmann's mission to adapt the use of carbon monoxide for the murder of the Jews by the *Einsatzgruppen* began. Given the high mobility of the units, mobile installations were used for the gassing: in principle it was a question of relatively small gas chambers on four wheels, which used the gas from the vehicle's motor. By December 1941 the first of a total of thirty gas vans, swiftly developed from models tested during the 'Euthanasia Programme', were 'in use'. Guns remained the principal instrument of murder used by the Security Police in the east, but such vans (which were referred to as *Sonderwagen, Spezialwagen* or simply *S-Wagen*) were used by *Einsatzgruppen* A, B, C, and D, to kill at least 100,000 Jews and for the extermination of the Jews of Yugoslavia, which was carried out on the spot without prior evacuation.

Apart from such deviations, which tended to arise by chance, the leaders of the SS and the police planned the murder of two other large groups in parallel to the gassing of the Jews in the Government General: on the one hand those German Jews who had emigrated to countries since occupied by Nazi Germany, from Norway and Denmark, via Slovakia, Yugoslavia and Romania, to Greece, and those who had gone from the Netherlands, via Belgium, Luxembourg and France, to Italy; and it quickly became clear that the masterminds in Berlin also had in their sights the Jewish inhabitants of states which were not yet within their reach, whether Great Britain or Switzerland, Spain Portugal or Turkey. The second, and numerically rather smaller group consisted of those Jews who were still living in the territory of the 'Greater German Reich': in the so-called *Altreich*, and in Austria and the Sudetenland; in the 'Protectorate of Bohemia and Moravia'; in the territories annexed from Poland (now designated *Reichsgau* Danzig–West Prussia and *Reichsgau* Wartheland); and in regions of indeterminate status, such as Alsace-Lorraine. The orders to annihilate both these groups were issued at the same time as the order for Operation Reinhard, and preparations also took place simultaneously.

Sometime in the summer of 1941 SS *Sturmbannführer* Rudolf Höss was instructed to report to Himmler. Höss had distinguished himself during the first World War, had subsequently served in the *Freikorps*, and from 1924 to 1928 had served a prison sentence for his part in a lynching. He joined the Nazi party in November 1922 and the SS in September 1933, and since the end of 1934 had worked in concentration camps (Dachau,

Sachsenhausen). In May 1940 he became First Commandant of the concentration camp at Auschwitz, situated to the west of Cracow on the confluence of the rivers Sola and Vistula, next to the recently annexed town of Oswiecim (Auschwitz), which had a population of 12,000. The new concentration camp had claimed an area of 40 square kilometres as its immediate 'sphere of interest' at the time of its erection and first phase of expansion. This necessitated the evacuation of seven Polish villages and the 'resettlement' of 15,000 Poles altogether.

The first prisoners were predominantly Poles who had been arrested for some 'political' reason or other. On 1 March 1941 Himmler had visited Auschwitz and instructed Höss to prepare for an enormous expansion of the camp, among other things in order to receive about 100,000 Soviet prisoners of war. As Slavs, these prisoners were to be used by the SS for agricultural work and in an IG Farben Buna works. Now, in the summer of 1941, Himmler revealed to the commandant of Auschwitz that the 'Führer' had ordered the 'final solution of the Jewish question', and that this meant the annihilation of 'all the Jews within reach'; Auschwitz concentration camp was to play a central role in all of this, not least on account of its fortunate position in the transport network.[35] Without revealing the intended function of the camp and its prisoners, its planned expansion must now be orientated to the requirements of the 'final solution' decided by the Führer. Shortly afterwards Höss learned from Eichmann that Auschwitz would have to 'process' the Jews living in states occupied and controlled by Germany, such as Holland, Belgium and France.

Accordingly in the autumn of 1941 Höss constructed Auschwitz II-Birkenau. This second camp formed part of a complex which was also to include Auschwitz III-Monowitz, with work slaves for IG Farben, and was ready for use by the end of 1941 at the latest. Meanwhile, from 3 September 1941, experiments were conducted in the main camp with a preparation of prussic acid called Zyklon B, experiments which cost the lives of at least nine hundred Soviet prisoners of war before it was decided that the chosen gas was a suitable method of killing. Eichmann himself, whose position in Department IV of the RSHA put him very largely in control of the imminent mass deportation of European Jews, had also been informed of Hitler's order in the summer of 1941 by Heydrich and Müller, the head of the Gestapo, and he subsequently made enquiries about the places where the mass murder was to take place. He visited Höss in Auschwitz, and Globocnik in Lublin in the the autumn of 1941, where he studied the developing installations of Operation Reinhard, probably in order to find out whether their capacity could also be used for non-Polish Jews.

At the same time the RSHA began to cover occupied Europe and other areas controlled by Germany with a network of 'Commissioners for Jewish Affairs', some of whom were attached to departments of the military and civilian occupation administrations, and some to diplomatic missions. In the occupied regions the co-operation of local forces had to be ensured, and this meant above all the police and railway personnel; in the satellite the support and active assistance of the respective governments had to be won.

When Eichmann was discussing the matter with Höss at Auschwitz he pointed out to the commandant that his camp would initially be the destination of transports from the neighbouring districts of the Government General and above all from the Reich itself – starting with Upper Silesia. This reflected the dominant opinion in the RSHA that it was neither possible nor worthwhile to separate clearly the three spheres of operation involved in the antisemitic war of annihilation, and the apparent intention to make Auschwitz a central point of all three spheres. It was above all an indication that the Security Police were prepared to adopt the priorities of *Gauleiter* such as Goebbels in Berlin or Schirach in Vienna, and to follow the wishes of the Führer himself – as Himmler wrote to *Gauleiter* Arthur Greiser in Posen on 18 September 1941 – in speeding up as much as possible the process of making the Reich 'free of Jews'.[36]

Significantly, when demanding the first contribution from the satellite states to the Europe-wide 'solution to the Jewish problem' in the autumn of 1941, the German embassies in Bratislava (Pressburg), Budapest, Bucharest and Sofia also requested permission from the respective governments for the RSHA to 'evacuate to the east' Slovak, Hungarian and Romanian Jews living in the Reich itself. Auschwitz, of course, would not be the only destination of Jews deported from the Reich, because of its geographical position and its other functions. Consequently, as far as we can tell from circumstantial evidence, the rapid construction of additional camps was planned in conquered Soviet territory after the defeat of the Soviet Union, while in October and November 1941 a gassing station was erected by a T4 team in collaboration with the Łodz police between Łodz and Posen in the Warthegau. It was ready for use in December and intended for the Jewish population of the annexed Soviet territories. Since September, staff of the Buchenwald concentration camp had been building a further camp, Majdanek, further to the east, near Lublin. Although Majdanek was intended as a support base for Operation Reinhard its main function was to be the murder of Jews – with Zyklon B, as in Auschwitz – from the newly incorporated parts of the Reich, the annexed district of Bialystok in East Prussia, and Slovakia – which the RSHA treated virtually as a *Reichsgau* with a measure of local autonomy.

Entrance to the gas chamber at Majdanek concentration camp in Poland
(Imperial War Museum, London)

There were also preparations of quite a different kind. On 1 September 1941 a police order was issued, to come into force in eighteen days, making it compulsory for all Jews in the Reich and in the 'Protectorate of Bohemia and Moravia', to wear a 'Jewish star', i.e. 'a hand-sized six-pointed yellow star with a black border and the inscription "Jew", also in black'.[37] On 25 November 1941 there followed an Eleventh Supplementary Decree to the Reich Citizenship Law, which deprived deported Jews, or those destined for deportation, of their nationality, and empowered the Reich to confiscate their remaining material possessions.

On the other hand the RSHA produced a plan to exclude older Jews of German nationality from the 'evacuation to the east' for the time being, if they had either distinguished themselves in the First World War or performed some other, comparable service to the nation, and to place them in separate camps with preferential treatment and their own cultural life. Theresienstadt, north-west of Prague, was selected as the locality. The declared motive was a tactical one. The RSHA simply wanted to pre-empt the multitude of interventions on behalf of individual Jews which it must have feared as a result of removing this fully assimilated group of Jews from German society.

Nevertheless the plans went somewhat awry. Even before the Eleventh Supplementary Decree to the Reich Citizenship Law, and certainly before the victorious conclusion of the campaign against the Soviet Union and the planned construction of death camps in Russia, transports of Jews began to move eastwards out of the Reich. Apart from the events of December 1939 and February 1940, *Gauleiter* Robert Wagner and Josef Bürckel had deported 6,500 Jews from the *Gaue* Baden and Saarland Palatinate to Vichy France on 22 and 23 October, without having informed the Vichy authorities; and in February and March 1941 more than 5,000 Jews had been dragged off from Vienna to the Government General. But these were individual initiatives; no connection was assumed or discovered between the general deportation plans of Nazi princelings and the respective orientation points of Nazi Jewish policy.

On 14 and 24 October 1941, however, two deportation orders signed by Kurt Daluege, head of the Ordnungspolizei, set in motion mass transports of Jews, and this was recognized by all Nazi offices as the first act in a process which would end – soon – in the deportation of all Jews from the German Reich. Obviously SS and police leaders were placed under so much pressure by the increasing impatience with which senior Nazi functionaries such as Goebbels, and even Hitler himself, expressed their wish for a Reich 'free of Jews' that in the end they had started the annihilation of the Jews remaining in the Reich without waiting for the preparatory work to be completed. Presumably Himmler and Heydrich considered such initiatives defensible since they were still under the illusion that the war in Russia would soon be over. After all, the double battle of Vyazma-Bryansk had eliminated Marshal Timoshenko's army between 2 and 13 October, and Moscow seemed to be at the mercy of a German attack. On 9 October Reich Press Chief Otto Dietrich publicly announced that 'the military turning point in the east' had been passed, and Russia was finished.[38] In such a mood the police chiefs convinced themselves that if such a great favour was being done for the Führer a certain measure of improvisation and inconsistency could be tolerated for a few months.

Between 16 October and 13 November 1941, therefore, the Reichsbahn (German National Railway) delivered about 20,000 Jews to Łodz in trainloads of about a thousand, above all from Berlin, Hamburg, Hanover, Münster, Dortmund, Düsseldorf, Cologne, Frankfurt-on-Main, Kassel, Stuttgart, Nuremberg, Munich and Breslau (Wrocław), and in addition from Vienna, Prague, Theresienstadt, Brünn (Brno), and Luxembourg. In Łodz the deportees were confined in ghettos which Himmler considered 'still capable of taking more people'.[39] The officiating head of the local authority in Łodz, SS *Brigadeführer* Friedrich Uebelhör, disagreed completely and protested strongly against the increasing burden. Himmler consoled the functionaries of the Warthegau with the assurance that Łodz was merely a staging post for the Jews from the Reich, which they would have to leave again in the spring, in order to travel 'further east';[40] the

Reich Leader of the SS knew, of course, that the death camp at Chelmno would soon be ready to take the Jews of the Warthegau, and in particular those of the Łodz ghetto.

However, the second wave of deportees, numbering around 40,000 Jews, was directed not to the incorporated eastern territories but rather, apart from a few transports to Warsaw, predominantly to Riga, Minsk and Kovno. Only a few of these were afforded a brief stay of execution in the respective ghettos; a considerable number of them were shot immediately on arrival by the *Einsatzgruppen*. When, on 29 November, Himmler ordered one of the transports to Riga to be excluded from the liquidation, apparently because the deportation of Berlin Jews had begun to attract the attention of American journalists and they were asking unwelcome questions, the order came too late: on 30 November so many Jews, both local and deported, were shot by the *Einsatzkommando* units that the day itself gained a bleak reputation in that area as 'Riga's Bloody Sunday'.

On 16 November 1941 Goebbels had commented on these deportations from Germany, Austria and Czechoslovakia with cynical satisfaction. Under the title 'The Jews are to blame!' he published a leading article in an intellectually pretentious journal he had set up, *Das Reich*, in which he recalled Hitler's prophecy of 30 January 1939 that the war would bring 'the annihilation of the Jewish race in Europe', and then – anticipating critics – he said:

> We are experiencing the fulfilment of that prophecy, and it delivers the Jews to a fate which is perhaps severe, but which is more than deserved. Pity, even regret, are totally inappropriate . . . The Jews are a parasitical race, which lies like a festering mould on the cultures of healthy . . . nations. There is only one remedy: a swift excision, and away with it.

The premature start to the operation in the Reich was, however, only a minor irritation in the planning and preparation for the Europe-wide 'final solution'. The preparations which, according to a letter from Eichmann to the 'Jewish experts' of the Foreign Ministry, had already been well under way in August, proceeded remorselessly, and the organizers of mass murder, far from being afraid of its sheer dimensions, began, on the contrary, to worry that some Jews might slip through their net. On 17 October 1941 Heydrich reacted sharply against an offer from Madrid to take back some 2,000 Spanish Jews living in France, some of whom were interned there. He explained that these Jews would 'all too easily escape the grasp of the measures to be taken after the end of the war as a fundamental solution to the Jewish problem';[41] on 23 October a decree from the RSHA prohibited all further Jewish emigration. In addition, two events of that autumn indicate clearly how far things had already gone. When the German administration in Belgrade requested information from Berlin on 12 September 1941 as to whether Serbian Jews should be deported to Russia or the Government General, the official responsible in the RSHA replied by return of post that this was impossible, but recommended another solution to the problem: 'Eichmann suggests shooting them.'[42]

On 25 October 1941 Dr Ernst Wetzel, the civil servant responsible for 'Jewish questions' in the Reich Ministry for the Occupied Eastern Territories, wrote a letter for his minister to Hinrich Lohse, Reich Commissar for the Baltic ('Ostland') in which he emphasized that Jews arriving from the Reich could be killed immediately by gassing if they were unfit for work, and that the necessary apparatus would be provided by the Führer chancellery's T4 teams.[43] That officials belonging to various departments, and of no particularly high rank, could set in motion such numerically significant murder operations is indisputable proof that a general murder decree, applicable to all Jews, must have long been issued by the highest authority in the regime, and already come into force. Only with the backing of a 'Führer order' would third-rank officials have dared to act in such a way, resolving local problems so casually when, for whatever reason, it seemed necessary. Admittedly, such a casual approach also betrayed the acquiescence and conviction with which the Nazi *apparatchiks* concerned had accepted both the ends and the means, how deeply they had become immersed in the mentality of genocide.

In addition, there was no small number of accessories and witnesses outside the SS and police apparatus even in the autumn months of 1941, as was inevitable to a certain extent. Apart from the many who knew of the murders committed by the *Einsatzgruppen* in the Soviet Union, and did not keep the knowledge to themselves, the waves of deportations from the Reich, along with smaller murder operations in Serbia, created further witnesses and accomplices in the state bureaucracy and the armed forces. Yet the attempt to maintain secrecy, understandable in itself, was undermined by the necessity of transmitting information, which could not be suppressed by the leading functionaries of the Nazi movement. Given its sinsister character, the extermination of the European Jews, which they welcomed as a 'historic mission', demanded a secrecy of equally historic dimensions. Instead, they felt compelled from the beginning to boast repeatedly of the monstrous 'greatness' of their enterprise. Paul Wurm, a member of the editorial board of Streicher's *Stürmer* wrote to his friend Rademacher in the Foreign Ministry on 23 October 1941 after meeting on a train journey an old 'party comrade' who had 'been working in the east on the solution of the Jewish question': 'Some of the Jewish vermin are shortly to be exterminated by exceptional measures.'[44]

Alfred Rosenberg felt obliged, on 18 November 1941, to use a press conference to reveal that that the 'Jewish question' would now be solved by the 'biological eradication of all the Jews in Europe',[45] and a week earlier, on 11 November Himmler himself had not been able to resist confiding to his masseur that the annihilation of the Jews was imminent.[46] Nor did Hans Frank mince his words when he announced the imminent disappearance of the Jews both from the Reich and from Poland to an audience of leading functionaries from the administration of the Government General on 16 December 1941. 'But what is to happen to the Jews?' he asked, and answered his own question with the rhetorical observation: 'Do you believe they are to be accommodated in resettlement villages in the east?' Although he trembled as he continued, and was evidently not entirely free of doubt as to whether such a gigantic operation could ever succeed, he also spoke with an awareness of the historic task, of 'intervention' which would 'somehow have to lead to successful annihilation'.[47]

As Frank was outlining such perspectives in Cracow's Wawel it was already clear that the concept of *Blitzkrieg* had gone wrong in Russia, and that the Wehrmacht, having mastered the difficult crisis of the Russian winter, had its work cut out in 1942. Furthermore, the Japanese attack on Pearl Harbor on 7 December 1941 had brought the United States into the war and transformed what had hitherto been a European conflict into a world war which threw all Berlin's calculations into total confusion. In fact, however, neither of these developments had made much difference to the regime's war of annihilation against the Jews. They certainly had no effect on the inclusion of all the Jews in German-occupied Europe in the initial stages of the 'final solution', begun several months previously by the *Einsatzgruppen*, nor on the resolve of those implementing the programme.

The programme itself neither faltered nor accelerated; the resolve of its executors was neither weakened nor intensified. Himmler and Heydrich, with Hitler's approval, now abandoned the existing formula for the introduction of the comprehensive murder programme 'after the end of the war' and replaced it with the decision to complete the 'removal of the Jews', as Himmler now occasionally called it, during the war itself. That the war could be lost, and the Nazi regime itself liquidated, was still an unimaginable eventuality. When the Ministry for the East attempted to rescue the formula 'after the end of the war' for the Nazi bureaucracy's catalogue of guidelines in January 1942, thereby postponing the more large-scale operations against the Jews, Himmler vehemently opposed the proposal. In fact gassing began in Chelmno on 8 December 1941. Jews from the neighbourhood of the camp itself were the first victims, and they were followed, systematically by Jews from all parts of the Warthegau,

*New arrivals, still wearing civilian clothes, parading at an unidentified concentration
camp*
(Imperial War Museum, London)

including the Łodz ghetto. The machinery of murder in Auschwitz-Birkenau went into operation at about the same time, and at the latest by January 1942.

In questions of detail it was increasingly significant, in any event, that the 'final solution' was implemented during wartime, and in fact during a war which became harder and drained more and more of Germany's resources as the months went by. First of all, there was the transport problem, which had already become noticeable by the autumn of 1941, during the first deportations from the Reich, and led to indignant protests from the military. As the scale of the operation came to encompass the whole of Europe, the problem took on considerably greater dimensions, and the greater the demands on a shrinking transport system from countless interests, during a war which developed into a single crisis, the more difficult they were to overcome.

That the organizer of the deportations, Adolf Eichmann, did not always succeed in coping with these difficulties on his own, and that occasionally Himmler, as *Reichsführer SS* had to intervene personally, for example when he wrote to the State Secretary in the Reich Transport Ministry on 20 January 1943, indicates clearly that the shortage of transport did have the effect of slowing the operation down. On the other hand the eagerness of

Women and children herded together in one of the barrack blocks
(Imperial War Museum, London)

Eichmann and his assistants, and above all their disregard of military interests brought so much human raw material into the camps in the east that the capacity of the death factories was always in full use. The level of their efficiency is illustrated by the fact that in August 1944, when twelve hundred Jews were deported from Rhodes in the middle of a German retreat in the Balkans which often degenerated into a rout, they could still be smuggled to Auschwitz, where about a thousand of them died. The German armies, on the other hand, could not manage to reconquer the island of Rhodes itself.

The leaders of the SS and the police were faced with even more difficult obstacles through a second consequence of the prolongation of the war. These hindrances were also evident by the autumn of 1941, when the intention to murder all Jews indiscriminately was first challenged and impeded by those who argued that it was not only senseless but impossible to dispense with the labour of Jewish slaves. Goebbels was both astonished and angry to discover that Berlin could not simply be made 'free of Jews', since of some 70,000 Jews living in Berlin no fewer than 15,000 were in reserved occupations. As the war dragged on and all hope of an early peace receded the value of this Jewish labour could only increase, more so in Poland and Russia than in western Europe or the Reich, since a considerable proportion of the skilled workforce and artisans were Jews. When Reich Commissar Lohse asked the Ministry for the East in December 1941 whether 'all the Jews in the east were to be liquidated without regard to age, sex or economic interests' (for, example, the army of skilled workers in munitions factories), the ministry replied that 'Economic interests should be disregarded when dealing with this problem.'[48] Increasingly in reality, however, economic interests had all too often to be borne in mind.

On 29 November 1941 Heydrich had invited the highest authorities in the Reich, the Party Chancellery and the administration of the Government General to a conference of state secretaries on 9 December, in order to secure the co-operation of the state apparatus and the leadership of the Reich Security Head Office (RSHA) as co-ordinator of the operation in the 'final solution'. Postponed for reasons now unclear, the meeting finally took place on 20 January 1942 in the Berlin headquarters of Interpol at 56–8, Grosses Wannsee, hence the designation 'Wannsee Conference'. Although it was without any real significance for the planning, initiation and implementation of genocide, the Wannsee Conference nevertheless deserves our attention for two reasons. Firstly, that it took place at all at this time with its original and unaltered agenda as the simple co-ordinating conference of an operation which was already decided on, and even partly begun, was a sign to all the offices which were to take part in the 'final solution' that the leadership of the SS and the police, and behind them Hitler himself, had no intention of being prevented from murdering the Jews by the postponement of victory in the war.

On the other hand, Heydrich's presentation at the beginning of the conference made it clear that the decision of the previous summer to kill as many Jews as possible in the course of a swift operation, had now been modified. According to Heydrich's plan, those Jews who were unfit for work, such as the elderly, the sick and many women and children, were still to be murdered, while those capable of work would be employed as slaves in the interests of Germany, albeit only for a short time, since they would be working under conditions in which 'a majority will doubtless be lost through natural wastage.' Those who survived would meet the same fate as the ones who had been unfit for work.[49]

The personnel of the 'final solution' were very unwilling to abandon their own conception of *Blitzkrieg* against the Jews in favour of the diluted solution of 'annihilation through work', and did so only under the extreme pressure of circumstances. The new situation meant that Goering could peremptorily forbid the evacuation of Jews employed in a concern which was important to the war effort. Even before this order, which was issued in March 1942, he had indicated the desirability of such a measure, but his wishes had not been sufficiently respected by the Security Police. Even this latest measure had only been able to slow down the police rather than stop them altogether. When Hitler lifted Goering's restrictions in the autumn of 1942 and ordered the evacuation of even those Jews in reserved occupations, the requirements of the war effort and the vital needs of many individual firms similarly prevented the rigorous or complete implementation of the 'Führer order'. The conflict between the executors of the 'final solution' and the representatives of military or business interests followed the same pattern throughout the German Reich: police attempts to seize Jewish slave labourers provoked protests, and the protests led to delays; after a time Himmler, who had intervened increasingly in the details of the 'final solution' since Heydrich's death on 4 June 1942, issued new orders for the decimation or even total evacuation of ghettos or other places where Jewish slave labour was concentrated, and the protests of offices or managers affected by the measure again forced him to stop, or at least to make compromises.

Even in the more restricted sphere of annihilation, the principle that Jews must be deployed as slave labour, which had been raised to the level of a directive at the Wannsee Conference, was implemented only half-heartedly: in the death camps at Auschwitz-Birkenau and Lublin-Majdanek 'normal' concentration camps had always existed, in which the Jews who worked for the SS or the IG Farben Buna works at Monowitz enjoyed only a brief stay of execution. Here, when the transport trains arrived at the 'selection point' on the ramp, SS doctors such as Josef Mengele divided the deported Jews into those who were fit for work and those who were to be gassed immediately. That Himmler nevertheless succeeded in making terrible inroads into the armies of Jewish slaves, and managed, in the course of time, to reduce both the remaining nests of Jewish labour in the Reich and the ghettos in Polish or Soviet territory to insignificant numbers, was not least due to the fact that whenever he followed his instincts and gave ideological mania priority over considerations of economic usefulness, he had the backing of Hitler.

Himmler noted in his diary on 19 June 1943, after delivering a report on the state of the 'final solution' on the Obersalzberg, that the Führer had clearly determined that 'the evacuation of the Jews must be radically implemented and that the unrest arising over the next three or four months must be resisted.'[50] Six months previously, on 9 December 1942, Hans

Frank, who had since discovered the blessing of efficiency for his Government General, bemoaned his lot in an address to a large audience:

> We have lost valuable labour resources from our long-standing teams of Jews. Clearly, work is made more difficult if an order is issued in the middle of the war work programme, instructing that all Jews are to be handed over for annihilation. The responsibility for this does not lie with the administration of the Government General. The instructions to destroy the Jews have come from our superiors.[51]

Yet the only superior the Governor General in Cracow had ever recognized was the Führer.

A third factor connected with the prolongation of the war led to an even more serious impediment to the work of the staff of the 'final solution'. Hitler's foreign policy had involved Germany in a war on several fronts, and there was no sign of victory on the horizon. As a consequence, Berlin was forced, despite the contrary inclination inherent in the Nazi mentality, to take into account the formal independence of the satellite states, and this created unexpected difficulties for the Security Police in their attempts to extend the 'final solution' to southern, western and northern Europe. Even in the occupied states of western Europe and Scandinavia there were surprising problems. In Belgium, for example, it proved to be impossible to secure the keen co-operation on the part of the authorities which would have been necessary for the police of the occupying power to track down all the Belgian Jews, the majority of whom were fully assimilated; consequently 40,000 out of a total of 65,000 managed to survive. In Holland the public even reacted initially to the deportation of their Jewish compatriots with strikes, which temporarily led to a more cautious approach, although the operation was not completely abandoned, and 100,000 of the country's 125,000 – strong Jewish population were killed. In Norway, too, which lost 728 of its 1,728 Jewish inhabitants, there were obstacles, and in Denmark only about a hundred Jews fell into the hands of Himmler's henchmen. When the deportations to Auschwitz began at the end of September and the beginning of October 1943 the non-Jewish population, in one of the most remarkable operations of the Second World War, hid no fewer than 7,000 of their Jewish compatriots, and then, with the agreement of the authorities in Stockholm, smuggled them in small groups to Sweden over the next few weeks.

In all these countries the German police encountered a resistance which was fuelled by hatred of a brutal occupying power, by western political principles, and by a humanism founded on Christianity or the principles of the Enlightenment; these factors combined to create a strong feeling of solidarity with the persecuted Jews. In Denmark, admittedly, German solidarity with the local population also played a part. The opposition of the military commander, General Hermann von Hannecken, to the deportations was sufficient to create the necessary delay, and Georg Ferdinand Duckwitz, the representative of a shipping company, managed to warn the endangered Jews at the last minute. After the war Duckwitz pursued a successful career in the West German diplomatic service.

Although the possibility of such solidarity was much more restricted in the satellite states, the governments themselves had more political effect. Pressure from Berlin certainly forced those governments under German control to pass antisemitic legislation along Nazi lines, from the authoritarian conservative regime of Marshal Pétain in Vichy France and Mussolini's fascist Italy, to reactionary dictatorships with fascist elements in Croatia, Slovakia, Hungary and Romania. But Nazi antisemites were forced to acknowledge with increasing displeasure that such laws were applied only very loosely in states such as Italy and Hungary – often, in fact, with a reluctance which could scarcely be distinguished from sabotage – and that even the enthusiastic support of local antisemitic movements was not enough to achieve a more rigorous application of the laws. The political leaders of the satellite states proved to be even more unmanageable when the Nazi leadership initiated the 'final solution'. Such states did largely accept the 'evacuation' of their Jewish citizens 'to the east' by the RSHA, and the government in Pressburg (Bratislava) also initially agreed to the deportation of other Jews living within its borders.

However, when it became known, in the autumn of 1942, that the Germans were not moving the Jews to camps in the east where conditions were more or less bearable, but for the most part murdering them as soon as they arrived, the Slovakian government of Monsignore Jozef Tiso became more stubborn, not least as result of the Vatican's reservations, which were communicated by the papal nuncio. By then, admittedly, only 25,000 of a total 58,000 were left, of whom a further 8,000 died following their arrest in the wake of the Slovakian uprising of the autumn of 1942. In Bucharest Marshal Antonescu initially agreed, after the invasion of the Soviet Union, to the deployment of Romanian police and army units in a dreadful war of annihilation against the Jews in Bessarabia, Bukovina and – together with *Einsatzgruppe* D – in southern Russia, an exercise which claimed 350,000 victims. Yet the Romanian head of state refused to deport Jews from Romania proper, and from the summer of 1942 some 300,000 owed their lives to this resistance. In France, too, politicians like Pierre Laval managed to resist both demands from Berlin and pressure from local antisemites. However, the Vichy government protected French Jews above all, while handing over the many Jewish emigrants in France to the Germans as a sign of their good will. Of the 90,000 or so Jews who were thrown to the wolves of French or German antisemitism, an estimated 8,000 were born in France.

Yet it was the attitude of the Italians and the Hungarians which most attracted the wrath of the organizers of the 'final solution'. That the governments in Rome and Budapest were particularly deaf to the deportation requests from Berlin, occasionally even from Hitler himself, was a source of irritation for two reasons. First of all, these were the states most closely allied to Germany, and in Italy's case, at least for the Nazis, the closest in ideological terms. Secondly, there was a quantitative dimension: there were 650,000 Jews in Hungary, including many refugees from Germany, Austria and Czecholovakia; and the protection of the Jews by Italy also covered the Italian occupation zones in Greece, the Balkans and the south of France.

Of course, there was a good measure of opportunism involved. Neither Marshal Antonescu nor Hungary's Admiral Nikolaus von Horthy were prepared to burn all their bridges to the West by participating in the murder of the Jews, especially as Nazi Germany's future was increasingly in doubt. But religious or moral scruples also had an effect; unlike their German counterparts, the Italian fascists, with notable exceptions, had never completely cut themselves off from the European tradition of morality and humanitarianism, and not least for that reason had never really abandoned their open contempt for the race mania of their northern ally in the 1930s.

In any event the RSHA could really begin operations only after political power had fallen into German hands. When this happened in Italy after the fall of the fascist government in July 1943 and the defection to the Allies under Marshal Pietro Badoglio at the beginning of September, military developments prevented any real change. Only 8,000 Jews were 'evacuated' from Italy out of a total of some 40,000. In Hungary, admittedly, the RSHA used the German military occupation, established on 19 March 1944, to implement the largest and swiftest single operation of the 'final solution'. The operation was organized personally by Eichmann, who arrived in Budapest on 19 March, and led to the deportation of at least 430,000 Hungarian Jews, of whom no fewer than 280,000 died in the gas chambers.

Eichmann's success in Hungary indicates that the commando units of the RSHA, who rounded up Jews in the states within Germany's sphere of control to be sent off to the death camps in the east, did not encounter only resistance and obstruction, but were also able to rely on the co-operation of willing collaborators. So the Hungarian success derived not least from the support Eichmann found among willing helpers in the

Hungarian administration and police force, local sympathizers no longer restricted by the conservative elites; the latter were able to reassert themselves only in Budapest in the summer of 1944, when they managed to bring the deportations to an end. French antisemites played a similar part in occupied France.

There was also a second factor, of equal importance. As in all countries sheltering Jews, the efficiency of Eichmann's apparatus in Hungary would have been severly impaired if the RSHA emissaries had not succeeded in forcing the existing administrative organs of the Jewish community – set up by the Nazis themselves, as in the early days of emigration and expulsion – to assist in the organization of the operation. There were similar organs in the death camps, and it is not surprising that the SS was able to force many Jews to assist with the gassing and with the disposal of corpses in the crematoria; every chance of escaping total alienation was lost on arrival in such camps. Yet the motives of leading members of Jewish communities and other prominent Jews in co-operating with the Nazi Security Police on so-called Jewish Councils, and particularly in function-ing as efficient executive organs in the tracing, rounding up and deporta-tion of the victims, are not easy to explain.

One reason, certainly, must have been the conviction that it was senseless or pointless to resist the orders of Himmler's armed thugs, who were always able to call for reinforcements from the Reich and request assistance from a regime which remained extraordinarily powerful right up until the last phase of the war. Jewish leaders were all the more prey to such fatalism given the historical experience of southern and east Eurpean Jews, which was characterized by centuries of periodically recurrent persecution, a fate the Jews seemed unable to escape. It was also felt that it might be possible to soften the process.

The determining factor was often a feeling of responsibility, which demands some respect. As long as their action was dominated by the assumption that deportation ended 'only' in slavery, this feeling of responsibility could be used to justify bargaining with the representatives of the RSHA both on behalf of individual Jews and in order to win an increased range – even a great number – of concessions; and even when such Jewish administrators learnt that the operation with which they were co-operating led in the majority of cases to immediate death, it seemed justifiable to continue in the hope of saving at least smaller groups. Bribery helped, as was always the case when faced with a combination of political powerlessness and financial strength, and in both Slovakia and Hungary money found its way into the pockets of individual members of the SS and the police, as well as into the coffers of the SS. The results were, admittedly, modest. In June 1944, forty-five members of probably one of the richest

Jewish families in Hungary, the Weiss industrial dynasty, were allowed to emigrate to Portugal, and in August and December 1944 two trains carrying relatives of Hungarian Zionist leaders left for Switzerland.

The largest such project, which involved the exchange of a million Jews in return for ten thousand lorries from Allied production, was unsuccessful. Since the idea was launched by Eichmann himself in discussions with Jewish leaders in Budapest at the end of April and beginning of May 1944, it is not unreasonable to suppose that the representatives of the RSHA dangled the possibility of such a large-scale operation before Hungarian Jewish leaders because they needed Jewish co-operation for the smooth running of the deportations being carried out in the meantime. At least that was the effect of the offer to exchange 'Jews for lorries'. Jewish functionaries, who knew the fate of the deportees from reliable reports, were even misled, by the possibility of doing business with the SS, into suppressing the information, and thereby contributing to the success of Eichmann's Hungarian operation, and this has led to the common but unfounded charge that members of Jewish organs of self-administration also co-operated with their persecutors in return for exemption from deportation and gassing as long as they made themselves useful to the SS.

This charge is not infrequently accompanied by the supposition that there would have been resistance to the deportations if the majority of Jews had understood the fate Nazi Germany had prepared for them, and that such resistance would have brought the machinery of the 'final solution' to a standstill. It is certainly true that the passivity of most European Jews in obeying the deportation orders made the job of the SS and the police that much easier, and that this obedience came all the more readily because most of the deportees knew nothing of the murderous intentions behind the operation. The idea that they would be murdered either immediately in a gas chamber or gradually by hard work, hunger and sickness – an idea which simply demanded too much of the human power of comprehension – was still dismissed when rumours started to circulate, and even when more reliable information emerged. If one takes account of the natural human reaction to news of such a dreadful fate, which is to greet it with disbelief, and if one further remembers that the majority of the Jewish victims – particularly those living in central, southern and eastern Europe – while they did not share the credulousness of the Nazis when anti-Jewish orders were received from the authorities, were nevertheless prepared to obey the orders of the authorities, whether they understood and approved of them or not, then it becomes questionable, at least, whether reliable information would have done anything to shake that obedience.

The fact that in eastern European ghettos, unlike those of Hungary of western Europe, the true nature of camps such as Auschwitz and Majdanek was known relatively soon after the beginning of the final solution, but that there were still no mass flights or acts of resistance, should make us more cautious in our speculative assumptions. in the death camps themselves there were occasionally revolts by the prisoners, yet all of them towards the end of the murder programme or the camp's existence: in Auschwitz on 7 October 1944, and in Chelmno in January 1945. Although some of these insurgents managed to escape, the greatest uprising in the entire extermination process, that in the Warsaw ghetto, which also broke out only after hundreds of its inhabitants had been deported and murdered, ended in inevitable disaster. To be sure, police units had to be strengthened between 19 April 1943 and the middle of May and they suffered considerable losses in violent and bloody street and house-to-house fighting. Yet, since the Jews, heroic fighters though they were, were hopelessly inferior in arms, the result was never in doubt. After thousands of the ghetto's defenders had been killed, all resistance ceased. Of the 56,000 surviving Jews 7,000 were shot immediately, and all the others were taken to concentration camps. On 16 May 1943 the commander of police units deployed in Warsaw, SS *Brigadeführer* Jürgen Stroop was able to submit a report to his superiors entitled: 'There no longer exists a Jewish residential district in Warsaw!'[52]

Obviously nothing could stop the 'final solution'. Above all the organizers of mass murder never ran the danger of the Allies putting a spoke in the wheels, or of facing local resistance among their own people such as to make their murderous task impossible. In the course of 1943 and 1944 the Allies received reliable information that genocide was actually taking place, and even had a relatively clear idea of how it was being executed, at least as far as the existence and method of operation of Auschwitz was concerned. But they could do nothing with this knowledge. After the first reliable reports about Auschwitz the first demands were heard – to be repeated vehemently decades later – that British and American bombers should have put a stop to the mass murder, by attacking the camps and their lines of communication. Yet this idea was a chimera, which rested on the one hand on an overestimation of what aerial warfare could achieve, and particularly the extent of lasting damage bombardment could do, and on the other hand on an underestimation of the 'political' commitment, criminal energy and technical resources of the RSHA staff.

That no attempt was made to disrupt the process was no doubt based on the fact that many in Britain and the United States only too quickly, and only too readily, accepted the idea that intervention was futile and consequently an impermissible distraction from the main business of winning the war, indicating a lack of imagination, a selfish refusal to be distracted from their own sphere of interest, and no least an insensitivity to moral appeals. Occasionally there was a specific expression of indifference to the suffering of the Jews, or even, on the part of individual antisemites, a sneaking sympathy with the Nazis' activities. Nevertheless it was true that there was only one way to end the murder: to win the war and put an end to Nazi rule altogether. The extermination of the Jews was not even allowed priority in propaganda. Even though Allied leaders, in the hope of achieving some degree of deterrent effect, repeatedly declared their intention of punishing German war criminals, they felt constrained, in order to preserve unity at home, to avoid even the appearance of giving credence to the notion, proclaimed incessantly by the German media, that Britain and the United States were waging war on behalf of Jewish interests. Even President Fraklin D. Roosevelt and Prime Minister Winston Churchill, both of whom, in the course of their careers, had shown sympathy with Jewish complaints and readiness to offer political assistance, could not escape such constraints. When Churchill was informed in June 1944 that ten to twelve thousand Hungarian Jews were being deported to Auschwitz daily, he wrote in helpless desperation in the margin of the report: 'What can we do? What can we say?'[53]

As long as the population of Nazi Germany, from the industrialist to the worker, continued, undeterred, to work, as long as the German state apparatus continued to function reliably, and as long as the armed forces of the German Reich stood between Hitler's regime and the Allies, the machinery of the 'final solution' could not in fact be stopped from outside. While the process of extermination took its course, the population went about its work so indefatigably, the state apparatus functioned so reliably, and the armed forces, not least, fought with astonishing courage and stood so firmly before the 'Führer' and his system that the SS and police apparatus was threatened by disruption neither from within nor from outside.

The 'final solution' had meanwhile also become known in Germany itself. After the public persecution of the Jews up to 1941, and after observers of the rampages of the *Einsatzgruppen* in Russia had passed on their information – by no means always with discretion – enough of what was happening in the camps leaked out to provide anyone who was interested with a fairly reasonable general idea of what was going on. After all, a not inconsiderable section of the state apparatus was directly involved, from the Foreign Ministry, the Interior Ministry and countless local authorities to the state railways; and the vainglorious boasting of some leading figures of the regime, which had been evident at the start of the operation, re-emerged during its implementation. Particularly after Stalingrad and the turning-point of the war in North Africa, which otherwise had no discernible influence on the direction and tempo of the

'final solution', such boasting about the murders which had been committed erupted again and again, while at the same time RSHA commando units were already trying to remove every trace of the death
camps. Obviously a certain perverseness was developing in the Nazis who
were no longer able to suppress entirely the prospect of military defeat: if
the war for *Lebensraum* should be lost, then they wanted not only to
pursue their war of racist destruction – its importance undiminished in
their eyes – to the greatest possible success but also to let both the outside
world and posterity know of this success. Hitler and Himmler boasted of
their historic crime relatively openly, in a series of addresses to SS leaders,
party functionaries, officers and cadets; on 9 May 1943 Joseph Goebbels
did the same, more publicly, in a leading article in his weekly journal *Das
Reich*; Robert Ley, head of the German Labour Front, celebrated the
genocide in a pamphlet of 1944 entitled *Pesthauch der Welt* ('World
Plague').[54]

More was known and more discussed than the disturbed and burdened
consciences of the guilty would confess after the end of the war. In 1942,
for example, a Party Chancellery decree obliged NSDAP functionaries to
respond to popular rumours of 'very severe measures' against the Jews
either by playing down what was happening, or making a plea for
understanding,[55] and in 1943 the SD noted in a report on popular opinion
that attempts by the Nazi propaganda machine to use the discovery of the
corpses of thousands of Polish officers, murdered by Stalin's NKVD in the
forest of Katyn in order to arouse moral indigation against the Bolshevik
subhumans (Untermenschen), had not had the desired effect, because a
surprising number of Germans had expressed the opinion that Katyn was
nothing in comparison with what their own regime was doing to the
Jews.[56] Theophil Wurm, the Bishop of Württemberg, wrote on 16 July
1943 in a letter to Hitler protesting at the threatened inclusion of the
'privileged non-Aryans' in the 'evacuation to the east', that 'the non-
Aryans under attack by the Germans' had 'already for the most part been
got rid of' and these events, 'much discussed' in Germany, were a heavy
burden 'on the conscience and the fortitude of countless German men and
women'.[57]

Yet this knowledge had no effect, and least of all among that minority
of antisemitic Nazi supporters who, in so far as they did not actively
participate, were wholly sympathetic. However, even the vast numbers of
'ordinary' antisemites who would once have indignantly condemned the
murders (and even now reacted with furious disapproval or at least with
sceptical unease) displayed a horrifying readiness to come to terms with
what was happening. The difficulties of opposing the extreme and brutal
consequences of an insane ideology, if one accepts certain elements of that

ideology, were clearly demonstrated. It was also clear that the gradual intensification of persecution which had hitherto characterized the Nazis' 'Jewish policy', and the regime's string of economic, political, and military successes, which had a parallel effect, undermined the moral judgement of these otherwise upright civil servants, doctors and craftsmen, often to the point of destroying it totally. Given their partial identification with quite other objectives and characteristics of the Nazi state, even those less sympathetic to antisemitism reacted passively – not least after the tide of the war had turned – just as the majority of the army in Russia had reacted to the behaviour of the *Einsatzgruppen* in 1941.

If Hitler and the Nazi movement had bewitched the Germans with the glory of their victories, they now bent the nation to their will with the horrors of defeat, and defeat by the Bolsheviks at that. Since many equated 'Bolshevik' quite simply with 'Jewish', the prospect of a defeat in the wake of the mass murder of the Jews aroused fears of political punishment; the fact that many Germans considered themselves accomplices in the 'final solution', or expected, at least to be treated as such, benefited the regime. In addition the Allied aerial bombardment created among the Germans such an intense feeling of perpetual danger, and rendered so difficult the struggle to secure the minimum requirements of everyday life, that moral egocentricity and political apathy became more marked by the day. Himmler's terror apparatus took care of the rest. On the other hand, several thousand German Jews escaped deportation and gassing because German friends helped them to go underground until the end of the war; others again – as in the wake of the Polish atrocities of 1939 and 1940 – either were prompted by news of the murder of the Jews to resist the Nazis, or their resistance to the system was reinforced. Not a few of the conspirators involved in the attempted coup of 20 July 1944 said as much to their Gestapo interrogators.

It was in such an atmosphere that Himmler ordered the suspension of the gassing in Auschwitz and the destruction of all the death camps throughout all German-controlled territory on 27 November 1944, hoping thereby to buy his way into postwar Germany with an 'act of mercy'. The balance sheet of murder in the death factories was breathtaking:[58]

1   *Chelmno*: between December 1941 and July 1944 (with interruptions), 152,000 victims from the Warthegau, including the Jews deported to Łodz from the Reich itself.
2   *Belzec*: in operation from March 1942 to January 1943, at least 600,000 victims from the districts of Lublin, Cracow, Galicia and other, non-Polish areas.

3 *Sobibor* (a camp built during Operation Reinhard in 1942 to supplement Belzec; it employed a T4 team using carbon monoxide gas): in operation from May 1942 to August 1943, at least 250,000 victims from the district of Lublin, Slovakia, the Reich, Holland, France and the Soviet Union.

4 *Treblinka* (the third Operation Reinhard camp, built in the spring of 1942; it was also run by a T4 team using carbon monoxide): in operation from July 1942 to the autumn of 1943, some 900,000 victims from Warsaw, the district of Radom, Greece, the town and surrounding district of Bialystok, and in addition Czech and German Jews from the 'preferential treatment camp' (*Vorzugslager*) at Theresienstadt.

5 *Auschwitz-Birkenau*: in operation from December 1941/January 1942 to October 1944, at least a million victims from Upper Silesia and other parts of Germany, from Slovakia from all the states occupied by Germany, and from Hungary.

6 *Majdanek*: in operation from the summer of 1942 to July 1944, some 200,000 victims, including 60,000 Jews from the district of Lublin, the Warsaw ghetto, the Bialystok ghetto and from Slovakia.

When Himmler ordered the cessation of the operation, at least three million Jews had been murdered in the camps, along with hundreds of thousands of gypsies, sick prisoners and prisoners of war. In addition, more than two million Jews were killed in the Soviet Union (several hundred thousand of whom must be subtracted from the overall total, since they were not murdered by the police units operating in the USSR, but met their deaths in camps such as Sobibor and Treblinka, and are therefore included in the balance sheet of those camps); others died in 'normal' concentration camps, ghettos, other prisons or during transportation to the East, either in overcrowded railway wagons or in murderous marches on foot. Nazi Germany's attempt to exterminate the Jews of Europe had cost more than five million lives, the unprecedented result of an operation itself without precedent. The historical uniqueness of the process arose from the unique combination of a number of elements which were in themselves rare. Firstly, the government of a so-called 'civilized state' had ordered mass murder. Secondly, this government was not acting on impulse, but implementing a carefully considered plan in the absence of any provocation. Thirdly, the plan provided for the actual extermination of a major European ethnic group, defined according to rigid 'racial' criteria; the age and sex of the victims were totally irrelevant, nor did religious confession, social status or personal behaviour count. Forthly, these elements added a horrifying quantitative dimension to a qualitatively appalling enterprise. Fifthly, the deaths of more than five million Jews served neither the political nor economic interests of their murderers, but an insane *idée fixe*. Sixthly, this *Weltanschauung* was not only crudely primitive, but ridiculously abstruse.

The suffering produced when the disciples of this primitive, abstruse and absurd doctrine of salvation achieved power and launched their crusade against European Jewry is both immeasurable and indescribable. Nor could any attempt at such an account ever do justice to the memory of the survivors, who suffered injuries which can never be healed. Yet even an event like the 'final solution' has political consequences, and some of these consequences can be mentioned. It is a truism that the attempted extermination of the Jews of Europe has laid a historical burden on the Germans which is heavier than any in the history of any other nation, as is the observation that so serious a crime calls for laws restricting the freedom of movement of the guilty nation more severe than those for other nations, above all where Jewish feelings and interests are affected.

Yet the historical burden works in other ways too. The guilt or shame felt by the majority of Germans on waking from the Nazi nightmare and 'seeing' the 'world' with relatively normal vision again, naturally and rightly made of antisemitism something both impermissible and indecent. The stigma attached to antisemitism stigmatized in turn, albeit in diluted form, all the other political elements associated with its prophets: rabid nationalism as much as the fundamental rejection of liberalism, democracy and parliamentarism. This contributed to the positive development of the West German political system after the war.

As far as the victims themselves were concerned, and despite the void left by the murders, Hitler and his accomplices achieved exactly the opposite of what they had intended. Instead of 'seeing the term "Jew" extinguished', Hitler and Himmler had compelled even completely assimilated Jews to develop a self-confidence and a separate sense of Jewish identity, to become Jews again. Past attempts at assimilation came to be seen as unsuccessful, future attempts as politically impossible and morally questionable. This rejection of assimilation in turn gave rise to the feeling that the potentially endangered Jews dispersed across the world should be given a centre, a territorial state, which could serve all Jews as a private, cultural and political homeland. Was this a triumph for Zionism, or the consequence of the re-judaization of the Jews of Europe and the world, which was so violently forced by the Nazis? The racism of the Nazis increased the suffering of the Jews to such dimensions, that after the overthrow of the Nazi regime, it was rightly acknowledged throughout the world, and not least by the victorious powers of the Second World War, that greater attention must be paid to the aspirations and interests of the Jews, particularly since they had – willingly or unwillingly – been ignored during the war and the 'final solution'. In this twofold sense the founding of the state of Israel was made inevitable by the Nazis' persecution of the Jews.

Appendices

Appendix 1

Documents

1 Notes from the Diary of a German Jewish Doctor

The removal of the Jews' civil rights, their isolation and expropriation, implemented in the course of Nazi antisemitic policies long before the beginnings of the 'final solution', the everyday reality of inhuman persecution, and the injuries it caused day after day were vividly expressed in the diary of a German Jewish doctor, Hertha Nathorff, who was born in Württemberg into the Einstein family – she was actually a niece of the Nobel Prize winner – and practised in Berlin. She was able to emigrate in 1939, and therefore at least managed to survive the Holocaust.

Source: Wolfgang Benz (ed.), Das Tagebuch der Hertha Nathorff. Berlin, New York, Aufzeichnungen 1933 bis 1945 *(Munich, 1987).*

1 April 1933

Jewish Boycott.

This day is engraved in my heart in flames. To think that such things are still possible in the twentieth century. In front of all Jewish shops, lawyers' offices, doctors' surgeries and flats there are young boys with signs saying, 'Don't buy from Jews', 'Don't go to Jewish doctors', 'Anybody who buys from Jews is a traitor', 'Jews are the incarnation of lies and deceit.' Doctors' signs on the walls of houses are soiled, and sometimes damaged, and people have looked on, gawping in silence. They must have forgotten to stick anything over my sign. I think I would have reacted violently. It was afternoon before one of these young boys visited me at home and asked: 'Is this a Jewish business?' 'This isn't a business at all; it's a doctor's surgery',

I said. 'Are you sick?' After these ironic words the youth disappeared without posting anybody in front of my door. Of course some patients who had appointments did not turn up. One woman rang to say that of course she couldn't come today, and I said that it would be better if she didn't come any more at all. For my own part, I shopped deliberately in places where such pickets were posted. One of them wanted to stop me going into a little soap shop, but I pushed him to one side, saying, 'I'll spend my money where I want.' Why doesn't everybody do that? That would soon settle the boycott. But people are a cowardly lot, as I know only too well.

In the evening we were with friends at the Hohenzollerndamm, three couples, all doctors. They were all quite depressed. One of the company, Emil, the optimist, tried to convince us: 'It'll all be over in a few days.' They don't understand my anger when I say, 'They should strike us dead instead. It would be more humane than the psychological death they have in mind . . .' But my instincts have always proved right.

25 April 1933

A letter from Charlottenburg municipal authorities: 'You are requested to cease your activity as senior doctor at the women's advice centre!' Full stop.

Thrown out then – full stop. My poor women, whose hands will they fall into now? I've run that place for five years, expanded it and made it well known, and now? It's all over. I have to repeat it again and again, in order to be able to grasp it.

12 May 1933

A patient comes to me in tears. She has been to the usual works lecture, where she was told that anybody who had once had relations with a Jew can no longer bear pure Aryan children. And she used to have a Jewish boyfriend. It took me ages to persuade this rather simple creature that this was all nonsense. Then she breathed a sign of relief and said, 'Frau Doktor, I was just about to turn the gas taps on, and then at the last minute I came to you.' Yes, but how many have nobody they can turn to?

30 August 1933

Back from holidays in southern Germany. How tense the atmosphere is there. The situation is completely changed in my home town, where everyone knows everyone else.

My family have lived in that small town for two hundred years, looked up to, respected and now . . . My old father said to me in passing that he no longer goes to his local. Mother got rather worked up because nobody knows how to greet her properly any more.

A friend of my sister's, a lawyer's wife, comes to visit only in the evenings after dark, until my sister suggests she doesn't bother coming at all. The Catholics are beside themselves with fear and dread. Where will it all end?

2 October 1934

I have just come from the H. mental asylum. They rang to ask if I would come. A patient had arrived during the night who was calling for me. She had been picked up on the street, in front of a hospital. They thought she was drunk, the way she was behaving, talking, crying in the street, and giving away her possessions to passers-by. Then she was brought to the asylum. Did I know her? A young colleague who is not allowed to practise. Her licence has been taken away. A love affair with an Aryan colleague suddenly came to an end. Then she tried to work as a nurse, and it proved too much for her soul, for her intellect. As a result she had gone mad.

30 November 1934

I have been to southern Germany. My dear father was seriously ill. The things I had to do to get the doctor treating him – it would be unprofessional to comment on his medical ability – to agree to send him for a consultation with the capable specialist in Ulm! 'One can't consult a Jewish doctor!' He would rather treat the patient wrongly and badly! He should be grateful that he can get an Aryan doctor to come at all. There is no Jewish doctor left in the small town, and the other Nazi doctor does not treat Jews. It's almost like the camps where they have imprisoned innocent people. 'If one happens to be a Jew, one is either healthy or dead!'

One of the Catholic nurses looking after Father told me: 'Frau Doktor, we needn't fear hell any more. The devil is already abroad in the world.'

30 December 1934

Three more suicides by people who could no longer stand the continuing defamation and spite.

The boy is afraid to go on the ice rink. Yesterday Jewish children were chased away and beaten up.

9 October 1935

I met my former secretary today. She fixed me sharply with her short-sighted eyes, and then turned away. I was so nauseated I spat into my handkerchief. She was once a patient of mine. Later I met her in the street. Her boyfriend had left her and she was out of work and without money. I took her on, trained her for years and employed her in my clinic until the last day. Now she has changed so much that she can no longer greet me; me, who rescued her from the gutter!

I never go anywhere any more. I am so well known through my profession and my position; why should I make trouble for myself and for others? I'm happy to be at home in peace.

4 December 1935

Miss G. in the surgery, completely broken. She knows nothing of Jews and Jewry. Suddenly they've dug up her Jewish grandmother! She is no longer allowed to work as an artist, and she must give up her boyfriend, a senior officer. She wants something 'to end it all'. She can only groan pitifully, 'I can't go on living.' What can I do? I can no longer help my patients, it's a living death for me.

5 August 1938

There was a telephone call as we were sitting at the table with guests. I went to the telephone myself. A colleague, S., who asks: 'Have you been listening to the radio?' 'No', I say, 'what's happened now?' The colleague, usually so calm, says with a trembling, angry voice: 'What you always said would happen. They're taking away our licences, we are no longer allowed to practise – it's just been on the radio.' 'On the radio.' This is how we learn that they are taking away from us what we earned through years of study, what we were taught by eminent professors, famous universities . . . I can't take it in . . . All I could think at that moment was: 'And now I have to tell my husband.' How I went calmly back to the dining table, drew the meal to a close, and told my guests, 'It's nothing much', I don't know; I know only that I sat at the desk, my hands clenched and said to my husband: 'It's over – over – over.' He went to get a paper, and it had already been reported. This is how we Jewish doctors learnt of our death sentence. In the clinic they are all in a state of complete despair.

26 October 1938

I go to the clinic every day and help the nurses. In the afternoons I am in the practice with my husband, but it's dreadfully soul-destroying for me. It's a good thing most of the patients don't know me. To them I'm the new assistant, and that means I can make my psychological studies. 'Is the doctor still allowed to treat Aryan patients, then?' one woman asked me. My only answer was 'No.' I think the good lady perhaps thought I was a 'spy'.

Frau C. has just been here. They've locked up her husband, who works for a car firm and was showing a new car to a customer. At his employer's request he drove a little way with her down a quiet side street. The car was stopped, papers demanded, blonde Aryan woman, Jewish man, quiet street, semi-darkness – so 'racial disgrace' or at least suspicion of it. In any event the man was immediately arrested.

2 The 'Final solution' in the Diaries of Joseph Goebbels

The notes for the diary of Joseph Goebbels (Reich Minister for Popular Enlightenment and Propaganda and Reich Director of Propaganda for the NSDAP) which accompanied the Nazi persecution of the Jews are of interest not least because they reflect Hitler's opinions. Particularly during the war years and the 'final solution', the sources for Hitler's attitude to this question are scarce.

Source: Louis P Lochner (ed.), Goebbels Tagebücher aus den Jahren 1942/43 *(Zurich, 1948) pp. 87f. and 142f. (An unabridged copy of Lochner's work is in the archive of the Institut für Zeitgeschichte, Munich.)*

Notes, 14 February 1942 (Sunday)

Along with Bolshevism, Jewry is also about to experience its great disaster. The Führer again expresses the opinion that he is resolved to clean up the Jews of Europe without mercy. There is no room for sentimentality here. The Jews have deserved the catastrophe which they are experiencing today. They, too, will be annihilated, along with our enemies. We must speed up this process coldly and ruthlessly, and we are doing mankind, tortured by Jewry for thousands of years, an inestimable service. This clear anti-Jewish line must be impressed on our own people too, in the face of any opposition from reluctant quarters. The Führer expressly emphasizes all this again afterwards in the presence of officers, who can take it or leave it.

The great opportunities which this war offers us are known to the Führer with all their implications. He is aware today that he is fighting out a struggle of gigantic dimensions, and that the fate of all civilized humanity depends on the outcome of that struggle.

Entry 27 March 1942 (Friday)

The Jews are now being forced eastwards out of the Government General, starting with Lublin. A rather barbaric process is being used which cannot be described in further detail, and there is very little left of the Jews themselves. On the whole one can say that 60 per cent must be liquidated, while only 40 per cent can be set to work. The former *Gauleiter* of Vienna [Odilo Globocnik], who is responsible for running this operation, does his job with circumspection and by means of a process which does not attract too much attention. The Jews are being subjected to a judicial process which, although barbaric, is fully deserved. What the Führer prophesied for the Jews in the eventuality of a world war is beginning to be realized in the most dreadful way. One cannot afford sentimentality in a situation such as this. The Jews would destroy us if we did not defend ourselves. It's a life-and-death struggle between the Aryan race and the Jewish bacillus. No other government, and no other regime, could summon the strength for such a general solution to this question. Here too the Führer is the untiring pioneer and spokesman for the radical solution the situation demands, and which now appears inevitable. Thank God the war has presented us with a whole series of opportunities which we would not have in peacetime. We must make use of them. Those ghettos which have become vacant in the Government General will now be filled with Jews expelled from the Reich, and then after a certain time the process will repeat itself.

3 Reichsführer *SS Heinrich Himmler on the 'Final Solution'*

Himmler could not help talking about the murderous 'final solution' in several speeches before audiences ranging from SS leaders to Wehrmacht *generals. Although limited in numbers, such audiences nevertheless constituted a sort of public forum.*

Source: (A) from a speech at the conference of SS Gruppenführer, *4 October 1943, in IMT, vol. 29, pp. 145f; (B) from a speech to Reich leaders and* Gauleiter *in Posen (Poznán), 6 October 1943, in Bradley F. Smith and Agnes F. Peterson (eds),* Heinrich Himmler, Geheimreden 1933 bis 1945 und andere Ansprachen *(Frankfurt, 1974), pp. 169ff; (C) from a speech to generals in Sonthofen, 5 May 1944, ibid., p. 202; (D) from a speech to generals in Sonthofen, 24 May 1944, ibid., p. 203; (E) from a speech to generals in Sonthofen, 21 June 1944, ibid., pp. 203f.*

(A)

I should now like to speak to you quite openly about a very serious matter. We can speak of it quite openly among ourselves and yet we will never mention it in public, just as we did not hesitate on 30 June 1934 to obey our orders dutifully by taking those comrades who had gone astray, standing them against a wall and shooting them, and yet have never spoken of it, and will never speak of it. Thank God we are possessed of sufficient discretion to avoid mentioning it, talking about it among ourselves. Although everyone was horrified, everyone also knew that he would do the same again, should it be necessary, should the order be given.

I refer, of course, to the evacuation of the Jews, the extermination of the Jewish people. It's one of those things which is easy to say: every party comrade says, 'The Jewish people is to be exterminated.' Of course. It's in our party programme, elimination of the Jews, extermination. We'll do it. And then they come along, the eighty million good Germans, and every one of them knows a decent Jew. The others are swine, quite clearly, but this particular one is a splendid Jew. Not one of them who says that he has seen what is happening, not one of them has been through it. Most of you will know what it means to see a hundred corpses lying side by side, or five hundred, or a thousand. To have lived through that, and apart from a few cases of human weakness, to have remained decent: that is what has made us hard. This is a glorious page in our history, but one which has never been written, and can never be written. For we know how difficult it would have been for us if in every town, on top of the bombing raids, on top of the burdens and deprivations of war, we still had secret Jewish saboteurs, agitators and troublemakers. We would probably have reached the same stage as in 1916 and 1917, when the Jews were still part of the body of the German nation.

We have taken away such wealth as they had. I have given a strict order, which has been implemented by *Obergruppenführer* Pohl, that this wealth should, of course, become the property of the Reich, without exception. We have kept none of it for ourselves.

(B)

On this matter, and in this closest of circles, I shall permit myself to come to a question which you, my party comrades, have all naturally accepted, but which for me has become the most difficult question of my entire life: the Jewish question. You all happily take it for granted that there are no more Jews left in your *Gaue*. All Germans, certain exceptions apart, understand that we would not have survived the bombing raids and the burdens of the fourth – and perhaps the inevitable fifth and sixth – year of war, we would not be able to survive if we still had this destructive plague within the body of our nation. The sentence, 'The Jews must be exterminated', with its few words, is easy to say, gentlemen. For those who have to carry out what it requires, it is the hardest and most serious that there is. Of course it is Jews, quite clearly, only Jews. But consider how many – even party comrades – have come to me, or to some office, with their famous petition, arguing that all Jews are swine, of course, but that so-and-so is a decent Jew who should be left alone. I would venture to suggest that the number of petitions and the number of opinions on the matter indicate a greater number of decent Jews than the nominal total of all Jews. We have so many people in Germany who know a decent Jew that this number is already greater than the number of Jews. I only mention it because you know from experience in your own *Gaue* that even decent and respectable National Socialists all know a decent Jew.

I would ask you only to listen to what I have to say here in this company and never to speak of it. We have been asked: 'What about the women and children?' I have resolved to find a clear solution here as well. I did not feel justified in exterminating – pronounced 'killing' [!] – the men, or having them killed, only to let their avengers, in the form of their children, live to seek revenge from our children and grandchildren. The difficult decision had to be made to wipe this people out totally from the face of the earth. For the organization which had to implement this decision it was the most difficult commission we have ever been given. I believe I can say that it has been implemented without our men and their leaders having suffered any serious psychological or spiritual damage. There was a very great danger of this. The way between the two possibilities here, either to be too brutal, too heartless and pay no further regard to human life, or to be too weak, to dither to the point of nervous breakdown – the way between this Scylla and Charybdis is dreadfully narrow.

Every last penny of the wealth we confiscated from the Jews – and it reached unquantifiable proportions – has been handed over to the Reich Economics Minister. I have always insisted that we owe it to our people, to our race – if we want to win the war – we have a duty to the Führer, with whom our nation has been blessed only once in two thousand years, not to shrink back from our duty here, but to be consistent. We do not have the right to take even a single penny from the confiscated wealth of the Jews. From the outset I have insisted on the death sentence for any SS man who takes even a single Mark. I can tell you quite openly now that in the course of the last few days I have signed a number of death sentences – about a dozen – for that very reason. Severity is required here, or the whole operation will suffer. I have felt it my duty to speak to you, the supreme bearers of the will and the honour of the party, of this political order, of this instrument of the Führer, and to tell you how it has been. The Jewish question in countries occupied by us will be settled by the end of the year. There will remain only a residue of individual Jews who have slipped through the net. The question of Jews married to non-Jewish partners and the question of half-Jews will be examined rationally and appropriately, decided and then solved.

Believe me, I had considerable difficulty with many businesses. I cleaned up large Jewish ghettos in the staging posts. In Warsaw we had four weeks of street fighting in one Jewish ghetto. Four weeks! We dug out some 700 bunkers there. This ghetto made things like fur coats, clothes and the like. When we wanted to go in earlier we were told: 'Halt! you are disrupting the war economy! Halt! Munitions works!' Of course, that had nothing to do with party comrade Speer, you can do nothing about it. It is the part of ostensible munitions works which party comrade Speer and I want to clear in the course of the coming weeks and months. We will do this with the same disregard for sentimentality with which all things must be done in the fifth year of war, for love of Germany.

With that I would like to bring the Jewish question to a close. Now you know, and you must keep it to yourselves. We can consider much later whether it is necessary to say anything more to the German people. I believe it is better that we – all of us – have taken this on ourselves for our people, have taken on a responsibility (responsibility for a deed, not for an idea), and that we take the secret with us to the grave.

(C)

You can be sure of this: if we had not got rid of the Jews from Germany it would have been impossible to survive the bombing campaign, the decency of the German people notwithstanding. Of that I am certain. The Führer warned the Jews at the beginning of the war, or before the war: 'If you again incite the nations of Europe to wage war on one another, then the outcome will not be the extermination of the German people, but the extermination of all the Jews.' The Jewish question has been solved, both within Germany itself, and more generally in the countries occupied by Germany. It was solved without compromise, as befits our people's life-and-death struggle, in which the existence of our blood is at stake. I tell you that as comrades. We are all soldiers, irrespective of our uniforms. You can tell how difficult it was for me to carry out my orders as a soldier in this instance, orders which I implemented obediently and with conviction. If you say, 'We can understand as far as the men are concerned, but not the children', then I must remind you of what I said at the very beginning. In this struggle with Asia we must accustom ourselves to condemn to oblivion the rules and principles of the European warfare of the past, which we have come to prefer. It is my opinion that, whatever qualms we have in the depths of our hearts, we have no right, as Germans, to allow a generation of hate-filled avengers to grow up, with whom our children and grand-children will have to deal because we, their fathers or grandfathers, were too weak and cowardly and left it to them.

(D)

A further question, which was central to the internal security of the Reich and of Europe, was the Jewish question. Orders were obeyed without compromise, and with a rational understanding of the situation. [*Applause*] I believe, gentlemen, that you know me well enough to know that I am not a bloodthirsty person, and that I am not a man who derives any joy or fun from the hard things he is required to do. On the other hand, I think I can claim to have nerves which are strong enough, and a sense of duty which is great enough, that when I recognize that something is necessary, I carry it out without compromise. I did not feel justified – with regard to Jewish women and children – to allow their children to grow up to be avengers who would then kill our fathers and our grandchildren. I would have considered such a thing cowardly. Consequently, the question was solved without compromise.

(E)

It was also necessary to solve another great question. It was the most dreadful of tasks and the most dreadful of commissions which an organization can receive: the task of solving the Jewish question. Permit me again to say a few words frankly in this company. It is good that we were tough enough to exterminate the Jews on our territory. Do not ask how difficult it was. But, even in the course of the most critical examination of these events, only as soldiers thinking of Germany, draw the logical conclusion – that it was necessary. For we would not have withstood even the bombing campaign if we had still had the Jews in our cities. I am also convinced that the Lemberg [Lvov] front in the Government General could not have been held if we had still had the great ghettos in Lemberg, Cracow, Lublin and Warsaw.

4 The Testimony of the Commandant of Auschwitz

Rudolf Höss, commandant of the concentration and annihilation camp at Auschwitz from 1940 to 1943, describes the mass murder in a report compiled after the end of the war.

Source: Kommandant von Auschwitz. Autobiographische Aufzeichnungen von Rudolf Höss, *introduced and with a commentary by Martin Broszat (Stuttgart, 1958), pp. 155f. and 158f.*

I can no longer say when the annihilation of the Jews began. Probably already in September 1941, but perhaps only in January 1942. At first it was a matter of Jews from Upper Silesia. These Jews were imprisoned by the state police office in Kattowitz and transported by train along a parallel track to the west of the Auschwitz–Dziedzice line, and unloaded there. As far as I can remember there were never more than a thousand people in there transports.

A reception committee from the camp took over responsibility for the Jews from the police on the platform, and they were taken in two groups by the *Schutzhaftlagerführer* [head of the protective custody camp] to the bunker, as the annihilation apparatus was called. Luggage remained on the platform and was then taken to the sorting office – called Canada – between the DAW [*Deutsche Ausrüstungswerke*, German equipment works] and the building site. The Jews had to undress by the bunker, and were told that they must go into the designated rooms to be dismissed. All the rooms – there were five – were filled simultaneously. The airtight doors were closed and the contents of the gas containers were released into the rooms through special holes.

After half an hour the doors were opened again – there were two doors to each room – and the dead were taken out and transported by means of small wagons on a small track to the graves. Items of clothing were taken in lorries to the sorting office. All the work, assisting with undressing, filling the bunkers, clearing the bunkers, removing the bodies, and the digging and filling of the mass graves, was carried out by a special unit of Jews, who were accommodated separately, and in accordance with Eichmann's orders they were also annihilated after every large-scale operation. During the first transports Eichmann brought an order from the RFSS (*Reichsführer* SS Himmler) instructing us to remove gold teeth from the corpses and cut off the women's hair. This work was also carried out by the special unit. The annihilation was supervised either by the *Schutzhaftlagerführer* or the *Rapportführer* [administrative officers]. Sick people who could not be taken to the gas chambers were shot in the neck with a small-calibre weapon. An SS doctor also had to be present. The gas was released into the rooms by means of the disinfection units, the SDGs . . .

The selection of Jews fit for work was supposed to be carried out by SS doctors. But it happened repeatedly that this job was undertaken by *Schutzhaftlagerführer* or the leaders of work units, without my knowledge and without my approval. This led to friction between the SS doctors and the leaders of work groups. Differences of opinion had arisen among the leaders in Auschwitz and were consistently nourished by the different interpretations of the order of the RFSS by the highest offices in Berlin. The RSHA (Müller, Eichmann) had the greatest interest in destroying as many Jews as possible, for Security Police reasons. The Reich Doctor SS, who of course gave the SS doctors guidelines for selection, was of the opinion that only those Jews fully capable of work should be considered for the work groups, since those who were weaker, older or of only limited capacity would very quickly become incapable of work, causing the already overburdened health situation to deteriorate further and the sick-bays to multiply unnecessarily, and demanding further medical personnel and medicines, before they eventually had to be killed. The WVHA [*Wirtschafts- und Verwaltungshauptamt*, SS Economic and Administrative Head Office] had an interest in getting as much labour as possible, even if such workers later became unfit for the job, for deployment in the munitions units. These conflicts of interest were increased by the immeasurably increasing demands the Armaments Ministry or the Todt Organization made of the work units in the camps. The RFSS kept promising both offices numbers he could not supply. *Standartenführer* Maurer (head of Office D II) now had the difficult task of responding to these steady pressures from his superiors as well as he could, and it was through him that the leaders of the work units were encouraged to take as many workers as possible. It was impossible to get a clear decision from the RFSS. I myself was of the opinion that only the really healthy and strong Jews should be selected for work.

The selection was carried out as follows. The wagons were unloaded one after the other. After depositing their luggage, the Jews had to pass individually before an SS doctor, who decided whether they were appropriate as they walked past. Those capable of working were taken immediately in smaller groups into the camp. The proportion of those judged capable of work was between 25 and 30 per cent over all the transport, but fluctuated a great deal. Of Greek Jews, for example, only about 15 per cent were capable of work, while there were transports from Slovakia where 100 per cent were fit to work. Jewish doctors and medical personnel were taken to the camp without exception.

Appendix 2

Sources and Literature

The Nazi persecution of the Jews between 1933 and 1945, intensified to the extermination of European Jewry from 1941, became the subject of academic studies while it was still happening. The Institute of Jewish Affairs, founded in New York in 1940–1 and housed in London since 1966, immediately began to collect material on the events in Germany's sphere of power, and the first comprehensive accounts of Nazi persecution were published under the auspices of the institute in 1943 and 1944; the collective work, *Hitler's War on the Jews*, and Jacob Letschinsky, *The Jewish Catastrophe*.

After the end of the war the Yiddish Scientific Institute (YIVO), which had emigrated from Vilnius to New York in 1939, developed, as the 'YIVO Institute for Jewish Research', into one of the most important centres for research into the Holocaust, collecting in one archive sources of both German and Jewish provenance. Along with a number of detailed studies, published since 1946 in its *YIVO Annual of Jewish Social Science* or in the *YIVO-bleter*, which have appeared irregularly since 1931, it was able to publish, as early as 1946, a comprehensive report on annihilation of the Polish Jews: Joseph Tenenbaum, *In Search of a Lost People*. Founded in 1954, the Leo Baeck Institute, with branches in New York, London and Jerusalem, has managed to achieve similar status, however, with its organs, the *Yearbooks*, published in London since 1956, and the *Bulletin*, published in Jerusalem. In adition the YIVO Institute works closely with an institution in Jerusalem, called Yad Vashem (The Martyrs' and Heroes' Remembrance Authority), which has functioned since 1953 as a memorial and at the same time as the central Israeli archive and research institute for the history of the Holocaust.

The Centre de Documentation Juive Contemporaine in Paris has achieved similar significance for the persecution of the Jews in France. It was founded in 1943, during the German occupation, as an institution of the resistance movement. In Poland a Jewish Historical Commission was founded in Lublin in 1944. This was transferred to Łodz in 1945 and Warsaw in 1947. Then in 1948 the 'Zydowska Komisja Historýczna' became the Jewish Historical Institute ('Zydowska Instytut Historyczny w Polce'; Nachmann Blumenthal, Michail Bowricz and Filip Friedman had already published their three-volume collection 'Dokumenty i Materialy' in Łodz in 1946.

Research on the Holocaust on German soil also began immediately after the end of the war, when the Central Historical Commission of the Central Committee of the Liberated Jews in the US Zone, established in Munich, put together a number of memoirs and eyewitness reports and published them between 1946 and 1948 in a series entitled From the Last Extermination: Journal for the History of the Jewish People duing the Nazi Regime. Some time later, following the return of documents from Nazi institutions and organizations to Germany, where they were deposited in the Federal Archive, the Political Archive of the Foreign Office, the state archives of the federal states and archives belonging to special research institutes, such as the Institut für Zeitgeschichte (Institute of Contemporary History) in Munich, German historians too were able to begin to make their own contribution to the history and analysis of the Nazi persecution of the Jews.

In the meantime, moreover, special institutions were created, which have participated in this research in a most commendable way, such as the Institut für die Geschichte der deutschen Juden, which was founded in 1963 in Hamburg, and the Institut zur Erforschung der Schicksale der Jüdischen Bürger in Baden und Württemberg in den Jahren 1933 bis 1945, which was founded in 1962 by the Stuttgart archival commission.

The Jewish archives and research institutes contain deposits saved from Jewish communities and organizations along with important collections from the documents of the German authorities and offices, and from organizations affiliated to the Nazi party. Among their most priceless treasures, however, are the contemporary personal observations and individual memoirs written later. These have made it possible to reconstruct the fate of many Jewish communities and ghettos in Europe, along with the structure and development of the concentration camps and death camps. By 1949 an anthology of Jewish eyewitness reports, translated from the Yiddish into English and prepared by Leo W. Schwarz, had already appeared in New York under the title The Root and the Bough. Such notes were often not only of great scholarly significance, but were also very vivid and of high moral importance. A good example is the collection of diary notes on the history of the Warsaw ghetto, which the Jewish chronicler Emmanuel Ringelblum buried before its destruction, and parts of which were found in the ruins of Warsaw in 1946 and 1950; they are now to be seen in the Jewish Historical Institute in Warsaw.

The Diary of Anne Frank (Das Tagebuch der Anne Frank 12. Juni 1942–1 August 1944), which relates the fate of the Dutch Jews, attracted world-wide attention when it was first published in Heidelberg in 1949, and had reached print runs of 2,116–2,145 thousand as a Fischer paperback in 1986. In 1987 Wolfgang Benz edited the diary of Hertha Nathorrf (Das Tagebuch der Hertha Nathorff. Berlin, New York. Aufzeichnungen 1933 bis 1945) for the Institut für Zeitgeschichte in Munich, and it stands as an equally impressive testament both to the process by which the German Jews were deprived of their rights and isolated, and to the difficulties of Jewish emigrants.

The perpetrators themselves have also left sources of a personal nature, of course, and these are key documents for research into the Nazi persecution of the Jews. In 1953 Hans Rothfels published in the first volume of the Vierteljahreshefte für Zeitgeschichte the eyewitness report written by the SS leader Kurt Gerstein, 'Augenzeugenbericht zu den Massenvergasungen'. The Munich Institut für Zeitgeschichte, which publishes the Vierteljahreshefte also published, in 1975, the diary of the Governor General of Poland, Diensttagebuch des deutschen Generalgouverneurs in Polen 1939–1945, and followed this in 1958 with Kommandant in Auschwitz. Autobiographische Aufzeichnungen von Rudolf Höss, introduced and with a commentary by Martin Broszat.

One unusual form of sources and source collections arises out of the nature of the events. Since the Nazi persecution of the Jews in general, and the individual acts of which it was made up, were criminal in nature, criminal trials were necessary after the war both in Germany and in the states occupied by Germany between 1938 and 1945. The documents and testimonies which were collected for these trials, or were produced by them, formed collections of material which served purposes beyond the forensic aims for which they were produced, and are of particular value for the work of the historian, constituting as they do something of a replacement for the loss of large numbers of important German records, such as the records of the RSHA and the police. This process began in Germany with the Nuremberg War Crimes Trials and the numerous trials instituted by German courts against those members of the NSDAP and SA who had committed acts of violence against Jews, including those during the 'Night of Broken Glass', and they continued in the 1960s and 1970s with the trials of members of the Einsatzgruppen and the staff of the concentration camps and death camps; the best-known were the Auschwitz trial, the Treblinka trial and the Majdanek trial.

The *Zentrale Stelle der Landesjustizverwaltungen zur Verfolgung Nationalsozialistischer Gewaltverbrechen* (Central Office of State Justice Administration for the Prosecution of National Socialist Criminal Violence), established in Ludwigsburg in 1958, collected a mass of very valuable material for such cases for decades. The Warsaw High Commission for the Investigation of Hitlerite Crimes in Poland, which is accountable to the Polish Ministry of Justice, has a similar role in Poland, while a collection of documents and testimonies was put together in Israel in connection with the Eichmann trial, and is now kept in the Israeli state archives. It is an indispensable collection, particularly for scholarly research on the problems of the 'final solution'. Meanwhile institutions such as the Auschwitz State Museum have also gained considerable significance; the *Hefte von Auschwitz*, which have been published there in German since 1959, are indispensable for the researcher, as is the *Kalendarium der Ereignisse in Auschwitz*, produced since 1959 by Danuta Czech.

Since specialized collections began to be put together very early, and an almost unmanageably large number of detailed studies was very quickly produced, the Nazi persecution of the Jews is one of those areas of research in contemporary history where general accounts appeared very quickly, many of them still useful to this day.

In 1953 Gerald Reitlinger published his large-scale study, *The Final Solution. The Attempt to Exterminate the Jews of Europe 1939–1945* (the most recent German edition was published in Berlin in 1961 under the title *Die Endlösung. Hitlers Versuch der Ausrottung der Juden Europas 1939–1945*); Raul Hilberg's standard work, *The Destruction of the European Jews*, appeared in London in 1961, and a revised and extended new edition came out in New York in 1985 (German edition: *Die Vernichtung der europäischen Juden, Berlin, 1982).*

Following useful overviews such as Reinhard Henky, *Die nationalsozialistischen Gewaltverbrechen. Geschichte und Gericht* (Stuttgart, 1964), and Wolfgang Scheffler, *Judenverfolgung im Dritten Reich* (Frankfurt, 1961), Helmut Krausnick presented his 'Judenverfolgung', which had an important role as historical evidence in the Auschwitz trial, and together with other evidence at the trial was published in *Anatomie des SS-Staates*, vol. 2 (Olten and Freiburg, 1965). As a concise synthesis it remains unsurpassed to the present.

This was followed by Uwe Dietrich Adam, *Judenpolitik im Dritten Reich* (Düsseldorf, 1972), which went into much greater detail and raised important questions about the far from linear Nazi decision-making process, and Lucy S. Dawidowicz, *The War against the Jews 1933–1945*

(New York, 1975) (German edition: *Der Krieg gegen die Juden 1933–1945*, Munich, 1979), which combined subtlety of approach with precise scholarship. Finally, in 1986 Martin Gilbert, who had already produced a very useful *Atlas of the Holocaust* (London, 1982; German edition: *Endlösung. Die Vertreibung and Vernichtung der Juden. Ein Atlas*, Hamburg, 1982), published *The Holocaust. The Jewish Tragedy* (London, 1986), a clear and dramatic work for all its wealth of material and detail.

Naturally the later accounts – including Hilberg's new edition – have profited from the wealth of studies on particular aspects of the Nazi persecution of the Jews published since the 1950s, and have been able to make use of more rigorous approaches and a broader base of primary sources than the pioneering works written immediately after the war. First of all we know rather more today about antisemitism as a phenomenon. In this area, too, several pioneering essays were written during the 1950s which are still very useful, above all Eva G. Reichmann, *Die Flucht in den Hass. Die Ursachen der deutschen Judenkatastrophe* (Frankfurt, 1958); Alexander Bein, 'Der moderne Antisemitismus und seine Bedeutung für die Judenfrage', *Vierteljahreshefte für Zeitgeschichte*, 6 (1958), pp. 340–60, and Paul W. Massing, *Vorgeschichte des politischen Antisemitismus* (Frankfurt, 1959).

Since then, however, research in this area has ploughed deeper furrows and considerably extended its area of cultivation. To mention only the most important works: Eleonore Sterling, *Judenhass, Die Anfänge des politischen Antisemitismus in Deutschland* (Frankfurt, 1969; revised edition of the study published in Munich in 1956, *Er ist wie Du*); Peter G. Pulzer, *The Rise of Political Anti-semitism in Germany and Austria* (New York, 1964); Michael D. Bidess, *Father of Racist Ideology. The Social and Political Thought of Count Gobineau* (New York, 1970); Norman Cohn, *Warrant for Genocide. The Myth of the Jewish World-Conspiracy and the Protocols of the Elders of Zion* (New York, 1967; German edition: *Die Protokolle der Weisen von Zion*, Cologne, 1969); Reinhard Rürup, *Emanzipation und Antisemitismus* (Göttingen, 1975).

Two works deserve special mention because they approach something like a description and explanation of the intellectual and emotional crisis of the German nation: Fritz Stern, *The Politics of Cultural Despair. A Study in the Rise of the German Ideology* (Berkeley, 1961; German edition: Kulturpessimismus als politische Gefahr, Berne, 1964); George L. Mosse, *The Crisis of German Ideology. Intellectual Origins of the Third Reich* (New York, 1964).

Specifically on Nazi antisemitism, or on the significance of antisemitism in determining the political activity of the Nazis, there are now works available which go some way to answering questions which for long remained open, for example Rupert Breitling, *Die nationalsozialistische Rassenlehre. Entstehung, Ausbreitung, Nutzen und Schaden einer politischen Ideologie* (Meisenheim, 1971), and above all Erich Goldhagen, 'Weltanschauung und Endlösung. Zum Antisemitismus der nationalsozialistischen Führungsschicht', *Vierteljahreshefte für Zeitgeschichte*, 24 (1976), pp. 379–405. Robert Cecil has worked on the leading ideologues (after Hitler) of the Nazi movement in *The Myth of the Master Race. Alfred Rosenberg and Nazi Ideology* (London, 1972), and on Hitler himself Eberhard Jäckel has produced both the basic source material and the most precise analysis in *Hitler. Sämtliche Aufzeichnungen 1905–1924* (Stuttgart, 1980) and *Hitlers Weltanschauung* (2nd edn, Stuttgart, 1981).

In the meantime Shulamit Volkov has posed thought-provoking questions on the comparability of German antisemitism with other European antisemitisms and on the possible differences between Nazi antisemitism and that of Wilhelmine Germany: 'Kontinuität und Diskontinuität im deutschen Antisemitismus 1878–1945', *Vierteljahreshefte für Zeitgeschichte*, 33 (1985), pp. 221–43.

Two researchers are principally responsible for the light that has finally been shed on the attitude of the majority of the German people to the Nazi persecution of the Jews: along with other pertinent essays, Otto Dov Kulka has published 'Die Nürnberger Rassengesetze und die deutsche Bevölkerung im Leicht geheimer NS-Lage- und Stimmungsberichte', *Vierteljahreshefte für Zeitgeschichte*, 32 (1984), pp. 582–624; Ian Kershaw has published 'Antisemitismus und Volksmeinung. Reaktionen auf die Judenverfolgung', in Martin Broszat and Elke Fröhlich (eds), *Bayern in der NS-Zeit*, vol. 2, and also 'The Persecution of the Jews and German Popular Opinion in the Third Reich', *Leo Baeck Institute Yearbook*, 26 (1981), and Lawrence D. Stokes has published 'The German People and the Destruction of the European Jews', *Journal of Contemporary History*, 6 (1973).

In works on particular aspects of the Nazi persecution of the Jews the emphasis has naturally been on events in Germany. In 1951 Hans Lamm submitted a dissertation at Erlangen which constituted the first overview and is still useful: *Über die innere und äussere Entwicklung des deutschen Judentums im Dritten Reich*, on which several important works have since expanded.

On the position of the German Jews in the Weimar period, at the beginning of the persecution and during the first few years after 1933 there are the important studies of Kurt Jakob Ball-Kaduri, *Vor der Katastrophe. Juden in Deutschland 1934–1939* (Tel Aviv, 1967) and in the collection edited by Werner E. Mosse and Arnold Paucker, *Entscheidungsjahr 1932. Zur Judenfrage in der Endphase der Weimarer Republik* (Tübingen, 1965);

Werner E. Mosse has also edited the equally important volume *Deutsches Judentum in Krieg und Revolution 1916–1923* (Tübingen, 1971).

A wealth of material on the Nazi decision-making process is to be found in Karl A. Schleunes, *The Twisted Road to Auschwitz. The Nazi Policy toward German Jews 1933–1939* (Urbana, Ill., 1970), although the present author cannot agree with Schleunes's thesis of the aimlessness of Nazi policy-making.

Among the individual events, the November pogrom of 1938 has understandably commanded a great deal of attention, and works written in the 1950s are still useful: Hermann Graml, *Der 9. November 1938. Reichskristallnacht* (Bonn, 1953, 6th impression, 1962) and Lionel Kochan *Pogrom. 10 November 1938* (London, 1957).

Events on a rather larger scale have been dealt with in exemplary fashion by Hans G. Adler, *Der verwaltete Mensch. Studien zur Deportation der Juden aus Deutschland* (Tübingen, 1974) and Helmut Genschel, *Die Verdrängung der Juden aus der Wirtschaft im Dritten Reich* (Göttingen, 1966).

There are also numerous studies of the persecution of the Jews in different regions and localities across Germany; one of the first of these, Peter Hanke, *Zur Geschichte der Juden in München zwischen 1933 und 1945* (Munich, 1967), can be cited as representative.

Research into particular problems and groups on the Nazi side has also yielded significant results. On the SS and police, Hans Mommsen edited and published documentary material in 1962 which retains its importance today: 'Der nationalsozialistische Polizeistaat und die Judenverfolgung vor 1938', *Vierteljahreshefte für Zeitgeschichte*, 10 (1962), pp. 68–87; Robert M Kempner has dealt with a related theme, *Eichmann and his Accomplices* (Zürich, 1961).

Above all, however, two works should be mentioned here in which events central to the history of the Holocaust are recounted, and in which, moreover, the role of the old German elites is discussed without apologetics and without the accusing gestures of the public prosecutor, in the first the role of the army and in the second the role of the governmental apparatus: Helmut Krausnick and Hans-Heinrich Wilhelm, *Die Truppe des Weltanschauungskrieges. Die Einsatzgruppen der Sicherheitspolizei und des SD 1938–1942* (Stuttgart, 1981), and Christopher R. Browning, *The Final Solution and the German Foreign Office* (New York, 1978).

There are already important essays even on individuals involved in the persecution or on particularly important witnesses from the ranks of the persecutors, such as Saul Friedländer, *Kurt Gerstein oder die Zwiespaltigkeit des Guten* (Gütersloh, 1968) and Zdenek Zofka, 'Der KZ-Arzt Josef

Mengele. Zur Typologie eines NS-Verbrechers', *Vierteljahreshefte für Zeitgeschichte*, 34 (1986) pp. 245–68.

On the occupied countries, the literature on the events in Poland, one of the principal scenes of the mass murders, has reached considerable proportions. An instructive work, and one which is available in German libraries, should be mentioned here: *Faschismus – Getto – Massenmord. Dokumentation über die Ausrottung und Widerstand der Juden in Polen Während des 2. Weltkriegs* (Berlin, 1961).

But there have been studies of other countries as well; on Holland J. Presser, *Ondergang. De verfolging en verdelging van het Nederlandse Jodendom, 1940–1945* (2 vols, 's-Gravenhage, 1965); on Hungary there is Randolph N. Braham, *The Politics of Genocide. The Holocaust in Hungary* (2 vols, New York, 1981); on Serbia, Christopher R. Browning, 'Wehrmacht Reprisal Policy and the Murder of the Male Jews in Serbia' and 'The Semlin Gas Van and the Final Solution in Serbia', both in his *Fateful Months. Essays on the Emergence of the Final Solution* (New York and London, 1985); finally on France there is Michael Marrus and Robert Paxton, *Vichy France and the Jews* (New York, 1981).

The concentration camps and death camps themselves have, of course, been the subject of numerous studies; to name but three which are particularly precise and based on a wealth of material, while offering the best overview: Ino Arndt and Wolfgang Scheffler, 'Organisierter Massenmord an Juden in nationalsozialistischen Vernichtungslagern', *Vierteljahreshefte für Zeitgeschichte*, 24 (1976), pp. 105–35; Adalbert Rückerl (who was chief public prosecutor in the Ludwigsburg Central Office and was the first to use the document collection there), *Nationalsozialistische Vernichtungslager im Spiegel deutscher Strafprozesse. Belzec, Sobibor, Treblinka, Chelmno'* (Munich, 1977).

Finally there have been comprehensive accounts of the Jewish resistance to the Nazis, above all in Reuben Ainsztein's standard work, *Jewish Resistance in Nazi-occupied Europe, with a Historical Survey of the Jew as Fighter and Soldier in the Diaspora* (London, 1974).

There are three controversial questions in particular which have been discussed for decades and, given the nature of these questions and the difficulties with sources, there is no end in sight to the controversies. One of them dates back to Geneva in 1946 and the publication by Reszö Kastner, one of the principal participants, of *Der Bericht des jüdischen Rettungskomitees aus Budapest 1942–1945* on the behaviour of Jewish organs of self-government (counsellors, elders etc.) and groups of Zionist leaders. Hanna Arendt's book *Eichmann in Jerusalem. Von der Banalität des Bösen* (Munich, 1964) has moved the debate on to a solid basis of historical fact and rational consideration. Among the more convincing contributions to this debate are two essays by John S. Conway: 'Frühe Augenzeugenberichte aus Auschwitz. Glaubwürdigkeit und Wirkungsgeschichte', *Vierteljahreshefte für Zeitgeschichte*, 27 (1979), pp. 260–84, and 'Der Holocaust in Ungarn. Neue Kontroversen und Überlegungen', *Vierteljahreshefte für Zeitgeschichte*, 32 (1984), pp. 179–212. Alexander Schölch's essay, 'Das Dritte Reich, die zionistische Bewegung und der Palästina-Konflikt', *Vierteljahreshefte für Zeitgeschichte*, 30 (1982), pp. 646–74, is also noteworthy.

The second question did not arise until the end of the 1960s. After many years during which the discussion had been restricted to the victims and their persecutors, the question suddenly arose whether powers such as Britain or the United States should not bear at least some responsibility for the Holocaust, in that they had failed to promote Jewish emigration from Europe, above all to Palestine, or even obstructed it, and that in addition they had made no attempt in any way to stop the Holocaust – by aerial bombardment, for example. The debate began with Harry F. Feingold, *The Politics of Rescue. The Roosevelt Administration and the Holocaust 1938–1945* (New Brunswick, N.J., 1970) David S. Wyman, *Paper Walls. America and the Refugee Crisis 1938–1941* (Amherst, Mass., 1968), and Arthur Morse, *While Six Million Died* (New York, 1968). These were than followed by weighty contributions which were in part very critical of Allied policy: Walter Laqueur, *The Terrible Secret. An Investigation into the Suppression of Information about Hitler's Final Solution* (London, 1980); Bernard Wasserstein, *Britain and the Jews of Europe, 1939–1945* (Oxford, 1979); and Martin Gilbert, *Auschwitz and the Allies* (New York, 1981). Interesting contributions, leading to rather more cautious criticism are those of Shlomo Aronson, 'Die dreifache Falle. Hitlers Judenpolitik, die Alliierten und die Juden', *Vierteljahreshefte für Zeitgeschichte*, 32 (1984), pp. 29–65; and the essay by John S. Conway mentioned above, 'Der Holocaust in Ungarn'.

The prehistory of the 'final solution' has emerged as a third area of conflict. This does not refer to the persistent attempts of radical right propagandists to present the Nazi persecution of the Jews as the mere reaction to Jewish declarations of war on the German nation, or as a response to anti-German annihilation plans forged during the war by the ostensible Jewish puppet-masters of British and American politics; Wolfgang Benz has said all that is necessary on this subject in 'Judenvernichtung aus Notwehr? Die Legende um Theodore N. Kaufman', *Vierteljahreshefte für Zeitgeschichte*, 29 (1981), pp. 614–30. Nor does it refer to the historiographical waffle of David Irving, who asserts in his book *Hitler's War* (London, 1977) that Hitler learned of the mass murder of the Jews only in October 1943; again, Martin Broszat has delivered a fitting response in his 'Hitler und die Genesis der "Endlösung". Aus Anlass der Thesen von David Irving', *Vierteljahreshefte für Zeitgeschichte*, 25 (1977) pp. 739–75. And above all it does not refer to the occasionally necessary replies to the fundamentally rather ridiculous attempts of authors from the radical right to deny that the Holocaust took place at all. Such attempts by A. R. Butz, *The Hoax of the Twentieth Century* (Torrance, Cal., 1977) or Wilhelm Stäglich, *Der Auschwitz-Mythos. Legende oder Wirklichkeit? Eine kritische Bestandsaufnahme* (Tübingen, 1979) were dispatched, for example, by John S. Conway's 'Frühe Augenzeugenberichten aus Auschwitz' (see above) and Hermann Graml's 'Alte und neue Apologeten Hitlers' in Wolfgang Benz (ed.), *Rechtsextremismus in der Bundesrepublik. Voraussetzungen, Zusammenhänge, Wirkungen* (Frankfurt, 1984).

It has, rather, to do with serious problems of research arising from gaps in the sources, e.g. from the lack of a written 'Führer order' for the 'final solution'. In his dispute with Irving, Martin Broszat developed the thesis that we cannot suppose there was either an order or a plan at the beginning of the 'final solution'; rather, numerous separate murder operations, all of them consequences of the inability of the system to deal with the administrative problems of the deportation of German and European Jews to eastern Europe, gradually came together in a single process, which the leadership finally sanctioned as the 'final solution', or referred to as the 'final solution'. The Holocaust appears here as the improvisation of bureaucrats overwhelmed by the consequences of a similarly improvised deportation plan whose unforeseen and unintended dimension rendered it unmanageable.

Hans Mommsen has expressly defended Broszat's interpretation in his essay 'Die Realisierung des Utopischen. Die "Endlösung" der Judenfrage im Dritten Reich', *Geschichte und Gesellschaft*, 9 (1983), pp. 381–420; and he has gone a step further in suggesting that the 'genocide policy' must not be interpreted as the implementation of a programme, but must be understood as the 'perfect improvisation'. Here a particular understanding of the essence of Nazism and of the nature of the Nazi regime plays a part, as does the particular evaluation of the role of convictions and individuals in history. Both authors have been contradicted. The most telling arguments are those of Christopher R. Browning, 'Zur Genesis der "Endlösung". Eine Antwort an Martin Broszat', *Vierteljahreshefte für Zeitgeschichte*, 29 (1981), pp. 97–109, and 'The Decision concerning the Final Solution', in *The Fateful Months* (see above).

Gerald Fleming should also be mentioned here: *Hitler und die Endlösung* (Wiesbaden and Munich, 1982). The present author has also taken issue with Broszat and Mommsen: 'Zur Genesis der Endlösung; in Ursula Büttner (ed.), *Das Unrechtsregime. Internationale Forschung über den*

Nationalsozialismus, vol. 2: *Verfolgung – Exil – Belasteter Neubeginn. Festchrift für Werner Jochmann* (Hamburg, 1986). The present volume has been an attempt to develop this critique conclusively within a comprehensive account of the subject.

For all the controversies there is always the possibility of a more general overview and a deeper penetration of the issues, since they have all led to some very useful collections of essays and conference papers, in which all the points of view, as presented by leading researchers of the Holocaust, are given space. Four, above all, should be mentioned: Gerhard Hirschfeld (ed.), *The Policies of Genocide. Jews and Soviet Prisoners of War in Nazi Germany* (London, Boston and Sydney, 1986); Ursula Büttner (ed.), *Das Unrechtsregime*, vol. 1: *Ideologie – Herrschaftssystem – Wirkung in Europa* vol. 2: *Verfolgung – Exil – Belasteter Neubeginn* (Hamburg, 1986); Henry Friedländer and Sybil Milton (eds), *The Holocaust. Ideology, Bureaucracy, and Genocide* (New York, 1980); Eberhard Jäckel and Jürgen Rohwer (eds), *Der Mord an den Juden im Zweiten Weltkrieg* (Stuttgart, 1985).

Appendix 3

Chronological Table

1933

30 January	Adolf Hitler, leader of a radically antisemitic party, the NSDAP, becomes Reich Chancellor.
February/March	Numerous acts of violence against individual Jews and Jewish shops by members of the NSDAP and the SA.
March	Erection of the first 'official' concentration camps, Dachau and Oranienburg.
1–3 April	Nationwide boycott of Jewish shops.
7 April	Law for the Restoration of a Professional Civil Service decrees the compulsory retirement of Jewish civil servants; further laws and decrees (Durchführungsverordnungen) regulate the dismissal of Jewish workers and clerical staff employed in the public service.
25 April	Law against the Overcrowding of German Schools and Universities limits the proportion of Jewish pupils and students to 1.5 per cent.
14 July	Law on the Repeal of Citizenship and the Removal of German Nationality against 'eastern' Jews (Jewish immigrants, particularly from Russia and Poland).
29 September	Reich Entailed Farm Law requires proof of 'Aryan' ancestry dating back to 1800 from entailed farmers.

4 October	Editorial Law excludes German Jews from the Press.

1934

5 May	Examinations Order for doctors and dentists excludes Jewish students from examinations.
22 July	Examinations Order for law students excludes Jewish students from examinations.
8 December	Jewish students no longer admitted to pharmacy examinations.

1935

21 May	Army Law excludes Jews in principle from military service, and absolutely from serving as officers; on 25 July Jews are definitively excluded from all armed forces.
Spring/summer	Various acts of violence by party and SA units against Jews and Jewish shops, along with boycotts.
16 July	Reich Interior Minister Frick instructs registrars not to solemnize any more 'mixed marriages'.
15 September	Reich Citizenship Law deprives all Jews of their civil rights, the Law for the Protection of German Blood and German Honour makes marriages and extra-marital sexual relationship between Jews and so-called 'Aryans' (Deutschblütige) crimes punishable by imprisonment. Both laws are announced by Hitler at the Nuremberg party conference, and therefore come to be taken as the Nuremberg Laws.
14 November	First Supplementary Decree to the Reich Citizenship Law; Jews are now dismissed without exception from the public service and from all other public offices.

1936

11 January	Jews no longer permitted to work as tax assistants.

24 March	No further benefit payments for large Jewish families.
26 March	Jews are no longer permitted to run or lease a pharmacy.
15 April	Reich Press Chamber requires proof of 'Aryan' ancestry from its members.
26 May	Reich Chamber of Fine Arts requires proof of 'Aryan' ancestry from its members.
15 October	Jewish teachers are no longer allowed to give private lessons to 'Aryans'.

1937

15 April	Jews can no longer be awarded doctoral degrees.
12 June	Secret decree of Head of Security Police, Heydrich: after serving their prison sentences, Jews guilty of 'racial disgrace' (miscegenation) are to be sent to a concentration camp, as are female Jewish partners involved in such relationships.
8 September	All Jews without exception are prohibited from practising as insurance doctors.

1938

March	Anti-Jewish terror for a week in Austria following the *Anschluss*, including the compulsory 'Aryanization' of many Jewish firms and the driving of Jews over the border into neighbouring states.
Spring	Anti-Jewish violence across the entire Reich on the part of the NSDAP and SA, accompanied by the slogan 'Jews out of the economy!'
26 April	All Jewish assets over 5,000 RM have to be registered. The Commissioner for the Four-Year Plan (Goering) is empowered to deploy such assets 'in the interests of the German economy'.
9 June	Destruction of the synagogues in Munich.
15 June	Some 1,500 Jews arrested and taken to concentration camps: so-called June Operation against 'asocials'.
23 July	Jews are issued with separate identity cards.

25 July	Jewish doctors are restricted to treating only other Jews and must refer to themselves as *Krankenbehandler* (treaters of the sick).
10 August	Destruction of Nuremberg synagogues.
17 August	Jews must take the additional names of Sara and Israel.
27 September	Jewish lawyers are restricted to working for Jewish clients, and must refer to themselves as 'consultants'.
5 October	Jewish passports must be stamped with a large red 'J'.
26–8 October	17,000 Jews with Polish citizenship are expelled from the German Reich, and transported to the Polish border.
7 November	Herschel Grünspan assassinates legation secretary Ernst vom Rath in the German embassy in Paris.
8–13 November	Anti-Jewish acts of terror, extended by Hitler and Goebbels on the evening of 9 November to a nationwide pogrom, *Reichskristallnacht*, the 'night of broken glass'.
12 November	A compensation fee of a thousand million RM is imposed on German Jews. The exclusion of Jews from the economy begins, involving the compulsory 'Aryanization' of Jewish businesses and the confiscation of other Jewish assets (such as share certificates etc.).

1939

24 January	The Commissioner for the Four-Year Plan (Goering) instructs Reich Interior Minister Frick to establish a Reich Central Office for Jewish Emigration; Heydrich, head of the Security Police, is named as its director.
30 January	Hitler prophesies in the Reichstag that another war would mean the 'extermination of the Jewish race in Europe'.
20 September	Jews must hand in their radios.
21 September	Decree from Heydrich marks the beginning of the concentration and ghettoization of the Polish

	Jews; it contains references to a 'final objective' which will require 'a much greater time scale' and which must be kept 'strictly secret'.
September/October/ November	*Einsatzgruppen der Sicherheitspolizei* (special units of the Security Police) and other Nazi formations murder numerous Jews; some massacres on a larger scale.
24 October	German occupation authorities in Wloclawec introduce a Jewish 'identification badge'; the first such measure in the twentieth century.
23 November	General introduction of the 'Yellow Star' for Jews living in the 'Government General'.
December	87,000 Poles and Jews deported from the new *Reichsgau* Wartheland to the Government General.

1940

January	First gassing of mentally handicapped ('Euthanasia Programme', or 'Operation T4').
12–13 February	First deportations of Jews from Vienna, Mährisch-Ostrau, Teschen and Stettin to the Government General.
27 April	*Reichsführer* SS Heinrich Himmler orders the establishment of a concentration camp at Auschwitz.
June–August	Foreign Office and Reich Security Head Office (RSHA) work on a plan for the deportation of European Jews to Madagascar.
October	Jewish ghetto in Warsaw 'closed' (this had already happened in Łodz in April and in Cracow and Lublin in March and April).
22 October	7,500 Jews deported from the Saarland, Baden and Alsace-Lorraine to the unoccupied part of France, where they are interned in camps (Gurs).

1941

1 March	*Reichsführer* SS Heinrich Himmler orders the building of extensions to the concentration camp

	at Auschwitz, which is to be ready to receive about 100,000 Soviet prisoners of war.
Spring	Four *Einsatzgruppen* (special units) of the Security Police and the SD (Security Service of the SS) are created for the attack on the Soviet Union. These are given the task of murdering Soviet functionaries and Jews living in the Soviet Union.
22 June	Beginning of the invasion of the Soviet Union: in the course of the following months there is systematic mass murder of soviet Jews by the *Einsatzgruppen* and other Nazi formations; between 28 and 30 September alone 33, 771 are shot near Kiev (Babi Yar).
31 July	Göring gives Heydrich the task of the 'final solution of the Jewish question'.
Summer	Himmler instructs commandant of Auschwitz concentration camp to prepare the camp to play a central part in the 'final solution' ordered by Hitler; at the same time Heydrich orders the Gestapo's 'Jewish expert', Eichmann, to prepare the deportation of the European Jews for the 'final solution to the Jewish question in Europe'; a further special commission from Himmler for the SS and police leader in Lublin, Globocnik, to murder the Polish Jews (Operation Reinhard); the 'Führer chancellery' provides staff from the 'Euthanasia Operation', which has been wound up as a result of popular pressure and church protests.
1 September	All Jews in the Reich from the age of six must now wear the 'Yellow Star'.
3 September	First trial gassing with Zyklon B at Auschwitz concentration camp; around 900 Soviet prisoners of war are victims of further experiments in September and October.
September–November	Planning, siting and beginning of construction of death camps at Chelmno, Belzec, Majdanek and Auschwitz-Birkenau in the winter of 1941–2. For Operation Reinhard, for which only Belzec is available at first, camps are built at Sobibor and Treblinka in the spring of 1942.

14/24 October	Start of the mass deportation of Jews from the Reich.
23 October	All Jewish emigration from German-controlled territory is forbidden.
30 November	Around 10,000 deported German and indigenous Jews shot near Riga.

1942

20 January	State Secretaries' Conference in Berlin under Heydrich's direction, for all government departments participating in the 'final solution' and the administration of the Government General (Wannsee Conference).
February	'Evacuation' of the Polish ghettos begins; continuous deportations to the death camps.
24 March	First deportations of south German Jews (Würzburg) to the death camp at Belzec.
26–27	March First transports of Jewish emigrants arrive from western Europe (Drancy, France) at Auschwitz.
May/June	Introduction of the 'Yellow Star' in occupied western Europe.
15–16 July	First transports of Dutch Jews from Westerbork to Auschwitz.
16–18 July	French police arrest 13,000 'stateless' Jews in Paris, 9,000 of whom (including 4,000 children) are taken to Auschwitz via Drancy.
19 July	Himmler insists that Poland must be 'free of Jews' by the end of 1942.
22 July	Mass transports from the Warsaw ghetto to Treblinka, where 67,000 Jews are gassed immediately after arrival, within a single month.
July–September	Mass deportations from western Europe to Auschwitz.
August	More than 200,000 Jews are gassed at Chelmno, Treblinka and Belzec during the last two weeks of the month.
Beginning of November	Himmler orders all concentration camps in the Reich to become 'free of Jews'.
25–6 November	Beginning of deportations from Norway.

1943

18 January	First organized Jewish resistance in the Warsaw ghetto.
27 February	Jewish munitions workers deported from Berlin to Auschwitz.
7 April	End of mass murder in Chelmno; gas chambers destroyed by the SS.
19 April	Beginning of the Jewish uprising in the Warsaw ghetto.
16 May	SS *Obergruppenführer* Stroop announces destruction of Jewish ghetto in Warsaw.
11 June	Himmler orders liquidation of all Polish ghettos.
19 June	Berlin *Gauleiter*, Reich Propaganda Minister Goebbels, declares Berlin 'free of Jews'.
21 June	Order to liquidate remaining ghettos on Soviet territory.
2 August	Prisoners' uprising in Treblinka; destruction of gas chambers.
August–December	Liquidation of Russian ghettos; inhabitants taken to death camps.
16–23 August	Deportation of about 8,000 Jews from the Bialystok ghetto leads to acts of resistance; the ghetto is liquidated.
September–October	Around 7,000 Danish Jews withdrawn from the deportations by their fellow citizens and smuggled to Sweden.
14 October	Prisoners' uprising in Sobibor; end of gassing there.
19 October	End of Operation Reinhard; between November 1941 and October 1943 1,750,000 Jews were murdered at Belzec, Sobibor and Treblinka.
October–November	Around 8,360 Jews deported from northern Italy to Auschwitz.

1944

March–April	More than 6,000 Greek Jews deported to Auschwitz. 1,500 Greek Jews manage to escape by boat to Turkey.

April–July	After Germany assumes governmental control in Hungary, Hungarian Jews are first of all concentrated in special ghetto areas and then deported to Auschwitz; of the 437,000 deported by July some 280,000 are gassed.
May–August	Resumption of mass gassing at Chelmno in connection with the final liquidation of the Lodz ghetto.
24 July	Soviet troops occupy Majdanek.
7 October	Revolt of Jewish special unit in Auschwitz.
27 November	Himmler orders cessation of gassing at Auschwitz.

1945

27 January	Soviet troops reach Auschwitz.
21–28 April	Last gassing of mainly sick concentration camp inmates at Ravensbrück and Mauthausen.
29 April	American troops occupy Dachau.
7–9 May	Unconditional surrender of armed forces of Nazi Germany.

Notes

Chapter 1 The 'Night of Broken Glass'

1 On this and the following paragraphs see Helmut Heiber, 'Der Fall Grünspan', *Vierteljahreshefte für Zeitgeschichte*, 5 (1957), pp. 134ff.
2 On the unleashing, implementation and course of the pogrom, see Hermann Graml, *Der 9 November 1938. 'Reichskristallnacht'*. (6th edn, Bonn, 1958); Lionel Kochan, *Pogrom. 10 November 1938* (London, 1957); Wolfgang Benz, 'Der Rückfall in der Barbarei. Bericht über den Pogrom', in Walter H Pehle (ed.), *Der Judenpogrom 1938* (Frankfurt, 1988), pp. 13ff.

Chapter 2 Modern Antisemitism in Germany

1 Here and on the following see Reinhard Rürup, *Emanzipation und Antisemitismus. Studien zur 'Judenfrage' der bürgerlichen Gesellschaft* (Göttingen, 1975).
2 On the history of antisemitism in Germany: Werner Jochmann, 'Struktur und Funktion des deutschen Antisemitismus', in Werner E. Mosse (ed.) with Arnold Paucker, *Juden im Wilhelminischen Deutschland 1890–1914* (Tübingen, 1976); George L. Mosse, *The Crisis of German Ideology. Intellectual Origins of the Third Reich* (New York, 1964); Fritz Stern, *Kulturpessimismus als politische Gefahr. Eine Analyse nationaler Ideologie in Deutschland* (Berne and Stuttgart, 1963); Lucy S, Dawidowicz, *The War against the Jews 1939–1945* (New York, 1975); Helmut Krausnick, 'Judenverfolgung', in *Martin Broszat and Helmut Krausnick (eds), Anatomie des SS-Staates*, vol. 2 (Freiburg, 1965).
3 *J. G. Fichtes Beitrag zur Berichtigung der Urteile des Publikums über die Französische Revolution* (new impression, Zürich, 1844).
4 Cited from Alexander Bein, 'Der moderne Antisemitismus und seine Bedeutung für die Judenfrage', *Vierteljahreshefte für Zeitgeschichte*, 6 (1958), p. 358.
5 See George L. Mosse, 'The Image of the Jew in German Popular Culture: Felix Dahn and Gustav Freytag', *Yearbook of the Leo Baeck Institute*, 2 (London, 1957), pp. 218–27.

6 Cf. Fritz Stern, *Gold and Iron. Bismarck, Bleichröder and the Building of the German Empire* (London, 1977), p. 438.

7 Heinrich von Treitschke, 'Unsere Aussichten', *Preussische Jahrbücher* (November 1879), reprinted in Walter Boehlich (ed.), *Der Berliner Antisemitismusstreit* (Frankfurt, 1965), pp. 5ff., at p. 8.

8 Theodor Mommsen, *Auch ein Wort über unser Judenthum* (Berlin, 1880), reprinted in Boehlich, *Antisemitismusstreit*, pp. 210ff., at p. 211.

9 Ibid., pp. 219f.

10 Paul de Lagarde, *Juden und Indogermanen. Eine Studie nach dem Leben* (Göttingen, 1887), pp. 339, 347.

11 August Rohling's pamphlet was translated into French by Eduard Drumont, and appeared a second time in Germany in 1890, translated back into German by Karl Paasch, and with a foreword by Drumont. It was published in Leipzig by Theodor Fritsch.

12 Eugen Dühring, *Die Judenfrage als Racen-, Sitten- und Culturfrage. Mit einer Weltgeschichtlichen Antwort* (Karlsruhe and Leipzig, 1881). The sixth, 'expanded' edition, prepared by Dühring in 1920, appeared in 1930 with the title *Die Judenfrage als Frage des Rassencharakters und seine Schädlichkeit für Existenz und Kultur der Völker* ('The Jewish Question as a Question of Racial Character and its Damaging Effects on the Existence and Culture of Nations').

13 Dühring, *Die Judenfrage*, p. 30.

14 Ibid., p. 109.

15 Ibid., p. 94.

16 Ibid., p. 3.

17 Ibid., p. 4.

18 Cf. Bein, *Der Moderne Antisemitismus*, p. 343; Mosse, *The Crisis of German Ideology*, pp. 89f.

19 Mosse, *The Crisis of German Ideology*, pp. 181f.

20 Ibid., pp. 75ff.

21 Cf. Martin Gregor-Dellin, *Richard Wagner. Sein Leben, sein Werk, sein Jahrhundert* (Munich and Zürich, 1980), especially pp. 766ff., Winfried Schüler, *Der Bayreuther Kreis von seiner Entstehung bis zum Ausgang der Wilhelminischen Ära. Wagnerkult und Kulturreform im Geiste völkischer Weltanschauung* (Münster, 1971).

22 Fritz Bolle, 'Darwinismus und Zeitgeist', *Zeitschrift für Religions – und Geistesgeschichte*, vol. 2, 14 (1962); Hedwig Conrad-Martius, *Utopien der Menschenzüchtung* (Munich, 1955); Hans-Günter Zmarzlik, 'Der Sozialdarwinismus in Deutschland als geschichtliches Problem', *Vierteljahreshefte für Zeitgeschichte*, 11 (1963), pp. 246ff.

23 Cf. Mosse, *The Crisis of German Ideology*, p. 99.

24 Hermann Ahlwardt, *Der Verzweiflungskampf der arischen Völker mit dem Judentum* (Berlin, 1890).

25 Stenographische Berichte über die Verhandlung des deutschen Reichstages, 53. Sitzung, 6 März 1895, pp. 1296ff.; Paul Massing, *Vorgeschichte des politischen Antisemitismus* (Frankfurt, 1959), p. 102 was the first to refer to this incident.

26 Karl Pasach, 'Eine Jüdische-Deutsche Gesandschaft und ihre Helfer', *Antisemiten Spiegel* (Danzig, 1892).

27 Dühring, *Die Judenfrage*, p. 108.

28 Cf. Alfred Kruck, *Geschichte des Alldeutschen Verbands* (Wiesbaden, 1954).

29 Daniel Frymann (Heinrich Class), *Wenn ich der Kaiser wär* (Leipzig, 1912; 5th impression, Leipzig, 1914).

30 Cf. Andrew G. Whiteside, 'Nationaler Sozialismus in Österreich vor 1918', *Viertel-*

jahreshefte für Zeitgeschichte, 9 (1961), pp. 333ff.; Ernst Nolte, *Der Faschismus in seiner Epoche* (Munich, 1963), pp. 364ff.

31 Nolte, *Der Faschismus in seiner Epoche*, p. 386.
32 Rudolf Jung, *Der nationale Sozialismus* (Munich, 1921).
33 Gottfried zur Beek (Ludwig Müller), *Die Geheimnisse der Weisen von Zion* (Charlottenburg, 1919; 5th impression, Berlin, 1920); also Alfred Rosenberg, *Die Protokolle der Weisen von Zion und die jüdische Weltpolitik* (Munich, 1923). See also Dawidowicz, *The War against the Jews*, p. 79; Mosse, *The Crisis of German Ideology*, pp. 128ff.; Norman Cohn, *Warrant for Genocide. The Myth of the Jewish World-Conspiracy and the 'Protocols of the Elders of Zion'* (New York, 1966).
34 Text in Ernst Deuerlein, 'Hitlers Eintritt in die Politik und die Reichswehr') *Vierteljahreshefte für Zeitgeschichte*, 7 (1959) pp. 177ff.
35 The text of the speech is in the collection Hauptarchiv der NSDAP, in the German Federal Archive (Bundesarchiv) in Koblenz. Cf. Reginald H. Phelps, 'Hitler als Parteiredner im Jahre 1920', *Vierteljahreshefte für Zeitgeschichte*, 11 (1963), pp. 274ff.
36 Information given to the author on 15 July 1956 by Ernst Frank, who was present at the time, and whose brother Karl Hermann, as Reich Protector of Bohemia and Moravia was later responsible for the 'Lidice incident'.
37 Hans Zöberlein, *Der Glaube an Deutschland* (Munich, 1931) and *Befehl des Gewissens* (Munich, 1937).
38 Gerhard Weinberg (ed.), *Hitlers Zweites Buch. Ein Dokument aus dem Jahre 1928* (Stuttgart, 1961), pp. 145f.
39 *Völkischer Beobachter*, 7 August 1929.
40 Teaching plan of the SS Head Office 1943–4, for the ideological training of the SS and police.
41 Martin Broszat, 'Soziale Motivation und Führerbindung des Nationalsozialismus', *Vierteljahreshefte für Zeitgechichte*, 18 (1970), pp. 392f.
42 Joseph Goebbels, *Die verfluchten Hakenkreuzler. Etwas zum Nachdenken* (Munich, 1930), pp. 15f.
43 Ibid., p. 16.
44 Ibid., p. 23.

Chapter 3   The Reversal of Emancipation

1 See Helmut Krausnick, 'Judenverfolgung', in *Anatomie des SS-Staates* (Olten and Freiburg, 1965), vol. 2, p. 311.
2 George Weiss (ed.), *Einige Dokumente zur Rechtstellung der Juden und zur Entziehung ihres Vermögens 1933–1945* (= *Schriftenreihe zum Berliner Rückerstattungsrecht*, vol. 7) n.p., n.d., pp. 11ff.
3 According to Werner T. Angress, 'Die "Judenfrage" im Spiegel amtlicher Berichte 1935', in Ursula Büttner (ed.) with Werner Johe and Angelika Voss, *Das Unrechtsregime. Internationale Forschung über den Nationalsozialismus*, vol. 2: *Verfolgung – Exil - Belasteter Neubeginn* (Hamburg, 1986) p. 26.
4 Quoted from Herbert Michaelis and Ernst Schraepler (eds), *Ursachen und Folgen. Vom deutschen Zusmmanebruch 1918 und 1945 bis zur staatlichen Neuordnung Deutschlands in der Gegenwart. Eine Urkunden- und Dokumentensammlung zur Zeitgeschichte* (Berlin, n.d.), vol 9, p. 393.

5 Ibid.

6 *Völkischer Beobachter*, 20 July 1933.

7 *Sechs Bekenntnisse zum neuen Deutschland* (Hamburg, 1933) pp. 15ff.

8 Thilo Vogelsang, 'Neue Dokumente zur Geschichte der Reichswehr 1930 bis 1933', *Vierteljahreshefte für Zeitgeschichte*, 2 (1954), pp. 204ff.

9 *Völkischer Beobachter*, 30 March 1933.

10 Nationalsozialistische Partei-Korrespondenz (NSK), no. 358, 30 March 1933.

11 *Deutsche Allgemeine Zeitung*, 4 April 1933.

12 *Ursachen und Folgen*, vol. 9, p. 383.

13 *Reichsgesetzblatt* (1933), vol. 1, 15 and 28 July 1933.

14 Sievert Lorenzen, *Die Juden und die Justiz* (Berlin, 1943) pp. 175ff.

15 See Krausnick, *Judenverfolgung*, pp. 316ff.; for the antisemitic laws and decrees see Bruno Blau, *Das Ausnahmerecht für die Juden in Deutschland 1933–1945* (Düsseldorf, 1954).

16 *Academia*, 46, no. 6/7 (1933).

17 *Deutsche Kultur-Wacht*, 9 (1933), p. 15.

18 After Lucy S. Dawidowicz, *The War against the Jews 1933–1945* (New York, 1975), p. 70.

19 *Kölnische Volkszeitung*, 27 March 1933.

20 After Angress, *Judenfrage, p. 23.*

21 *Ursachen und Folgen*, vol. 9, pp. 161f.

22 Ibid., pp. 159ff.

23 Fritz Stern, *Gold and Iron. Bismarck, Bleichröder and the Building of the German Empire* (London, 1977) p. 548.

24 *Ursachen und Folgen*, vol. 9. p. 155.

Chapter 4   Isolation

1 *Schultess' Europäischer Geschichtskalendar* (1934), p. 424.

2 Walter Strauss, 'Das Reichsministerium des Innern und die Judengesetzgebung. Aufzeichnungen von Dr Bernhard Lösener'. *Vierteljahreshefte für Zeitgeschichte*, 9 (1961), pp. 262ff.

3 Alfred Rosenberg, *Der Mythos des 20. Jahrhunderts. Eine Wertung der seelisch-geistigen Gestaltenkämpfe unserer Zeit* (4th edn, Munich 1932), p. 569.

4 After Lothar Gruchmann, '"Blutschutzgesetz" und Justiz zu Entstehung und Auswirkung des Nürnberger Gesetzes vom 15. September 1935, *Vierteljahreshefte für Zeitgeschichte*, 31 (1983), pp. 418ff.

5 *Nationalsozialistisches Strafrecht. Denkschrift des Preussischen Justizministers* (Berlin, 1933), pp. 47ff.

6 Strauss, 'Reichsministerium', pp. 277f.

7 See Gruchmann, '"Blutschutzgesetz" und Justiz', p. 425.

8 Ibid., p. 420.

9 Ibid., p. 419.

10 Ibid., p. 423

11 See Werner T. Angress, 'Die "Judenfrage" im Spiegel amtlicher Berichte 1935', in Ursula Büttner (ed.) with Werner Johe and Angelika Voss, *Das Unrechtsregime. Internationale Forschung über den Nationalsozialismus*, vol. 2: *Verfolgung – Exil – Belasteter Neubeginn* (Hamburg, 1986), p. 29.

12 See Gruchmann, '"Blutschutzgesetz" und Justiz', pp. 426f.
13 Ibid., p. 427.
14 Ibid., p. 430.
15 Angress, 'Judenfrage', p. 27.
16 See Gruchmann, '"Blutschutzgesetz" und Justiz', p. 428.
17 Ibid., p. 429.
18 Reichsgesetzblatt 1935, vol. 1, p. 1146.
19 Ibid.
20 Cf. Gruchmann, '"Blutschutzgesetz" und Justiz', p. 437.
21 Reichsgesetzblatt (1935), vol. 1, p. 1333.
22 Ibid., p. 1334
23 See Gruchmann. '"Blutschutzgesetz" und Justiz', pp. 435f.
24 Peter Deeg, Die Judengesetzgebung Grossdeutschlands, (Nuremberg, 1936).

Chapter 5 Expropriation

1 Julius Streicher, 'Der Kampf gegen den Teufel', Der Stürmer 14, no. 39, (1936).
2 Avraham Barkai 'Schicksalsjahr 1938', in Ursula Büttner (ed.) with Werner Johe and Angelika Voss, Das Unrechtsregime. Internationale Forschung über den National-sozialismus, vol. 2: Verfolgung - Exil - Belasteter Neubeginn (Hamburg, 1986), p. 50; also cited in Walter H. Pehle (ed.), Der Judenpogrom 1938 (Frankfurt, 1938), pp. 94ff.
3 See Barkai, 'Schicksalsjahr 1938', p. 51. The Hitler quotation which follows is based on notes by his adjutant, Fritz Wiedemann. Photocopy in the Institut für Zeitgeschichte, Munich.
4 Peter Hanke, Zur Geschichte der Juden in München zwischen 1933 und 1945 (Munich, 1967), pp. 154f.
5 Copy in the archive of the Institut für Zeitgeschichte, Munich.
6 See Barkai, 'Schicksalsjahr 1938', p. 48.
7 Foreign Relations of the United States. Diplomatic Papers 1938, vol. 2, p. 382.
8 Barkai, 'Schicksalsjahr 1938', p. 52.
9 IMT, vol. 17, p. 163.
10 Barkai, 'Schicksalsjahr 1938', p. 55.
11 Wilhelm Treue, 'Rede Hitlers vor der deutschen Presse (10. November 1938)', Vierteljahreshefte für Zeitgeschichte, 6 (1958), pp. 175ff.
12 Die Tagebücher von Joseph Goebbels, edited by Elke Fröhlich (Munich, 1987), Part I, vol. 3, p. 533.
13 Documents on British Foreign Policy 1919–1937, Third Series, vol. 3, p. 277.
14 'Protokoll einer Sitzung im Reichluftfahrtsministerium am 12.11.1938' in IMT, vol. 28, pp. 499ff.
15 Ibid., p. 540.

Chapter 6 Approach to Genocide

1 Die Tagebücher von Joseph Goebbels, edited by Elke Fröhlich (Munich, 1987), Part I, vol. 3, p. 532.

2 Ibid., p. 533.
3 IMT, vol. 28, pp. 538f.
4 Nuremberg Document NG-2586.
5 *Akten zur Deutschen Auswärtigen Politik 1918–1945*, Series D, vol. 5, pp. 780ff.
6 'Bericht des Obersten Parteigerichts der NSDAP vom 13. 2. 1939', in Nuremberg Document PS-3063.
7 *Die Tagebücher von Joseph Goebbels*. Part I, vol. 3, p. 536.
8 *Akten zur deutschen Auswärtigen Politik*, Series D, vol. 4, pp. 291ff.
9 Max Domarus, *Hitler. Reden und Proklamationen 1932–1945* (Würzburg, 1963), vol. 2, p. 1058.
10 *Akten zur Deutschen Auswärtigen Politik*, Series D, vol. 4, p. 170.
11 Ibid., pp. 566ff.
12 In a speech to *SS Grüppenführer* of 8 November 1938 Himmler said: 'The situation in Germany has now become impossible for the Jews . . . We will drive them out with increasing indifference [Rücksichtslosigkeit] . . . Of course, the other states . . . are not antisemitic today, but they will become so with time . . . so that in the end the world will have no place left to offer the Jews', Bradley F. Smith and Agnes F. Peterson (eds), *Heinrich Himmler. Geheimreden 1933 bis 1945.* (with an introduction by Joachim C. Fest) (Frankfurt, Berlin and Vienna, 1974), pp. 38f.
13 Nuremberg Document NC-2586.
14 *Akten zur deutschen Auswärtigen Politik*, Series D, vol. 8, p. 716.
15 Nuremberg Document PS-3363.
16 Document WB 2754 (Manstein Trial), microfilm at Institut für Zeitgeschichte, Munich.
17 *Die Tagebücher von Joseph Goebbels*. Part I, vol. 4, pp. 544.
18 Ibid., Part I, vol. 3, p. 628.
19 Ibid., p. 630.
20 Ibid., p. 612.
21 Nuremberg Document, NO-3011.
22 IMT, vol. 36 p. 89.
23 Nuremberg Document NO-3011.
24 Ibid.
25 Quoted by General Blaskowitz in his notes, Nuremberg Document NO-3011.
26 Helmut Krausnick, 'Hitler und die Morde in Polen. Ein Beitrag zum Konflikt zwischen Heer und SS um die Verwaltung der besetzten Gebiete', *Vierteljahreshefte für Zeitgeschichte*, 11 (1963), pp. 196ff.
27 Evidence of General Ulex (retired), Institut für Zeitgeschichte, Munich, ZS 626.
28 Hildegard von Kotze (ed.), *Heeresadjutant bei Hitler. Aufzeichnungen des Majors Engel* (Stuttgart, 1974), p. 68.
29 Nuremberg Document NO-3011
30 Eichmann Trial, document of evidence no. 464, photocopy in the Institut für Zeitgeschichte, Munich.
31 Nuremberg Documents NG-2586 and NG-5764.
32 Helmut Krausnick, 'Denkschrift über die Behandlung der Fremdvölkischen im Osten (Mai 1940)', *Vierteljahreshefte für Zeitgeschichte*, 5 (1957), pp. 194ff., 197.
33 *Die Tagebücher von Joseph Goebbels*, Part I, vol. 4, p. 253.
34 Werner Präg and Wolfgang Jacobmeyer (eds), *Das Diensttagebuch des deutschen Generalgouverneurs in Polen 1939 bis 1945* (Stuttgart, 1975), p. 252.

Chapter 7 Genocide

1 Helmut Krausnick, 'Denkschrift Himmlers über die Behandlung der Fremdvölkischen im Osten (Mai 1940)', *Vierteljahreshefte für Zeitgeschichte*, 5 (1957), p. 197.

2 Helmut Heiber, 'Der Generalplan Ost', *Vierteljahreshefte für Zeitgeschichte*, 6 (1958), pp. 281ff., at p. 308.

3 Felix Kersten, *Klerk en Beul* (Amsterdam, 1948), pp. 197ff. and *Totenkopf und Treue* (Hamburg, 1952), p. 201.

4 Elke Frölich (ed.), *Die Tagebücher von Joseph Goebbels* Part I, vol. 4 (Munich, 1987) p. 246.

5 Helmut Krausnick, 'Kommissarbefehl und "Gerichtsbarkeiterlass Barbarossa" in neuer Sicht', *Vierteljahreshefte für Zeitgeschichte*, 25 (1977), pp. 682ff.

6 On this and the following paragraphs see Helmut Krausnick and Hans-Heinrich Wilhelm, *Die Truppe des Weltanschauungskrieges. Die Einsatzgruppen der Sicherheitspolizei und des SD 1938–1942* (Stuttgart, 1981), particularly, pp. 150ff.; also Helmut Krausnick, 'Hitler und die Befehle an die Einsatzgruppen im Sommer 1941', in Eberhard Jäckel and Jürgen Rohwer, *Der Mord an den Juden im Zweiten Weltkrieg. Entschlussbildung und Verwirklichung* (Stuttgart, 1985), pp. 88ff.

7 Quoted from Krausnick, 'Hitler und die Befehle an die Einsatzgruppen', p. 96.

8 Nuremberg Document L-180.

9 Quoted from Krausnick, 'Hitler und die Befehle an die Einsatzgruppen', p. 100.

10 Ibid., p. 95.

11 Quoted from Krausnick, 'Judenverfolgung', in *Anatomie des SS-Staates* (Olten and Freiburg, 1965), vol. 2, p. 367.

12 Ibid., p. 367.

13 Quoted from Gerald Fleming, *Hitler und die Endlösung* (Munich, 1982), p. 142.

14 Even Goering occasionally said, 'We must assume that the Jews are indispensable.' Cf. Krausnick, 'Judenverfolgung', p. 424.

15 Krausnick and Wilhelm, *Die Truppe des Weltanschauungskrieges*, pp. 621f.

16 Krausnick, 'Hitler und die Befehle an die Einsatzgruppen', pp. 95f.

17 IMT, vol. 32, pp. 72ff.

18 Quoted from Krausnick and Wilhelm, *Die Truppe des Weltanschauungskrieges*, pp. 275f.

19 Ernst Jünger, *Strahlungen* (Tübingen, 1949), p. 250.

20 On this see Krausnick and Wilhelm, *Die Truppe des Weltanschauungskrieges*, pp. 258ff.

21 *Völkischer Beobachter*, 31 January 1942, p. 4.

22 Werner Präg and Wolfgang Jacobmeyer (eds), *Das Diensttagebuch des deutschen Generalgouverneurs in Polen 1939 bis 1945* (Stuttgart, 1975), pp. 335, 338.

23 Ibid., p. 389.

24 Quoted from Robert Kempner, *Eichmann und Komplizen* (Zurich, 1961), p. 97.

25 Nuremberg Document NG-1123.

26 Nuremberg Document NG-3104.

27 Heinrich Himmler in a speech to *SS-Gruppenführer* in Posen (Poznán), 4 October 1943.

28 Hermann Graml, 'Zur Genesis der "Endlösung"', in Ursula Büttner (ed.) with Werner Johe and Angelika Voss, *Das Unrechtsregime. Internationale Forschung über den Nationalsozialismus.* vol. 2: *Verfolgung – Exil – Belasteter Neubeginn* (Hamburg, 1986), pp. 13f.

29 *Generaloberst* Franz Halder, *Kriegstagebuch*, edited by Hans Adolf Jacobsen (3 vols, Stuttgart, 1962–4), vol. 3, p. 38.

30 Nuremberg Document NG-2586/PS-710.

31 Quoted from Raul Hilberg, 'Die Aktion Reinhard', in Eberhard Jäckel and Jürgen Rohwer (eds), *Der Mord an den Juden im Zweiten Weltkrieg. Entschlussbildung und Verwirklichung* (Stuttgart, 1985), p. 126).

32 After Eberhard Jäckel, in Jäckel and Rohwer, Der Mord an den Juden im Zweiten Weltkrieg, p. 137.

33 Statement by SS judge Dr Konrad Morgen in IMT, vol. 42, p. 564.

34 Mathias Beer, 'Die Entwicklung der Gaswagen beim Mord an den Juden', *Vierteljahreshefte für Zeitgeschichte*, 35 (1987), pp. 403f.

35 *Kommandant in Auschwitz Autobiographische Aufzeichnungen von Rudolf Höss*, with an introduction and commentary by Martin Broszat (Stuttgart, 1958).

36 Personal Staff RFSS, Archive of the Institut für Zeitgeschichte, Munich, MA 3/9, folder 94.

37 *Reichsgesetzblatt 1941*, vol. 1, p. 547.

38 Cf. Hitler's 'Tagesbefehl an die Soldaten der Ostfront' of 2 October 1941, *Völkischer Beobachter*, 11 October 1941.

39 'Noch aufnahmefähig': thus on 18 September 1941 to Greiser: Personal Staff RFSS, Archive of the Institut für Zeitgeschichte, Munich, MA 3/9, folder 94. The version 'kaum noch aufnahmefähig' (scarcely capable of taking more people) in Martin Broszat, 'Hitler und die Genesis der Endlösung. Aus Anlass der Thesen von David Irving', *Vierteljahreshefte für Zeitgeschichte*, 25 (1977), p. 750, arises from a mistake in reading the source.

40 Personal Staff RFSS, Archive of the Institut für Zeitgeschichte, Munich, MA 3/9, folder 94.

41 Quoted from Christopher R. Browning, *Fateful Months. Essays on the Emergence of the Final Solution* (New York and London, 1985), pp. 26f.

42 Browning, *Fateful Months*, p. 26.

43 Nuremberg Document NO-365.

44 Browning, *Fateful Months*, p. 27.

45 Ibid., p. 33.

46 Felix Kersten, *The Kersten Memoirs 1940–1945* (New York, 1957), p. 119.

47 *Das Diensttagebuch des deutschen Generalgouverneurs in Polen*, pp. 457f.

48 IMT, vol. 33, pp. 435ff.

49 Nuremberg Document NG-2586.

50 Quoted from Krausnick, 'Judenverfolgang', p. 447.

51 *Das Diensttagebuch des deutschen Generalgouverneurs in Polen*, p. 588.

52 IMT, vol. 26, p. 693.

53 Quoted from John S Conway, 'Der Holocaust in Ungarn. Neue Kontroversen und Überlegungen', *Vierteljahreshefte für Zeitgeschichte*, 32 (1984), p. 185.

54 See Hans-Heinrich Wilhelm, 'Wie geheim war die "Endlösung"?' in *Miscellanea. Festschrift für Helmut Krausnick zum 75. Geburtstag* (Stuttgart, 1980), pp. 131ff.

55 Verfügungen, Anordnungen, Bekanntgaben, published by the Party Chancellery (Munich, n.d.) vol. 3, pp. 131f.

56 Quoted from O. D. Kulka, 'The Churches in the Third Reich and the "Jewish Question" in the light of secret Nazi Reports on German 'Public Opinion', unpublished lecture to the congress organized by the Commission Internationale d'Histoire Comparée, Warsaw, 25 June–1 July 1978.

57 Heinrich Hermelink (ed.), *Kirche im Kampf* (Tübingen, 1950), pp. 654ff.
58 After Ino Arndt and Wolfgang Scheffler, 'Organisierter Massenmord an Juden in nationalsozialistischen Vernichtungslagern. Ein Beitrag Zur Richtigstellung apologetischer Literatur', *Vierteljahreshefte für Zeitgeschichte*, 24 (1976), pp. 105ff.; Hilberg, 'Die Aktion Reinhard', pp. 125ff.; Wolfgang Scheffler, 'Chelmno, Sobibor, Belzec und Majdanek', in Jäckel and Rohwer, *Der Mord an den Juden im Zweiten Weltkrieg*, pp. 145ff.; Gitta Sereny, 'Treblinka', ibid., pp. 157ff.; Yehuda Bauer, 'Auschwitz', ibid., pp. 164ff.

Glossary

Brigadeführer	SS rank, approximately equivalent to major-general.
CV	General Association of Catholic Students' Clubs.
DAP	*Deutsche Arbeiterpartei* (German Workers' Party), a precursor of the Nazi Party, founded in Bohemia in 1904.
DNVP	*Deutschnationale Volkspartei* (German National People's party), a right-wing conservative and nationalist party in Weimar Germany.
Einsatzkommando	A detachment of the Security Police and subdivision of an Einsatzgruppe, a task force for special missions in occupied territory.
Gau	Principal territorial division of the NSDAP. Germany was divided into forty-two such units.
Gauleiter	'Gau leader', highest-ranking Nazi official.
Generaloberst	German army rank with no exact equivalent in the British army. The literal meaning is 'colonel-general'.
Gestapo	Geheime Staatspolizei, secret state police.
GG	Generalgouvernement (Government General), those parts of German-occupied Poland not integrated directly into Reich.
Gründerjahre	'Founding years', the years of the German post-unification boom of the early 1870s.
Hauptsturmiührer	SS rank approximately equivalent to army captian.
IG Farben	German chemicals concern.
IMT	International Military Tribunal (for the trial of war criminals at Nuremberg.)
Kreisleiter	'District leader', intermediate-level Nazi official.

KTI	Kriminaltechnisches Institut (Technical Institute of Criminology), a subdivision of the RSHA.
Landesgruppenleiter	Leader of Nazi organization in a foreign country.
NSDAP	Nationalsozialistische Deutsche Arbeiterpartei (National Socialist German Workers' party, Nazi party).
NSKK	Nationalsozialistisches Kraftfahr-Korps (National Socialist Motor Corps).
Obergruppenführer	SS rank, approximately equivalent to general.
Obersturmbannführer	SS rank, approximately equivalent to lieutenant-colonel.
Obersturmführer	SS rank, approximately equivalent to lieutenant.
OKH	Oberkommando des Herres (Army High Command).
OKW	Oberkommando der Wehrmacht (High Command of the Armed Forces).
Ordnungspolizei	'Order police'. Regular uniformed police.
Ortsgruppe	Administrative division of the Nazi party based on a local community.
Ortsgruppenleiter	'Local group leader', Nazi party official subordinate to Kreisleiter in charge of a local community branch of the party.
RFSS	Reichsführer SS (Reich Leader of the SS, i.e. Heinrich Himmler).
RM	Reichsmark.
RSHA	Reichssicherheitshauptamt (Reich Security Head Office), the central security department of the Reich formed in 1939.
SA	Sturmabteilung (storm division), Nazi paramilitary units otherwise known as stormtroopers or 'brownshirts'.
SD	Sicherheitsdienst (Security Service), a department of the SS formed by Reinhard Heydrich as the intelligence service of the Nazi party.
SS	Schutzstaffel (Guard Detachment). Developed by Himmler, it became the most powerful party formation.
Reichsführer	Reich leader.
Scharführer	SS rank, approximately equivalent to staff sergeant.
Sonderkommando	SS task force used for police and political tasks.
Standartenführer	SS rank approximately equivalent to colonel.
Sturmbannführer	SS rank, approximately equivalent to major.
Sturmhauptführer	SA rank. Leader of a stormtrooper unit.
Truppenleiter	'Squad leader' leader of a stormtrooper (or SS) squad.
völkisch	racist-nationalist. (The German term conveys a sense of both, and usually refers to the ideology and organizations of the radical and proto-Nazi right in Germany and Austria.)
YIVO	Yiddish Scientific Institute.

Index

53-5

Antisemitism in the Third Reich